DINOSAURS

Fossils and Feathers

MK REED
JOE FLOOD

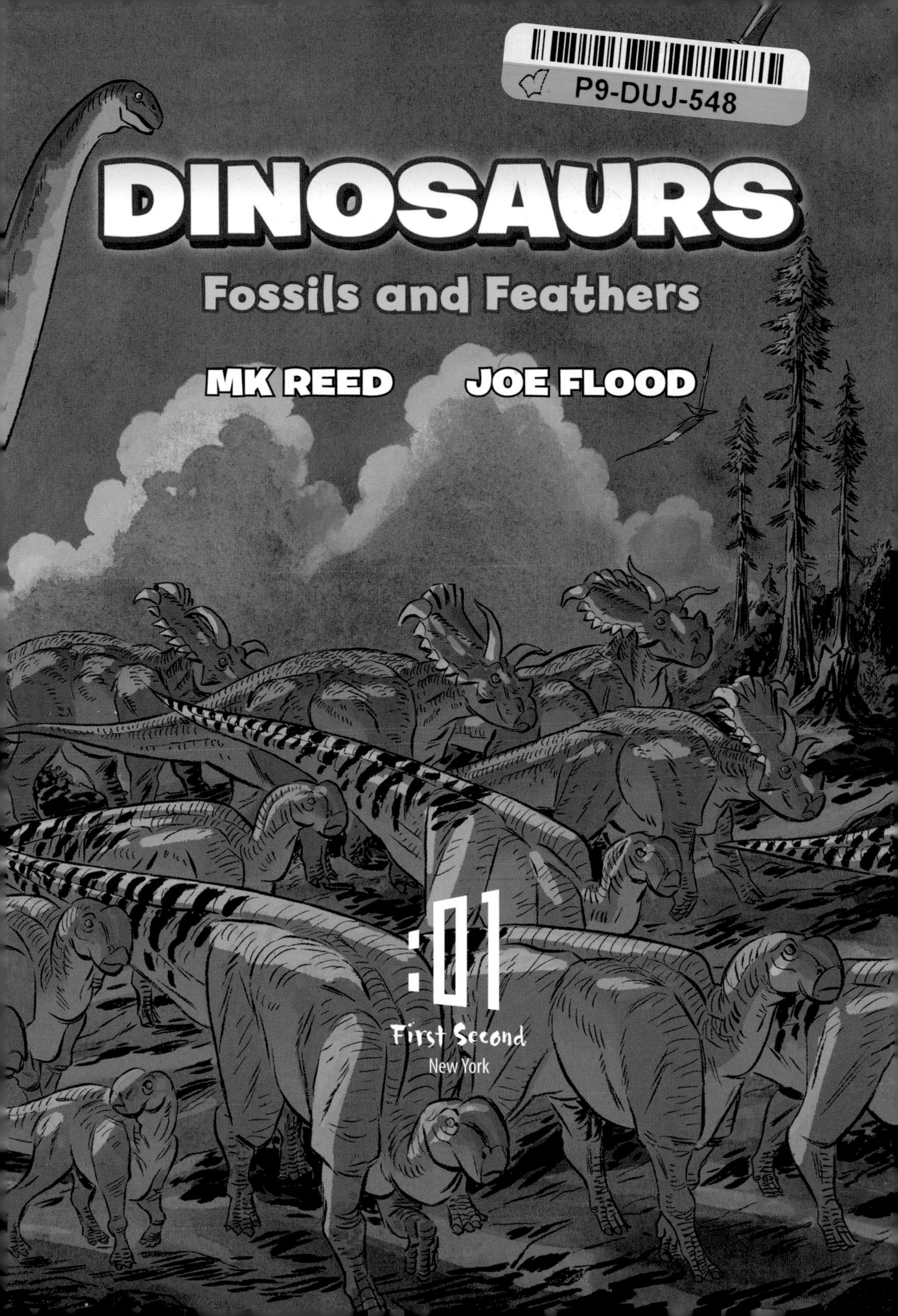

:01
First Second
New York

:01

First Second

Drawn with a Staedtler .07 mm mechanical pencil with Pilot Eno blue and light blue lead, inked with Dr Ph Martin's black India ink using a Raphael #8404 size 1 kolinsky sable brush and Nikko crow quill on Strathmore 500 series 2ply Vellum Bristol. Backgrounds colored with Schminke water colors on Farbriano Artistico paper. Remaining art colored digitally with Photoshop using Kyle Webster's digital brushes. Lettered in Comicrazy.

Published by First Second
First Second is an imprint of Roaring Brook Press,
a division of Holtzbrinck Publishing Holdings Limited Partnership
175 Fifth Avenue, New York, NY 10010

Cataloging-in-Publication Data is on file at the Library of Congress.

Paperback ISBN 978-1-62672-143-2
Hardcover ISBN 978-1-62672-144-9

FIRST EDITION

First edition 2016
Book design by John Green

Printed in China by Toppan Leefung Printing Ltd., Dongguan City, Guandong Province
10 9 8 7 6 5 4

BY ART WE LIVE

When I was a kid, I drew a picture of the dinosaur *Deinonychus*. This wasn't unusual for me. I loved dinosaurs by the time I could hold a pencil. I remember that particular *Deinonychus* so well because of how hard I tried to be imaginative when drawing it.

Why did this drawing require all the powers of my imagination? Because my *Deinonychus* had stripes! More shocking than that: the stripes were blue! Every dinosaur in every picture book I had ever seen was green, gray, or brown. I felt like a madman as I pulled the blue crayon from its box.

Looking back now, I know that I didn't go too far. In fact, I didn't go far enough. In all the years since I drew that picture, I've had one idea reinforced over and over: dinosaurs are fantastic.

The word "fantastic" literally means "appearing as if conceived from an unrestrained imagination." The most important discovery from the last few decades of paleontology is that we restrain our imaginations too much when we think about dinosaurs. In my wildest dreams I never dared to imagine the fuzzy coat on *Yutyrannus*, the buckteeth of *Incisivosaurus*, the comb-over on *Kosmoceratops*, the spiny neck of *Amargasaurus*, or *Microraptor*'s winged legs.

Go look up the most recent drawings of *Deinocheirus*. I'll bet your unrestrained imagination didn't see that one coming. No one's did.

The incredible new findings keep coming. Soft tissue in tyrannosaur bones and sauropod eggs. Color pigments in dromaeosaur feathers and hadrosaur scales. Burrowing ornithopods. Aquatic spinosaurs. Arctic dinosaurs. Antarctic dinosaurs. With each new discovery, we learn just how much we'd been restraining the way we imagined dinosaurs.

You might ask: Are we still restraining our imaginations when we think about dinosaurs? What fantastic new fact will literally rise up out of the Earth tomorrow? As you'll see, these are questions that paleontologists have been asking for centuries.

Reading their stories teaches us not only how dinosaurs lived, but also how we live.

We usually think of discovery as a process that limits possibilities. Think about looking for something—say, a dinosaur toy—in a messy room. When you start your search, you imagine that the toy might be in a number of different places: maybe under the bed or behind the dresser or buried under a bunch of other toys. But as you search, you eliminate possibilities. Once you discover where the toy is, you stop imagining other places it might be. This normal sort of discovery—discovery by process of elimination—is the kind that restrains our imaginations.

When I drew that *Deinonychus*, I wished that I could encounter a living dinosaur. I would sit in the backseat of my parents' car, searching in the passing trees for a glimpse of a dinosaur. I thought I'd see one if I could just find the right way to look. But even then, I believed finding a living dinosaur was just a fantasy.

Many years later, I took a class about the science and philosophy of evolution. The teacher had promised that I would learn about dinosaurs. And I did. I found out about a truly fantastic discovery, one that you'll read about later in this book. I learned that there are living dinosaurs that survived extinction. We call them "birds."

This discovery gave me new places to look for dinosaurs. I could look up from the rocks under my feet. I could look in a pond or on a tree branch or up in the sky. I had found the right way to look, and it changed the way I saw birds and the way I saw dinosaurs. It changed the way I saw everything.

The lesson that MK Reed and Joe Flood teach in this book is that scientific discovery is very different from normal discovery. Rather than limiting our imaginations, scientific discovery lets us imagine more about the world around us. Three hundred years ago, no one knew about dinosaurs at all. Two hundred years ago,

no one knew that dinosaurs had lived on every continent. One hundred years ago, no one knew that the continents themselves moved around. Those discoveries changed the way we understand our world. Someday, discoveries you make could unleash our imaginations, too. That is what science does: it shows us how fantastic the world can be.

We now imagine dinosaurs with feathers. We imagine them with colorful stripes. By the time you reach the back cover of this book, you'll imagine them in ways you've never imagined them before.

In this book, you'll find plenty of dinosaurs drawn the way today's paleontologists imagine them. One of those dinosaurs is an up-to-date *Deinonychus*. Joe Flood has drawn the animal covered in feathers, stalking the middle ground between modern reptiles and birds. If my younger counterpart thought himself a madman for pulling out that blue crayon, then what would he say about Joe?

I can say this much now: Joe's art and MK Reed's words are just as fantastic as the animals that served as their inspiration. Their balance of science, philosophy, and history is informative, funny, and, above all, imaginative. The spirit of discovery hovers over each page.

Remember that as you read this book. Keep it in mind as you lean in closer to the page to take in new details in the *Rhinorex* herds, or when you pause to digest the idea that *T. rex* might have had feathers. The spirit of discovery lies in finding what is fantastic. As you read, the spirit of discovery lies in you.

Sometimes people say that your imagination flies once it's set free. When you turn this page, you'll begin to see that this is true. Let your imagination soar. You will find the fantastic. You will be among the dinosaurs.

—Leonard Finkelman, Ph.D.
Assistant Professor in Philosophy of Science, Linfield College

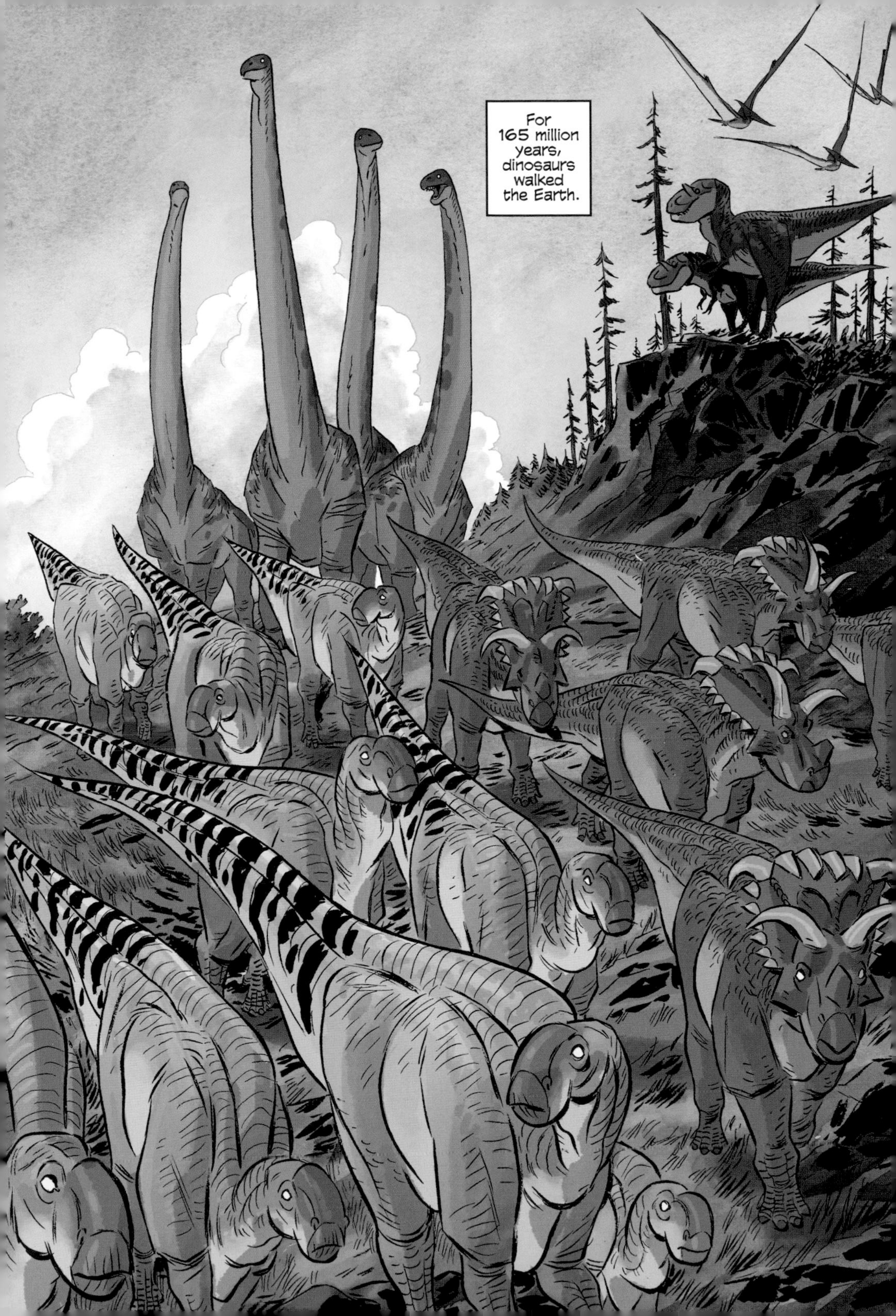
For 165 million years, dinosaurs walked the Earth.

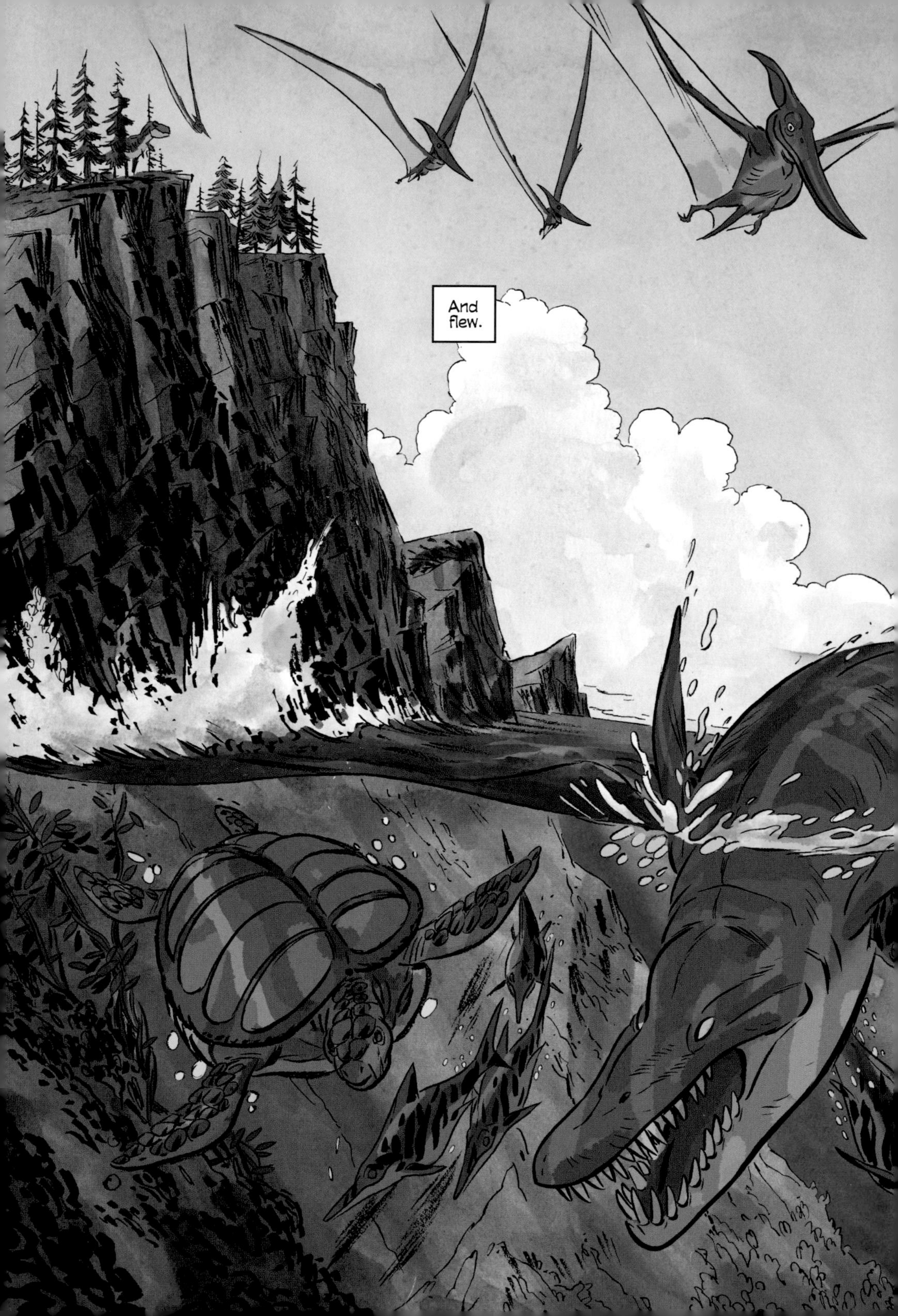
And flew.

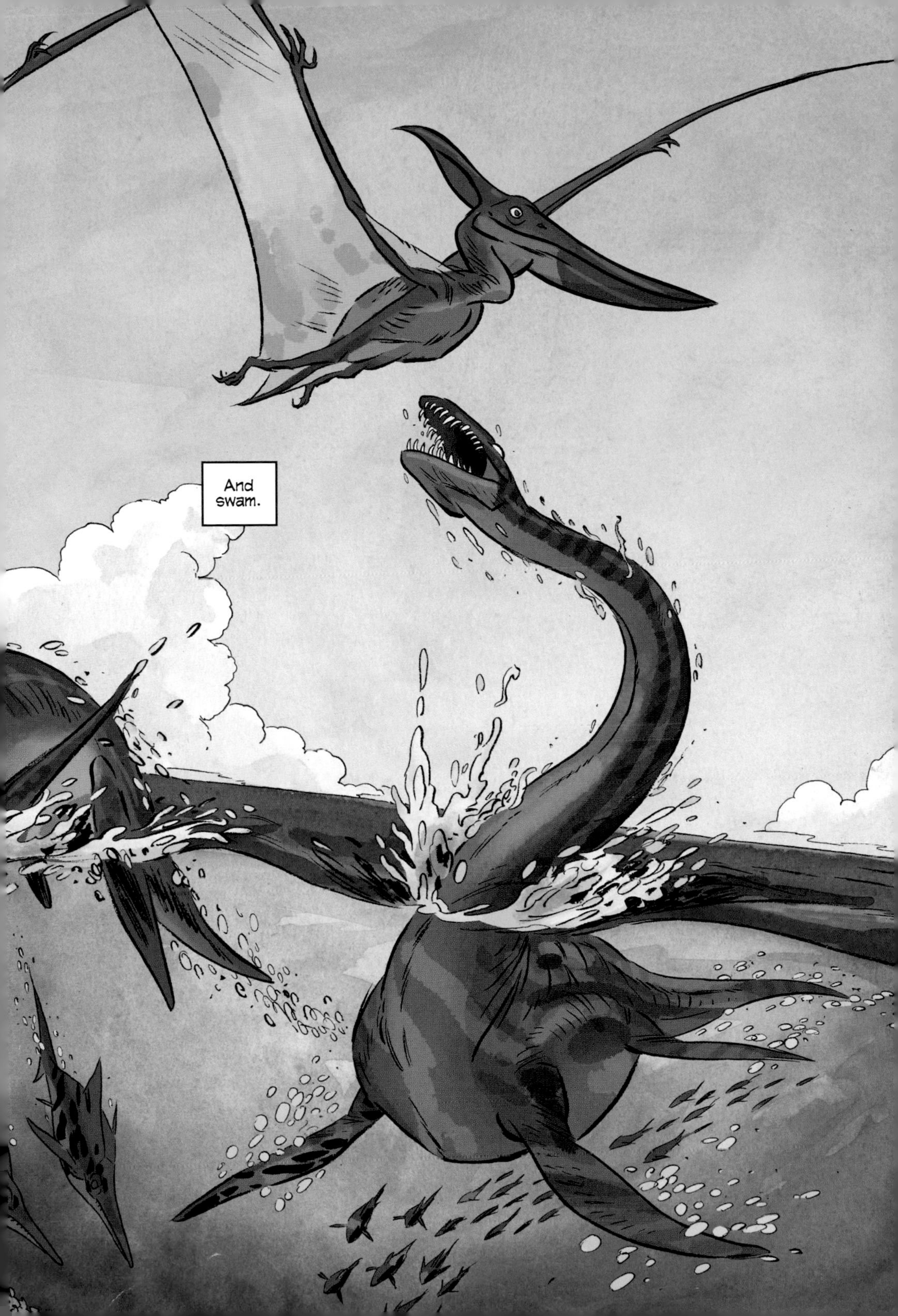
And swam.

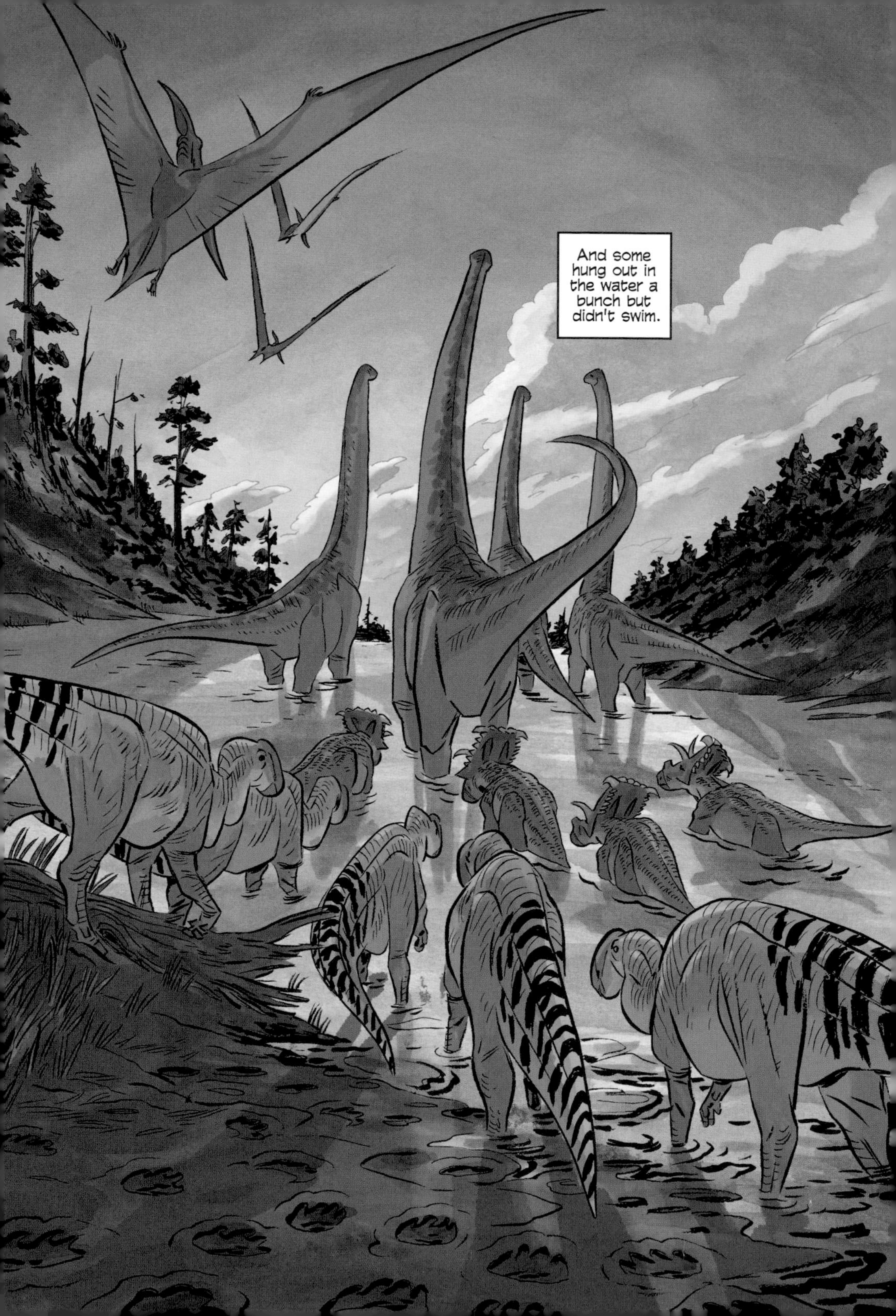
And some hung out in the water a bunch but didn't swim.

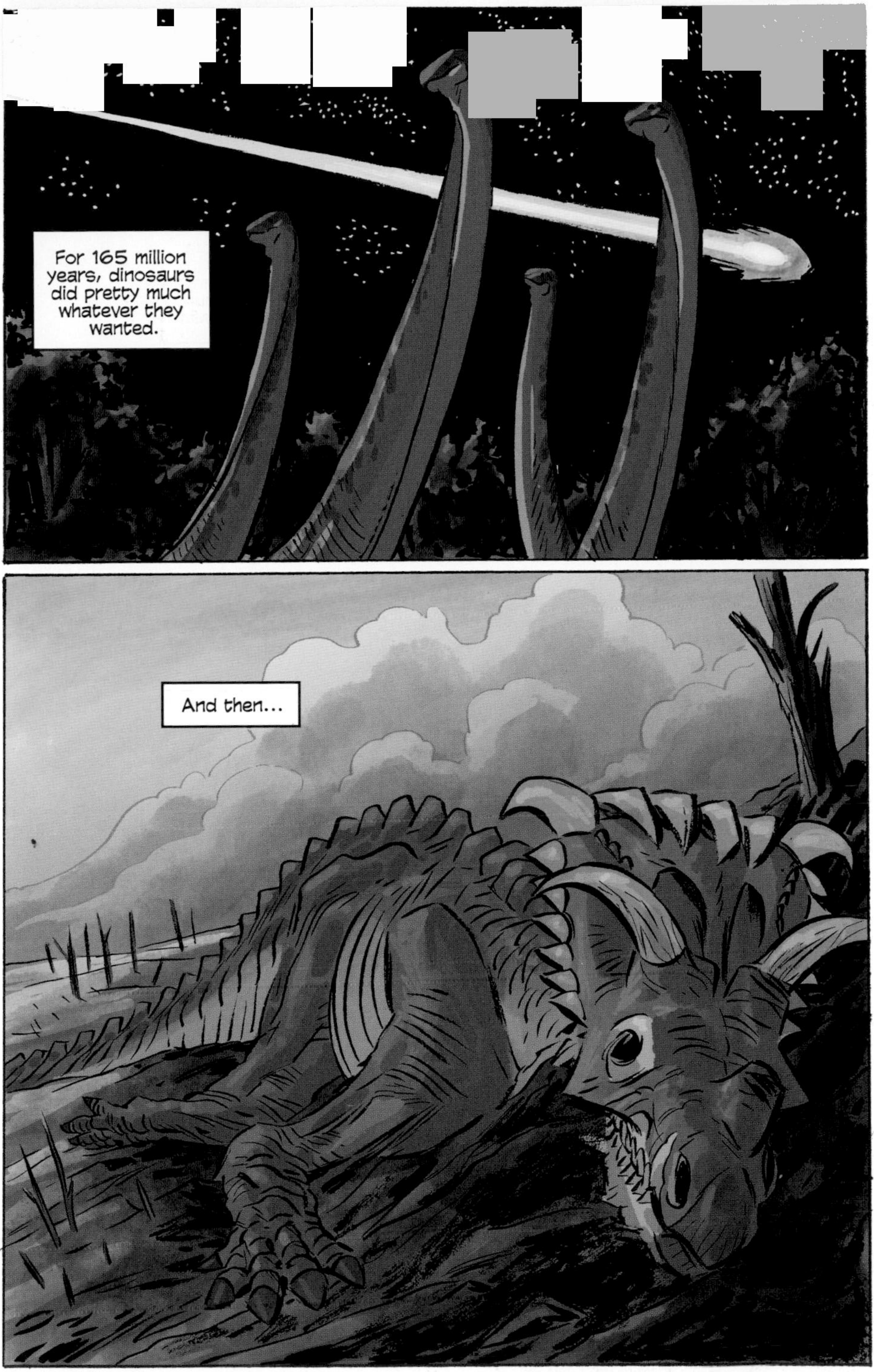
For 165 million years, dinosaurs did pretty much whatever they wanted.
And then...

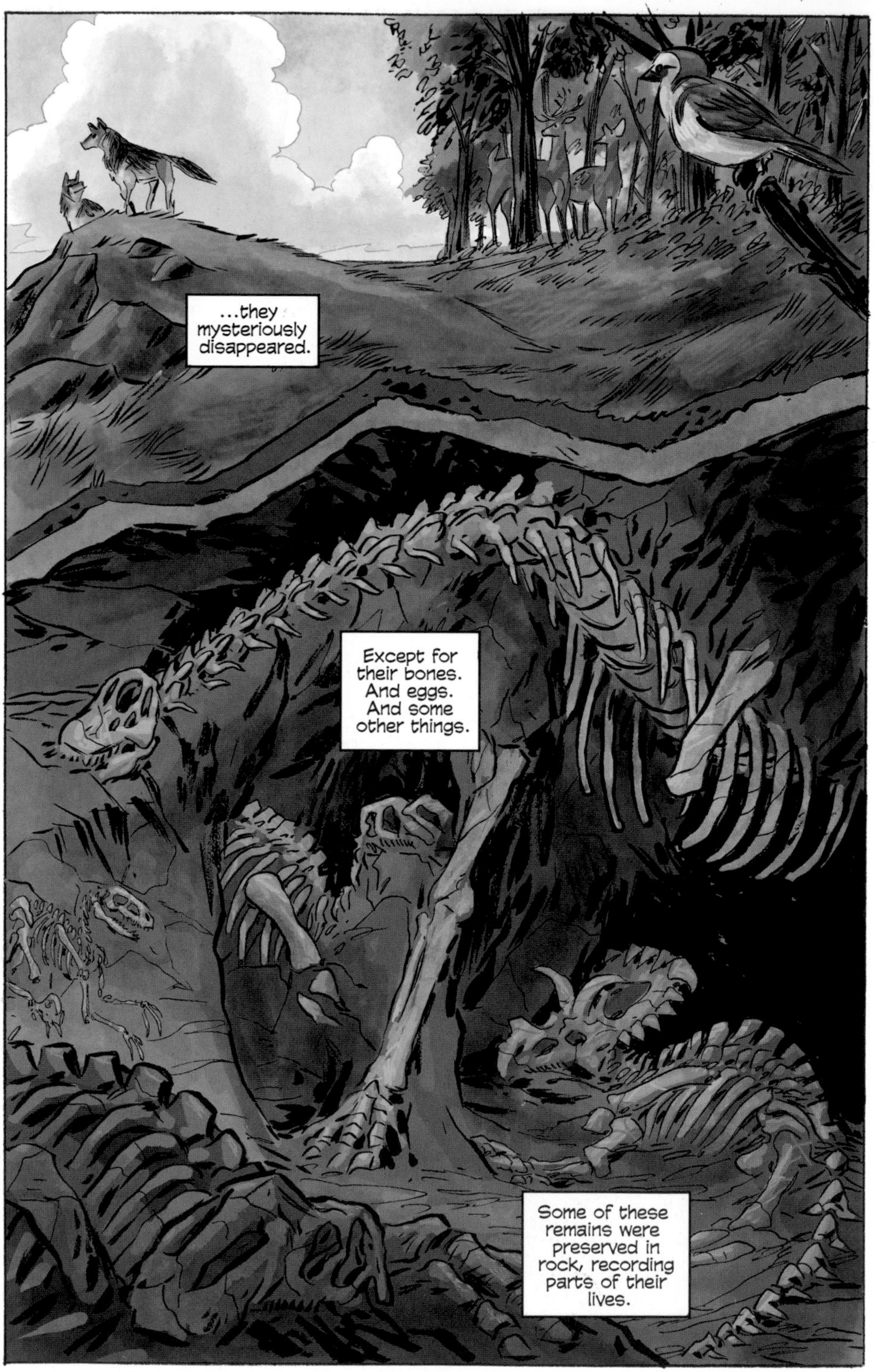
...they mysteriously disappeared.
Except for their bones. And eggs. And some other things.
Some of these remains were preserved in rock, recording parts of their lives.

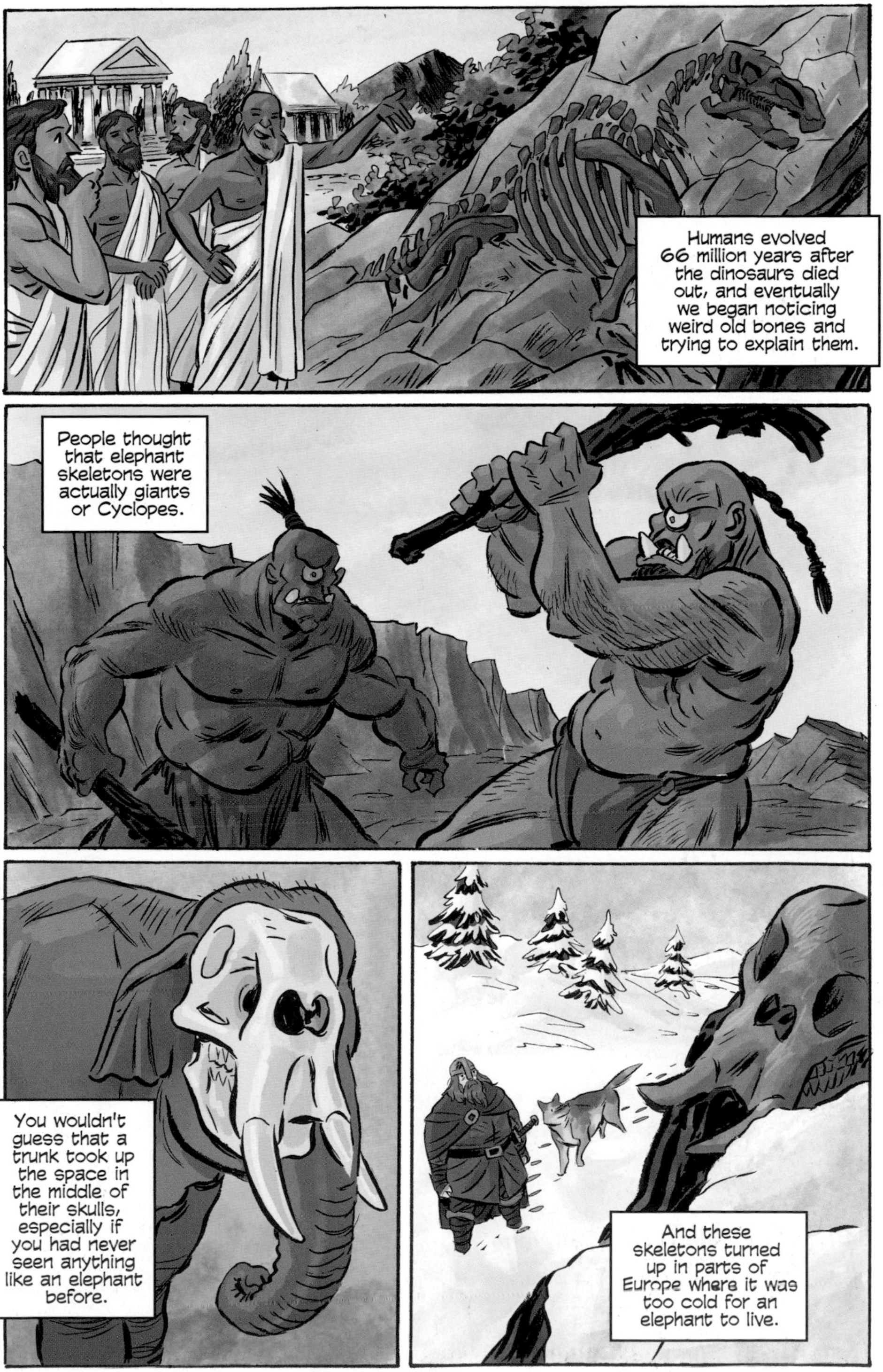
Humans evolved 66 million years after the dinosaurs died out, and eventually we began noticing weird old bones and trying to explain them.
People thought that elephant skeletons were actually giants or Cyclopes.
You wouldn't guess that a trunk took up the space in the middle of their skulls, especially if you had never seen anything like an elephant before.
And these skeletons turned up in parts of Europe where it was too cold for an elephant to live.

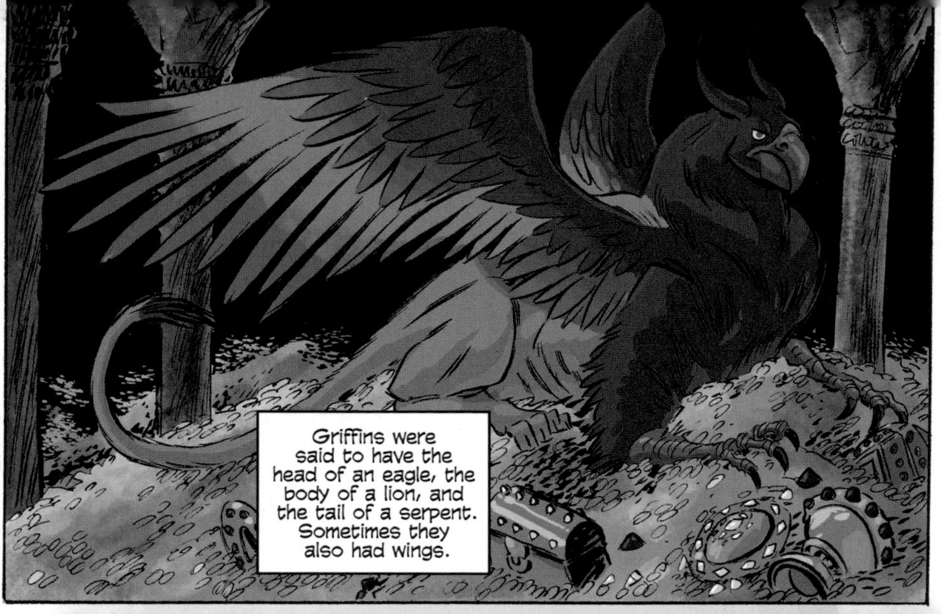
Griffins were said to have the head of an eagle, the body of a lion, and the tail of a serpent. Sometimes they also had wings.

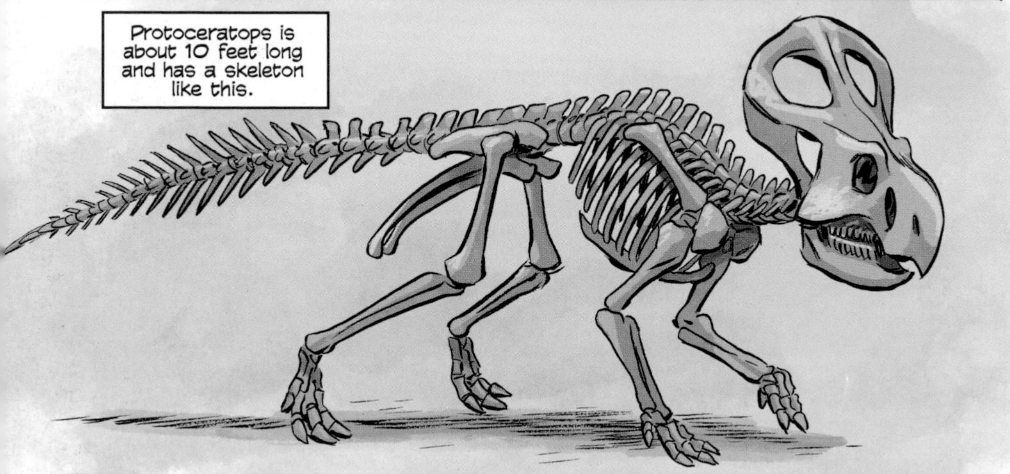
Protoceratops is about 10 feet long and has a skeleton like this.

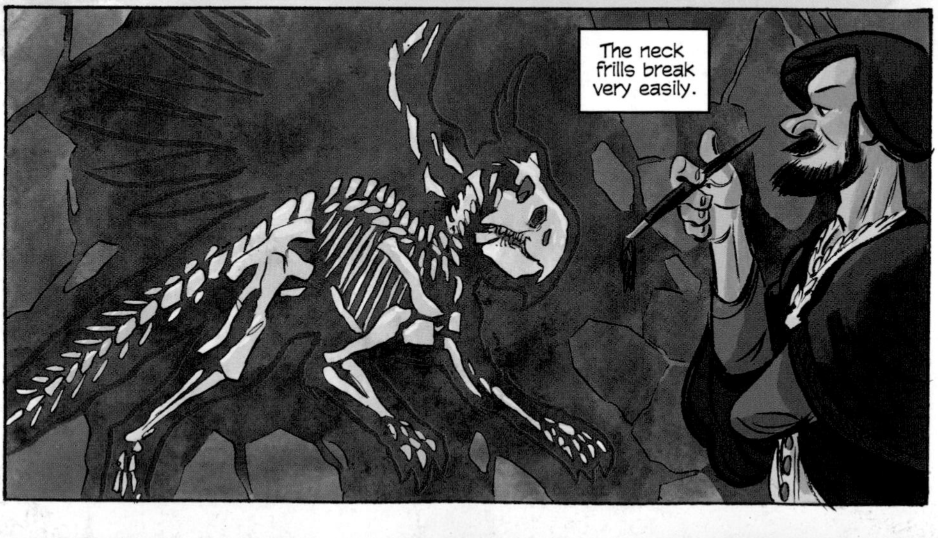
The neck frills break very easily.

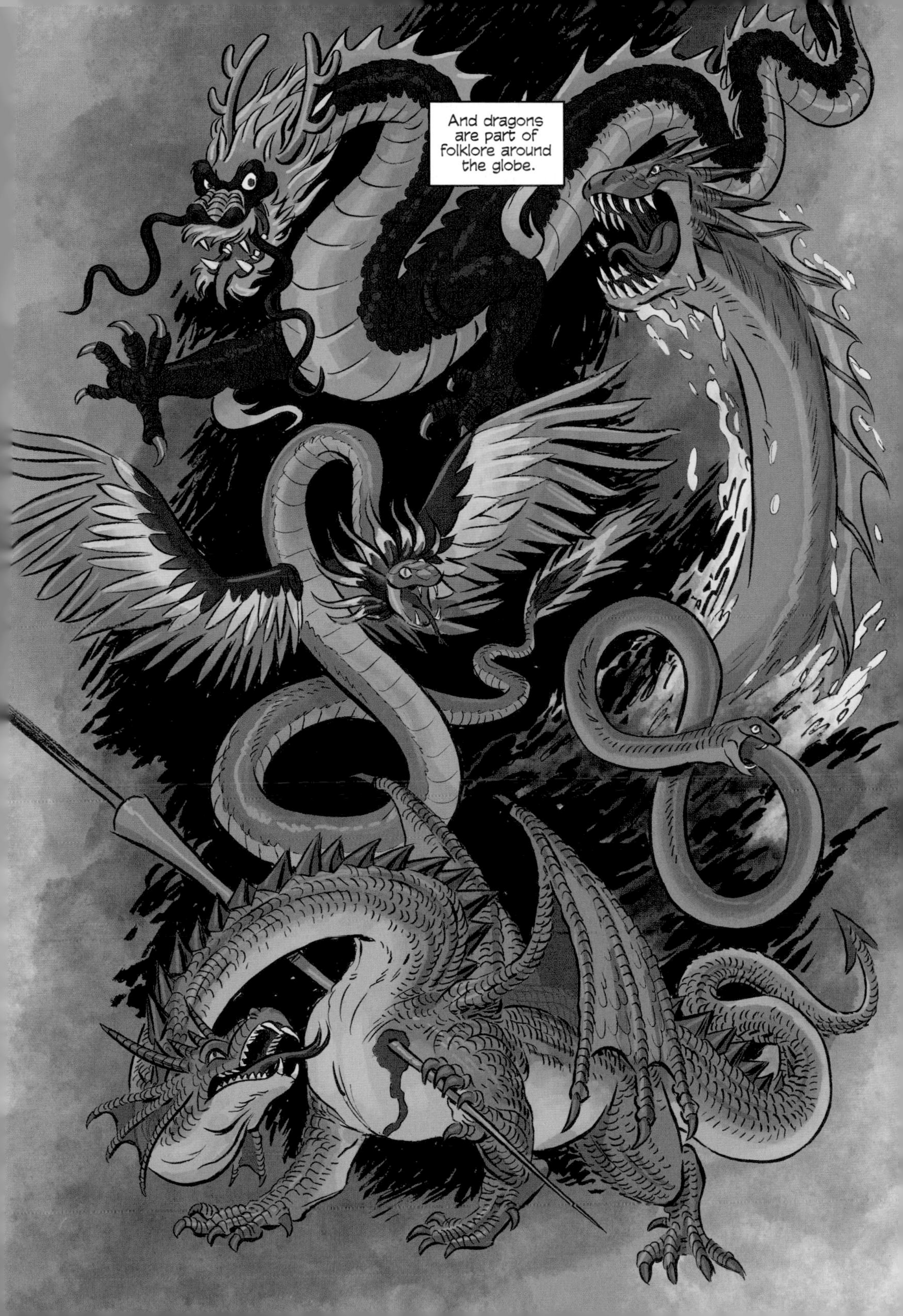
And dragons are part of folklore around the globe.

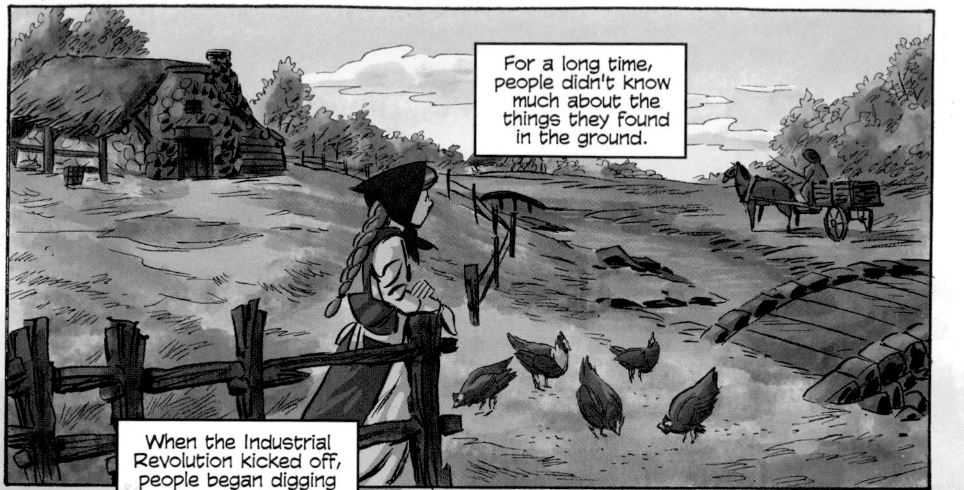
For a long time, people didn't know much about the things they found in the ground.
When the Industrial Revolution kicked off, people began digging more things out of the earth.

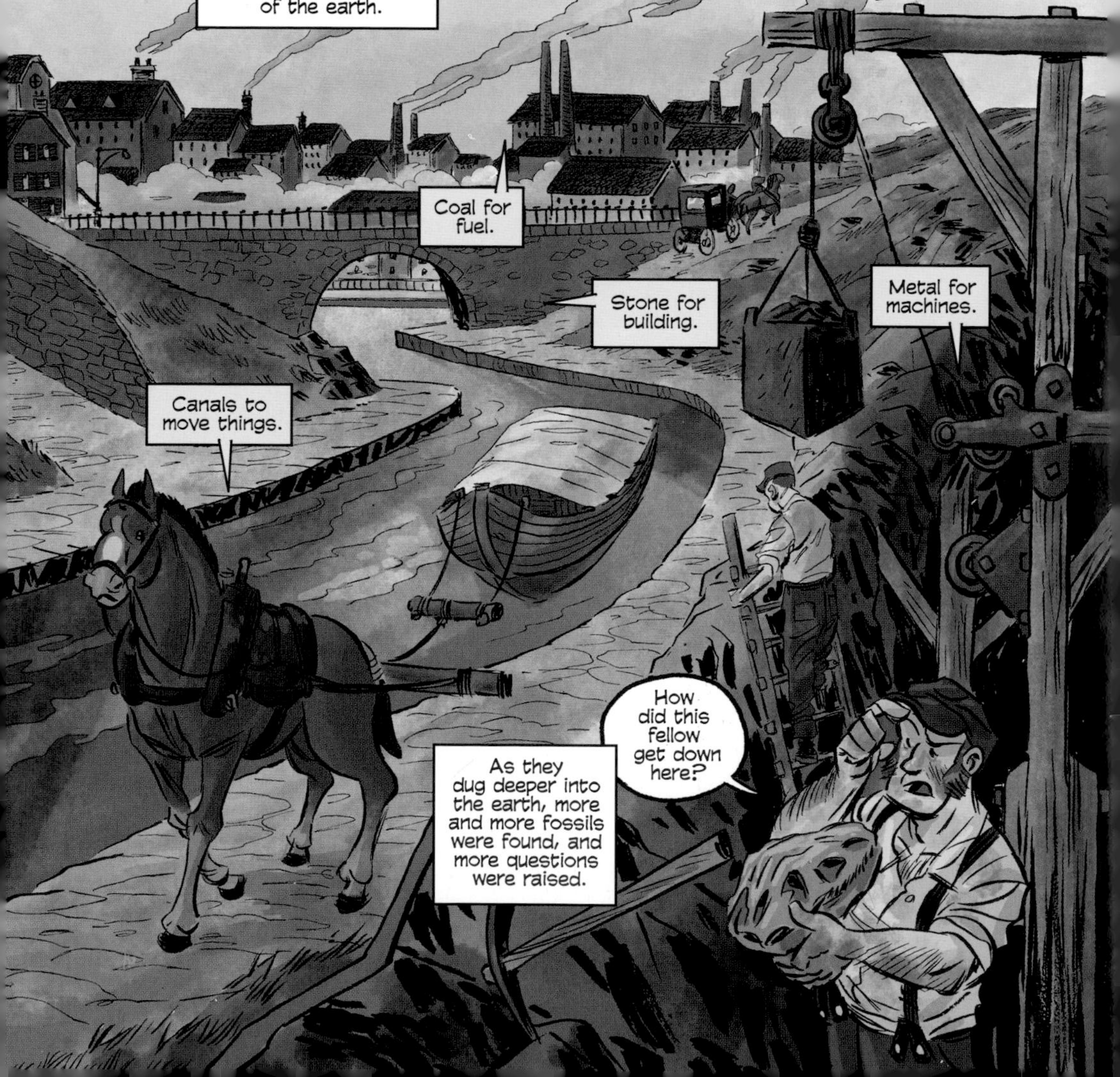
Coal for fuel.
Stone for building.
Metal for machines.
Canals to move things.
As they dug deeper into the earth, more and more fossils were found, and more questions were raised.
How did this fellow get down here?

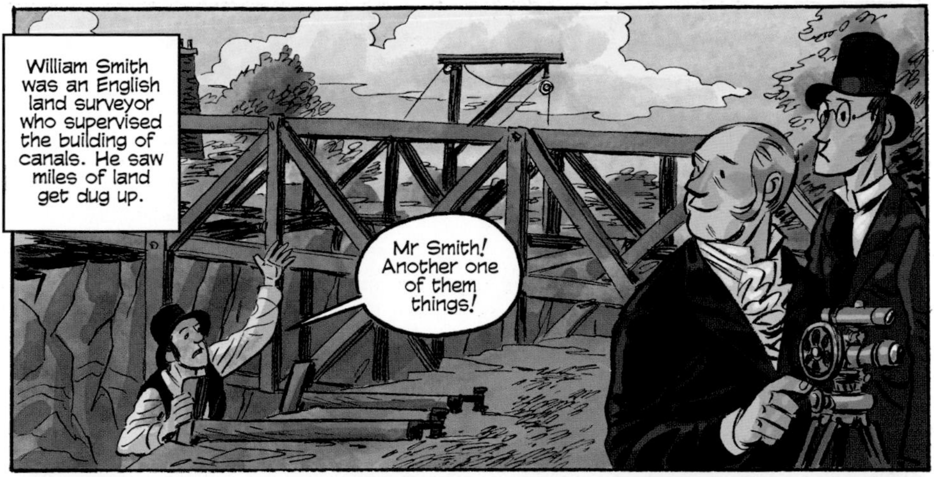
William Smith was an English land surveyor who supervised the building of canals. He saw miles of land get dug up.
Mr Smith! Another one of them things!

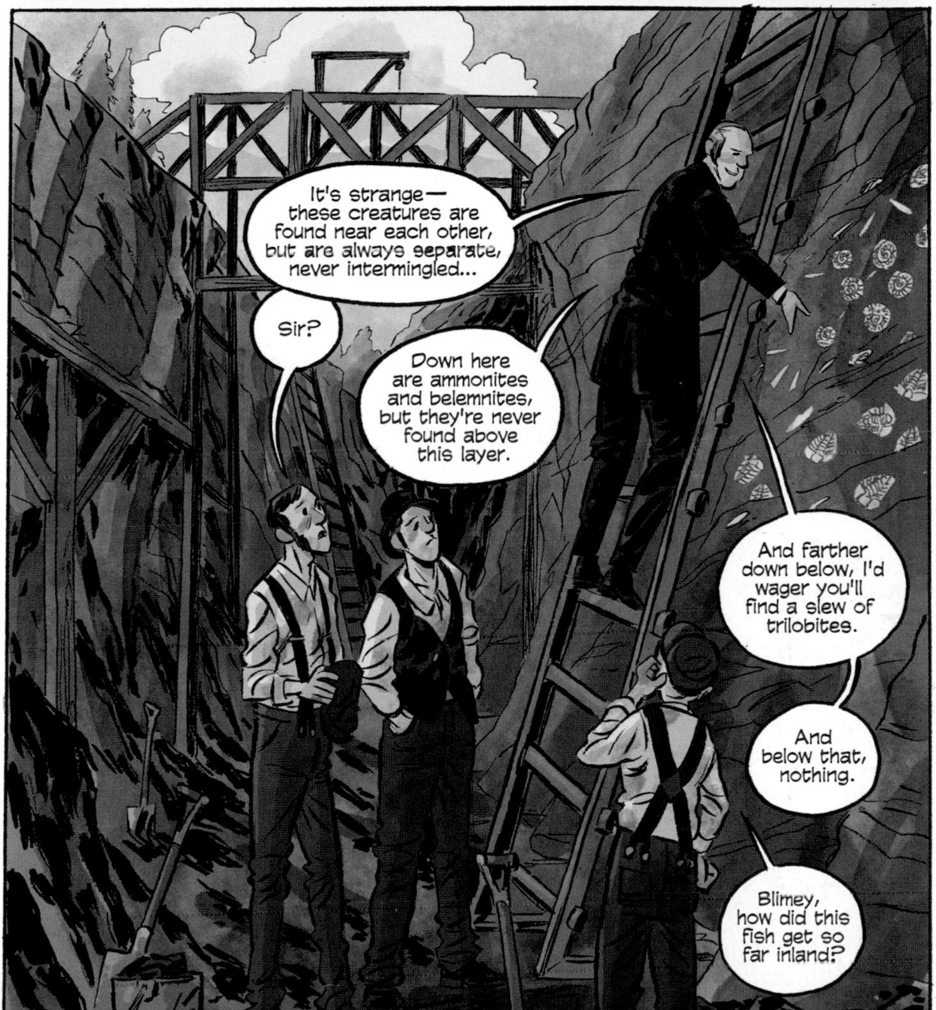
It's strange— these creatures are found near each other, but are always separate, never intermingled...
Sir?
Down here are ammonites and belemnites, but they're never found above this layer.
And farther down below, I'd wager you'll find a slew of trilobites.
And below that, nothing.
Blimey, how did this fish get so far inland?

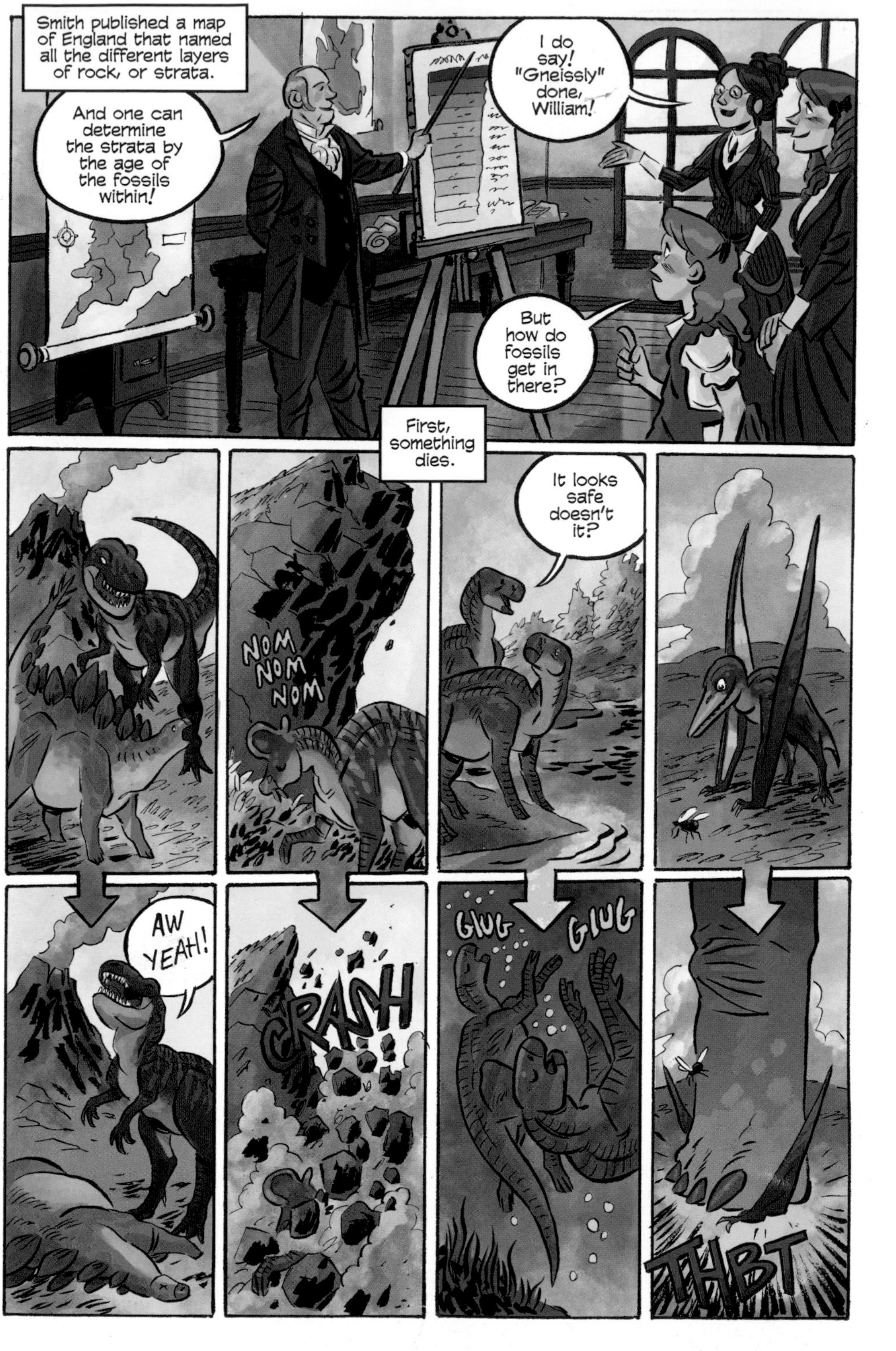
Smith published a map of England that named all the different layers of rock, or strata.
And one can determine the strata by the age of the fossils within!
I do say! "Gneissly" done, William!
But how do fossils get in there?
First, something dies.
NOM NOM NOM
It looks safe doesn't it?
AW YEAH!
CRASH
GLUG GLUG
THBT

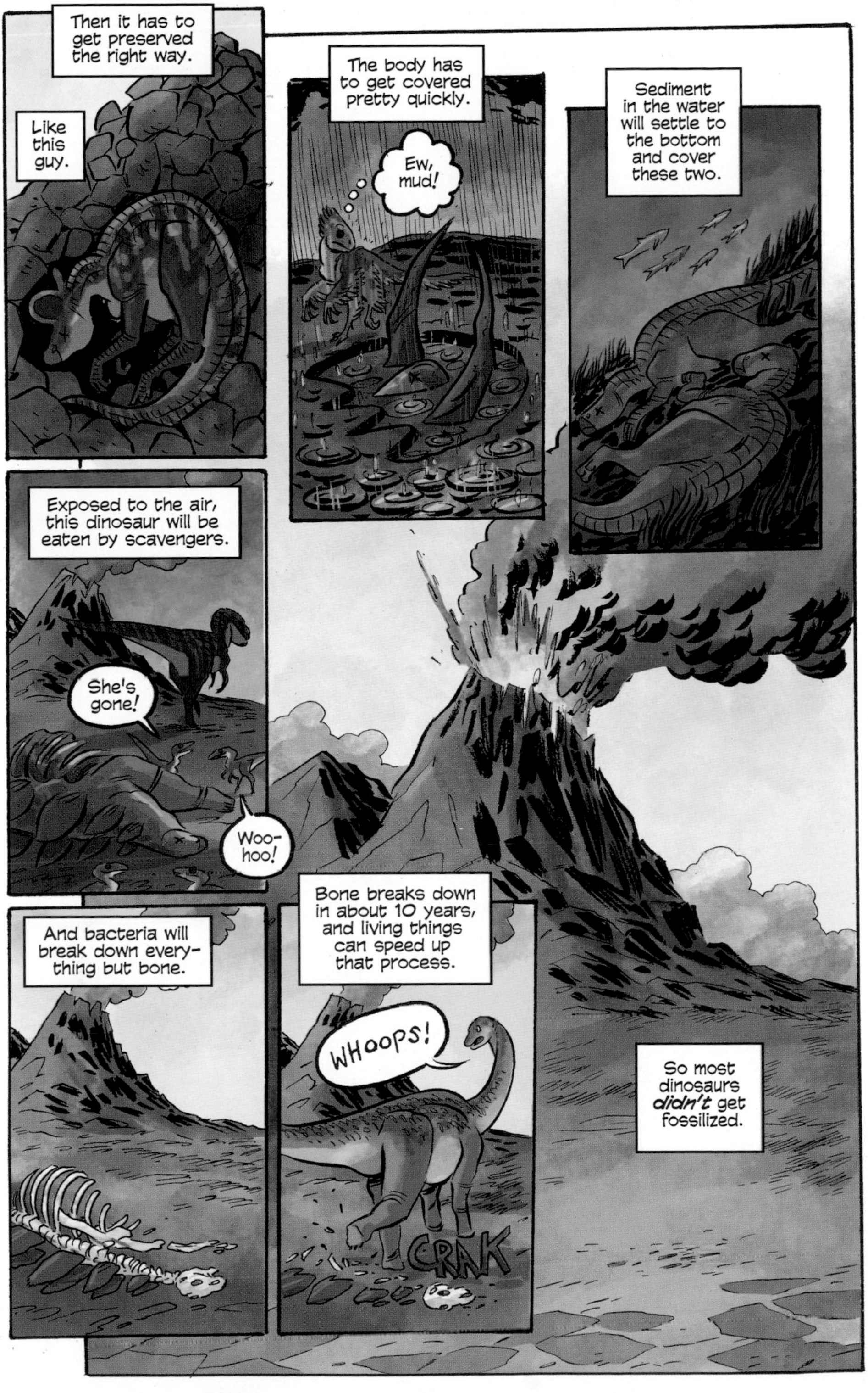
Then it has to get preserved the right way.
Like this guy.
The body has to get covered pretty quickly.
Ew, mud!
Sediment in the water will settle to the bottom and cover these two.
Exposed to the air, this dinosaur will be eaten by scavengers.
She's gone!
Woo-hoo!
And bacteria will break down every-thing but bone.
Bone breaks down in about 10 years, and living things can speed up that process.
WHOOPS!
CRAK
So most dinosaurs *didn't* get fossilized.

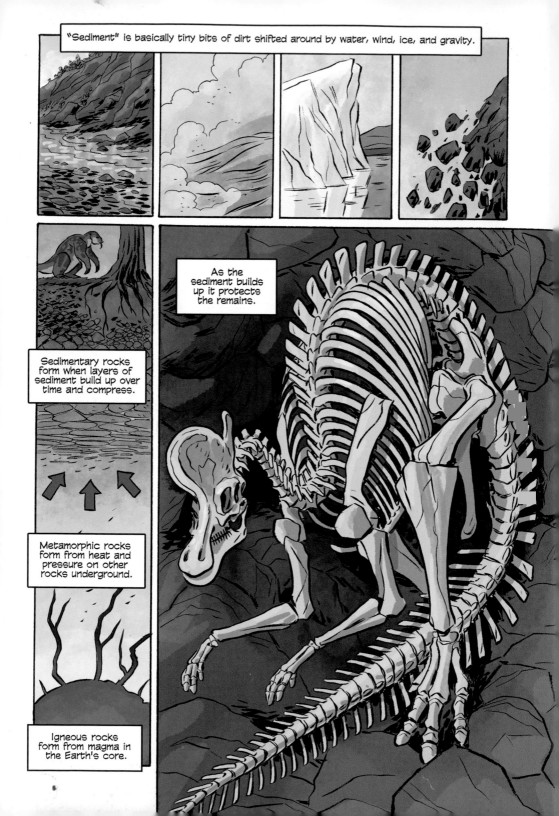

"Sediment" is basically tiny bits of dirt shifted around by water, wind, ice, and gravity.

As the sediment builds up it protects the remains.

Sedimentary rocks form when layers of sediment build up over time and compress.

Metamorphic rocks form from heat and pressure on other rocks underground.

Igneous rocks form from magma in the Earth's core.

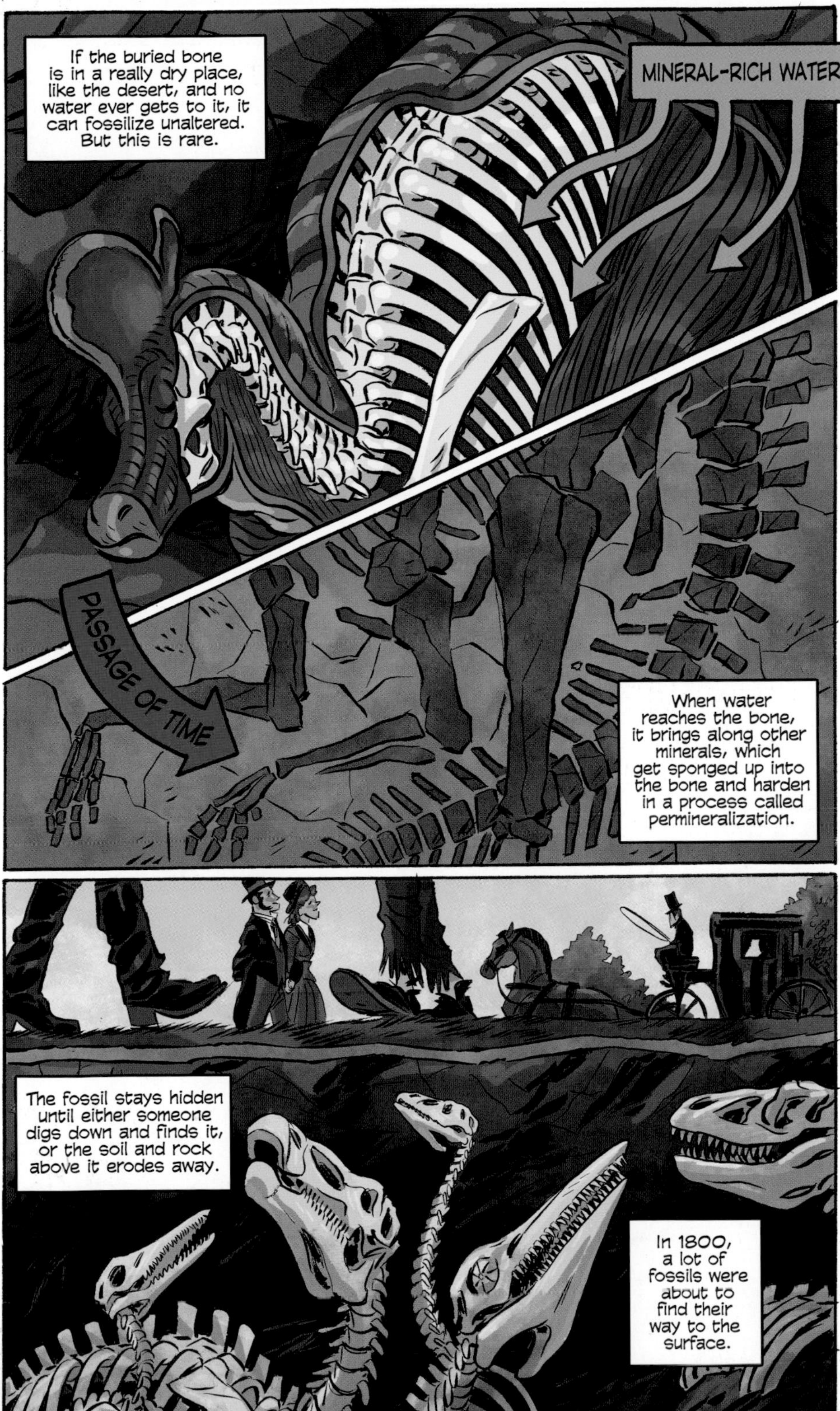
If the buried bone is in a really dry place, like the desert, and no water ever gets to it, it can fossilize unaltered. But this is rare.
MINERAL-RICH WATER
PASSAGE OF TIME
When water reaches the bone, it brings along other minerals, which get sponged up into the bone and harden in a process called permineralization.
The fossil stays hidden until either someone digs down and finds it, or the soil and rock above it erodes away.
In 1800, a lot of fossils were about to find their way to the surface.

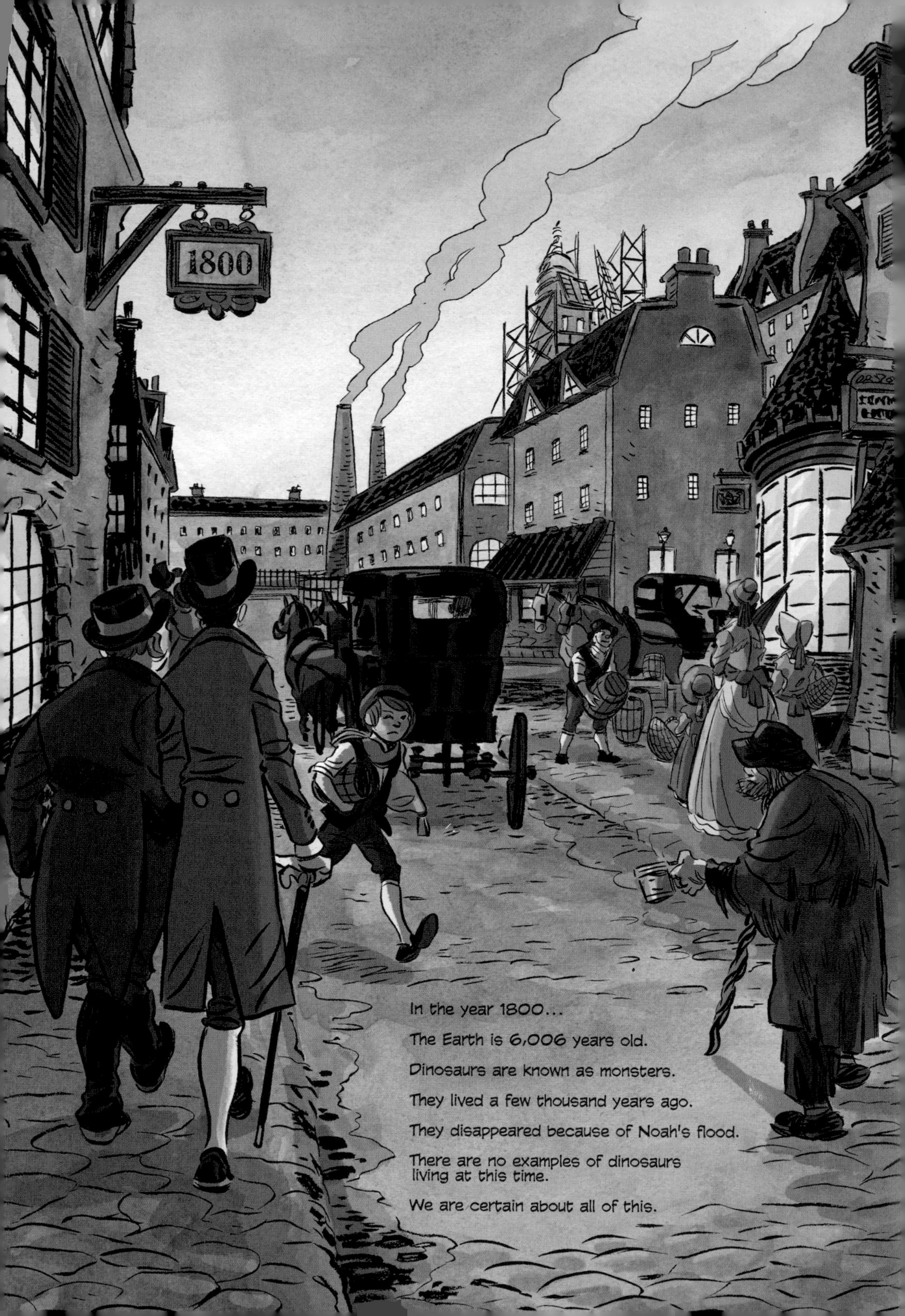
1800
In the year 1800...
The Earth is 6,006 years old.
Dinosaurs are known as monsters.
They lived a few thousand years ago.
They disappeared because of Noah's flood.
There are no examples of dinosaurs living at this time.
We are certain about all of this.

HOW DO I GET TO NAME A DINOSAUR?

1. Become a paleontologist,* then discover a new species and write about it.

2. Win a contest! In 2005, the Children's Museum of Indianapolis held a contest to name what became "*Dracorex hogwartsia*," which means the "Dragon King of Hogwarts."

*Amateurs can also find and study fossils, but you do have to know all the technical terms for everything and write a scientific paper.

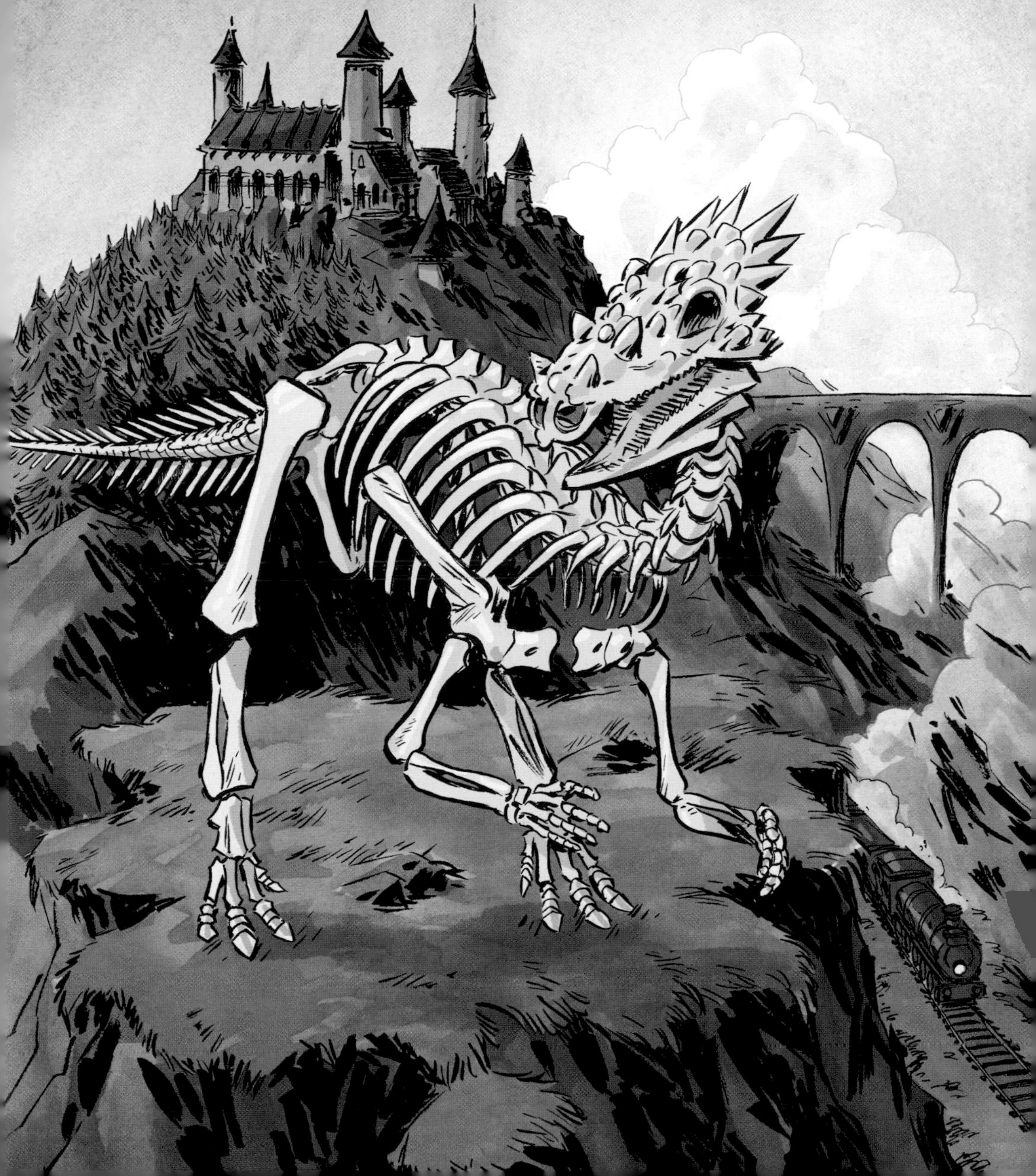

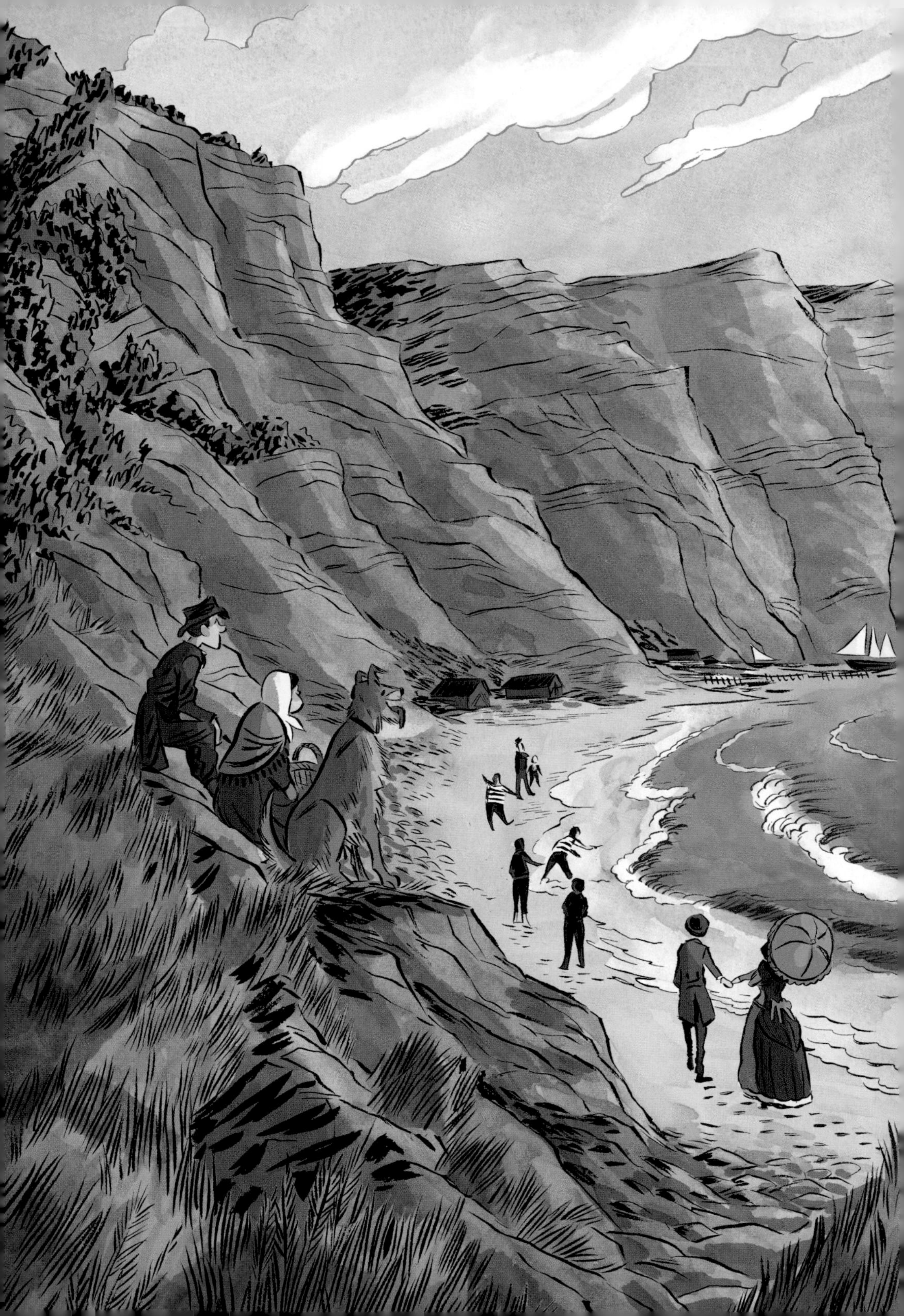

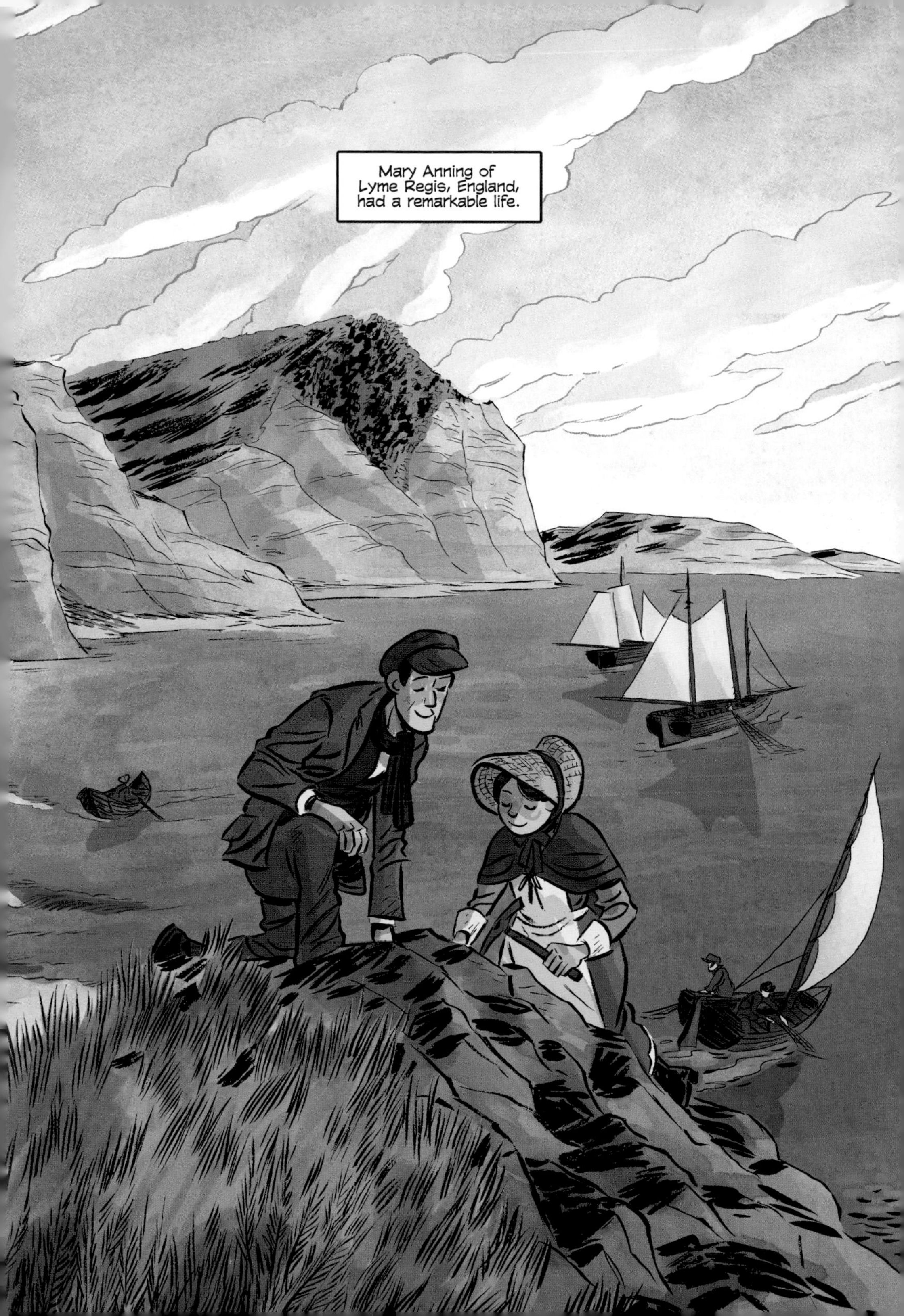
Mary Anning of
Lyme Regis, England,
had a remarkable life.

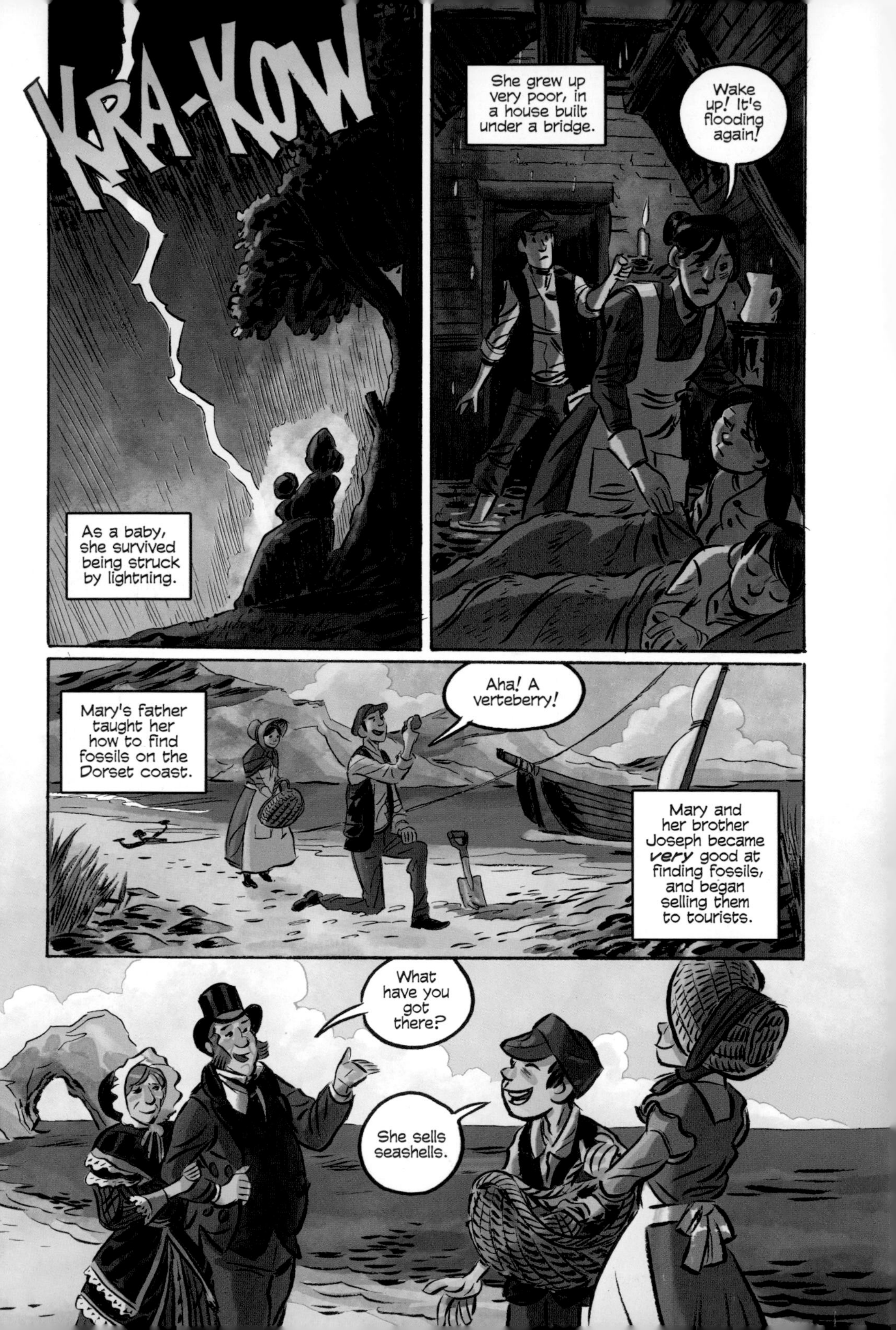
KRA-KOW
As a baby, she survived being struck by lightning.
She grew up very poor, in a house built under a bridge.
Wake up! It's flooding again!
Mary's father taught her how to find fossils on the Dorset coast.
Aha! A verteberry!
Mary and her brother Joseph became *very* good at finding fossils, and began selling them to tourists.
What have you got there?
She sells seashells.

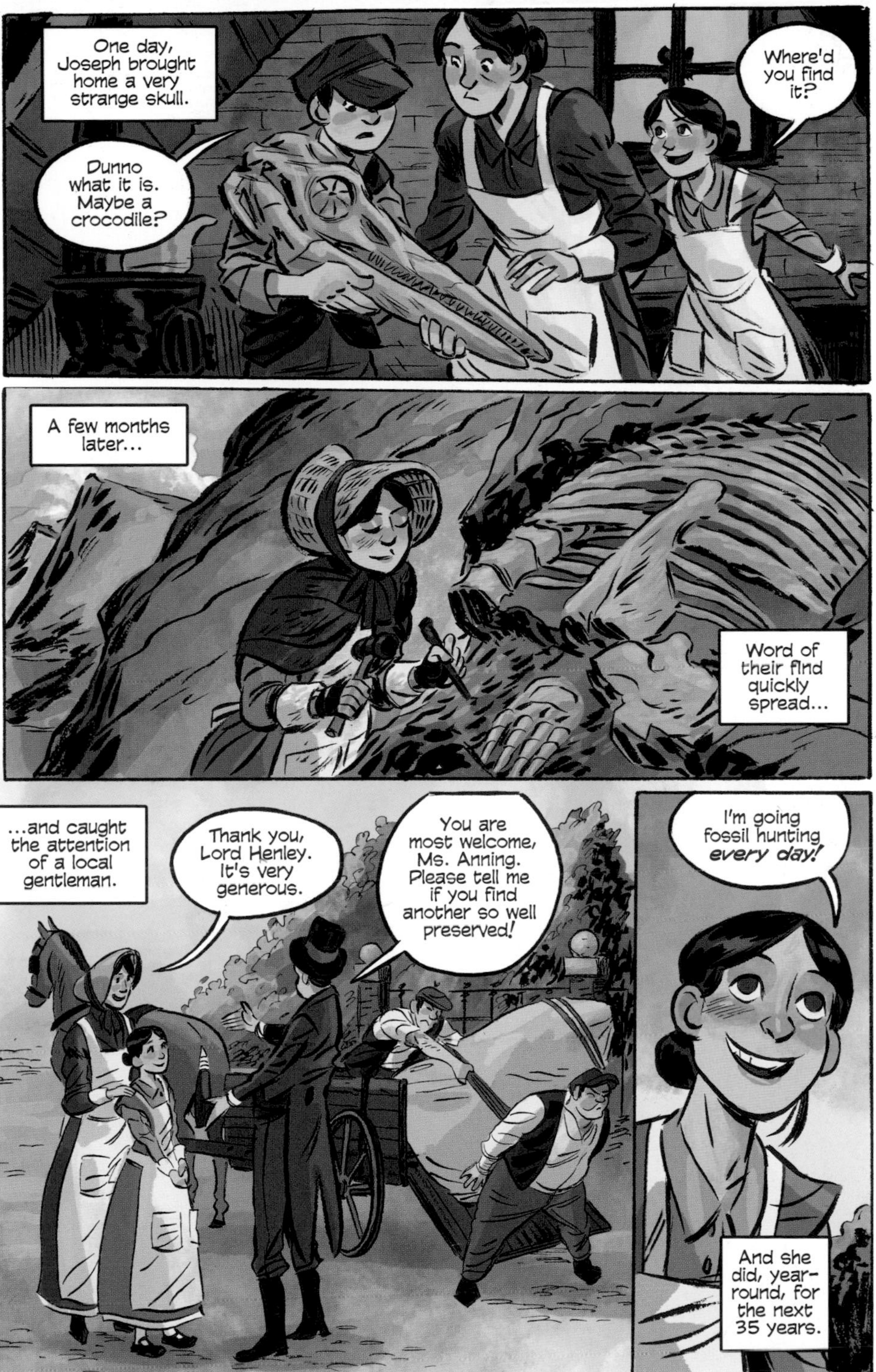
One day, Joseph brought home a very strange skull.
Dunno what it is. Maybe a crocodile?
Where'd you find it?
A few months later...
Word of their find quickly spread...
...and caught the attention of a local gentleman.
Thank you, Lord Henley. It's very generous.
You are most welcome, Ms. Anning. Please tell me if you find another so well preserved!
I'm going fossil hunting *every day!*
And she did, year-round, for the next 35 years.

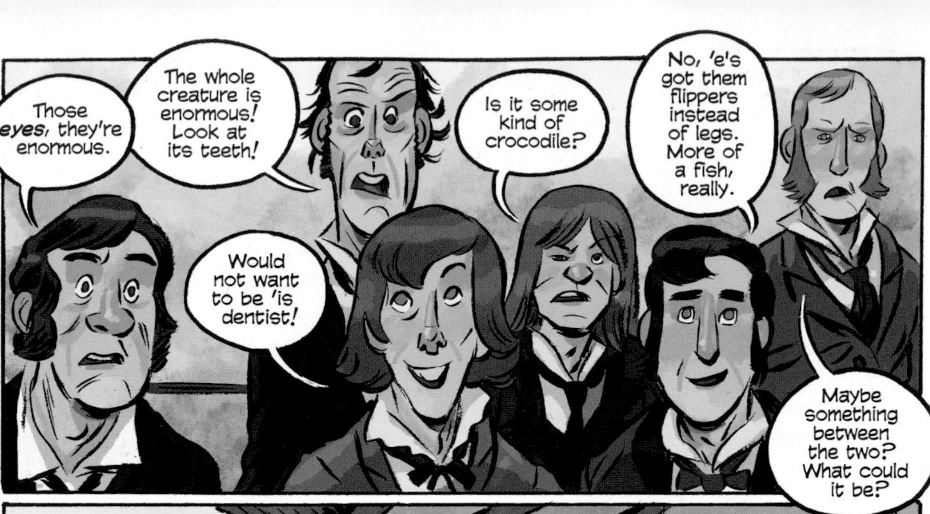
Those *eyes*, they're enormous.
The whole creature is enormous! Look at its teeth!
Would not want to be 'is dentist!
Is it some kind of crocodile?
No, 'e's got them flippers instead of legs. More of a fish, really.
Maybe something between the two? What could it be?

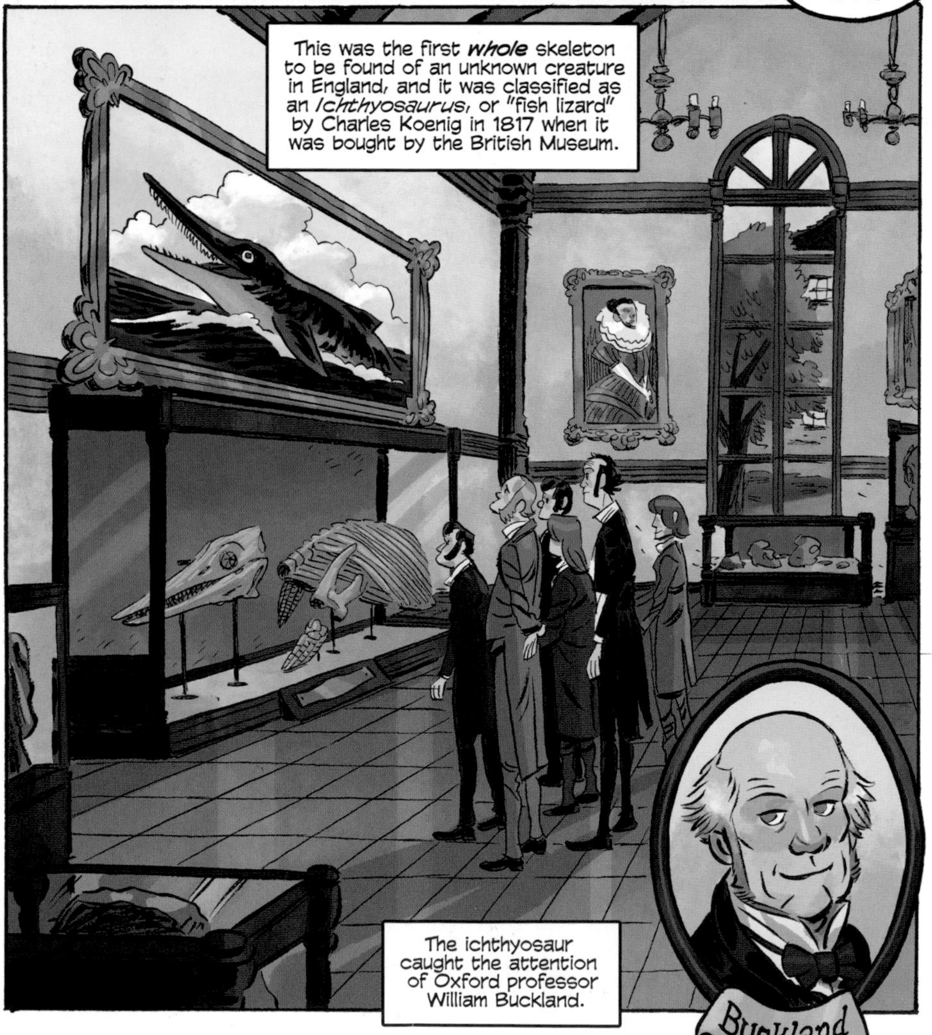
This was the first ***whole*** skeleton to be found of an unknown creature in England, and it was classified as an *Ichthyosaurus*, or "fish lizard" by Charles Koenig in 1817 when it was bought by the British Museum.
The ichthyosaur caught the attention of Oxford professor William Buckland.
Buckland

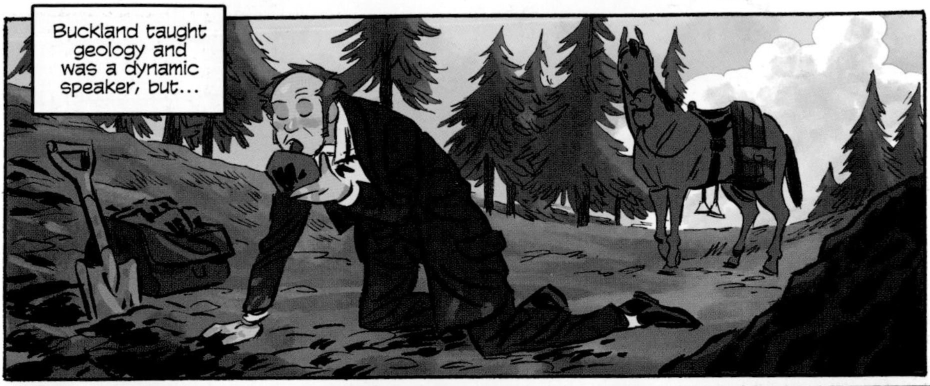
Buckland taught geology and was a dynamic speaker, but...

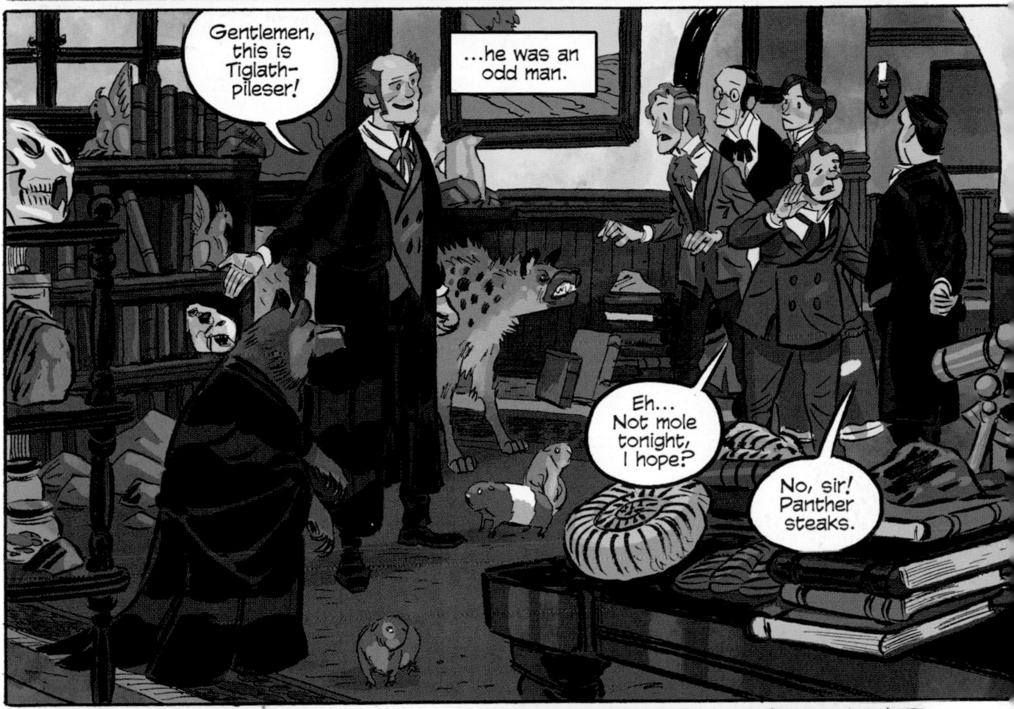
Gentlemen, this is Tiglath-pileser!
...he was an odd man.
Eh... Not mole tonight, I hope?
No, sir! Panther steaks.

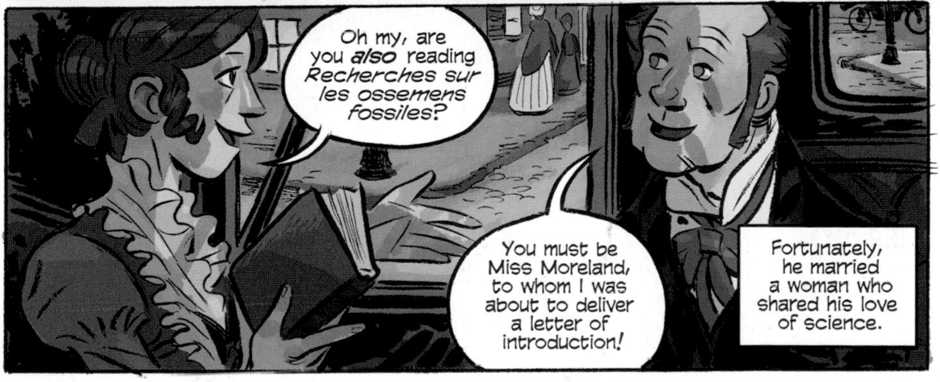
Oh my, are you *also* reading *Recherches sur les ossemens fossiles?*
You must be Miss Moreland, to whom I was about to deliver a letter of introduction!
Fortunately, he married a woman who shared his love of science.

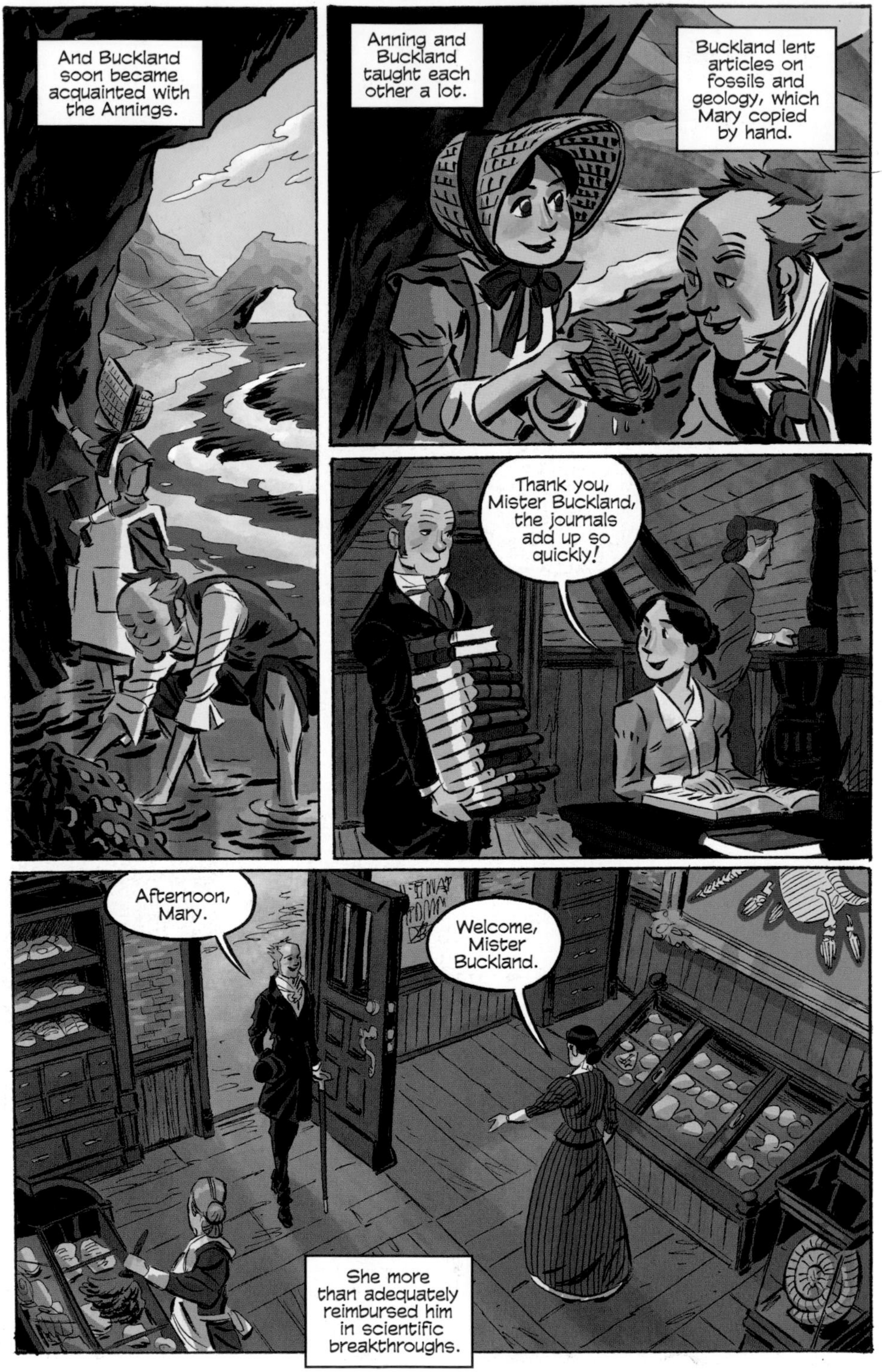

And Buckland soon became acquainted with the Annings.
Anning and Buckland taught each other a lot.
Buckland lent articles on fossils and geology, which Mary copied by hand.
Thank you, Mister Buckland, the journals add up so quickly!
Afternoon, Mary.
Welcome, Mister Buckland.
She more than adequately reimbursed him in scientific breakthroughs.

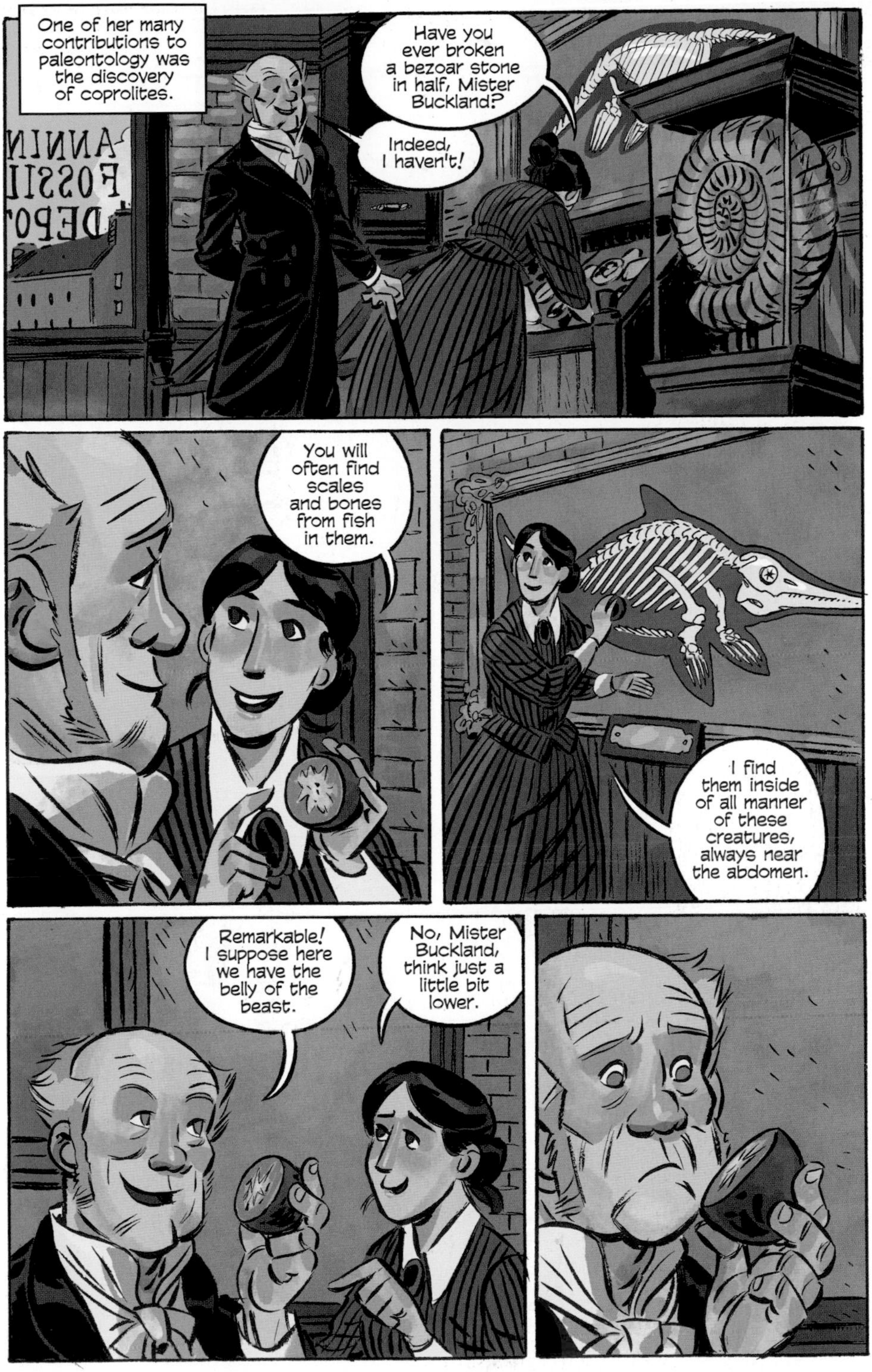
One of her many contributions to paleontology was the discovery of coprolites.
Have you ever broken a bezoar stone in half, Mister Buckland?
Indeed, I haven't!
ANNING FOSSIL DEPOT
You will often find scales and bones from fish in them.
I find them inside of all manner of these creatures, always near the abdomen.
Remarkable! I suppose here we have the belly of the beast.
No, Mister Buckland, think just a little bit lower.

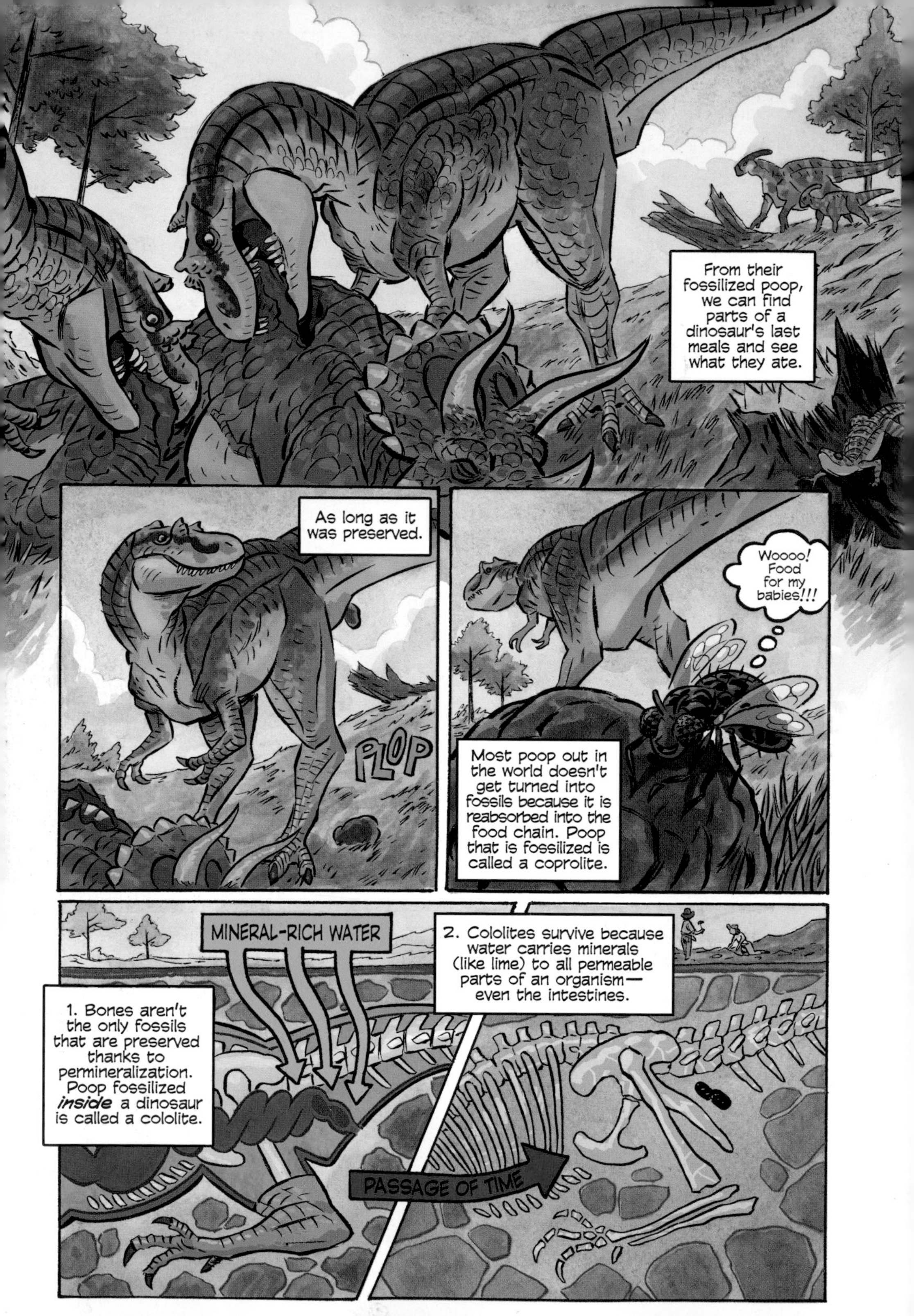
From their fossilized poop, we can find parts of a dinosaur's last meals and see what they ate.
As long as it was preserved.
PLOP
Woooo! Food for my babies!!!
Most poop out in the world doesn't get turned into fossils because it is reabsorbed into the food chain. Poop that is fossilized is called a coprolite.
MINERAL-RICH WATER
1. Bones aren't the only fossils that are preserved thanks to permineralization. Poop fossilized *inside* a dinosaur is called a cololite.
2. Cololites survive because water carries minerals (like lime) to all permeable parts of an organism— even the intestines.
PASSAGE OF TIME

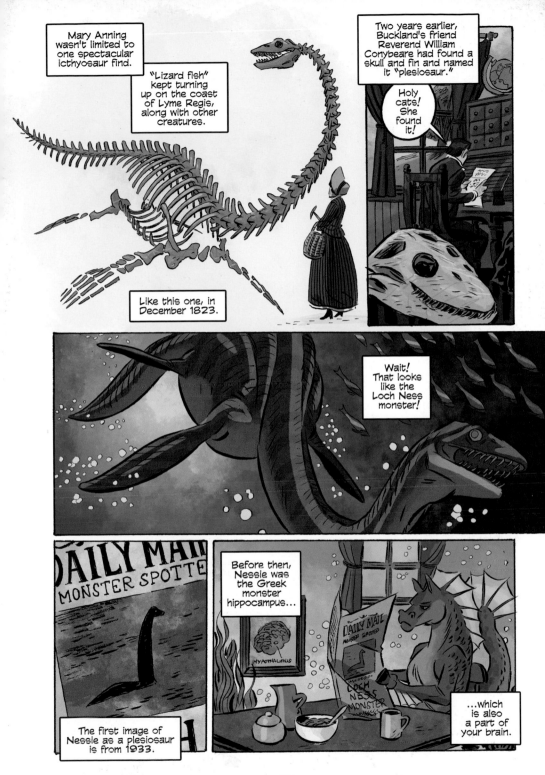

Mary Anning wasn't limited to one spectacular icthyosaur find.

"Lizard fish" kept turning up on the coast of Lyme Regis, along with other creatures.

Like this one, in December 1823.

Two years earlier, Buckland's friend Reverend William Conybeare had found a skull and fin and named it "plesiosaur."

Holy cats! She found it!

Wait! That looks like the Loch Ness monster!

DAILY MAIL
MONSTER SPOTTE

The first image of Nessie as a plesiosaur is from 1933.

Before then, Nessie was the Greek monster hippocampus...

HYPOTHALIMUS

DAILY MAIL
MONSTER SPOTTED

LOCH NESS MONSTER

...which is also a part of your brain.

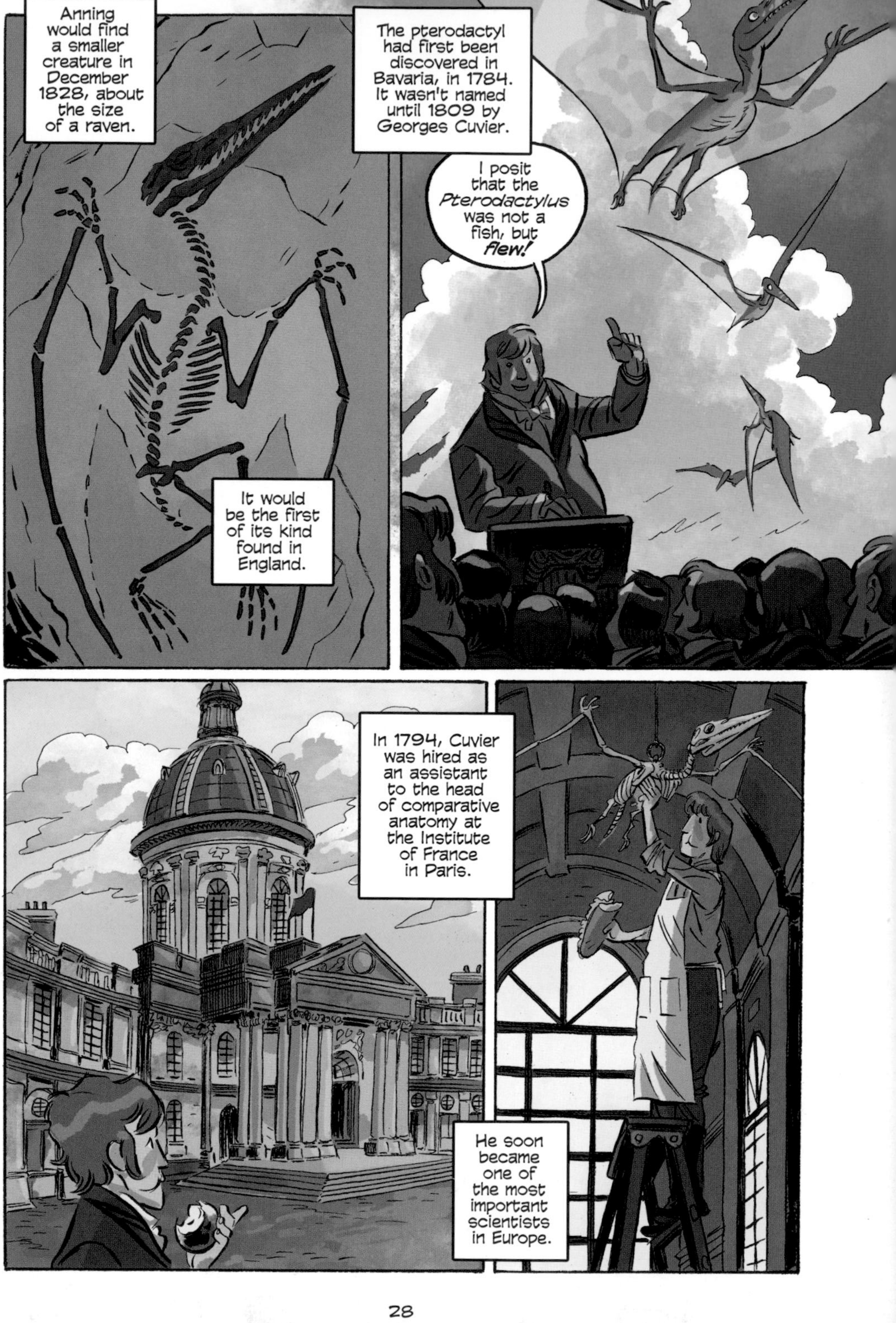
Anning would find a smaller creature in December 1828, about the size of a raven.
It would be the first of its kind found in England.
The pterodactyl had first been discovered in Bavaria, in 1784. It wasn't named until 1809 by Georges Cuvier.
I posit that the *Pterodactylus* was not a fish, but ***flew!***
In 1794, Cuvier was hired as an assistant to the head of comparative anatomy at the Institute of France in Paris.
He soon became one of the most important scientists in Europe.

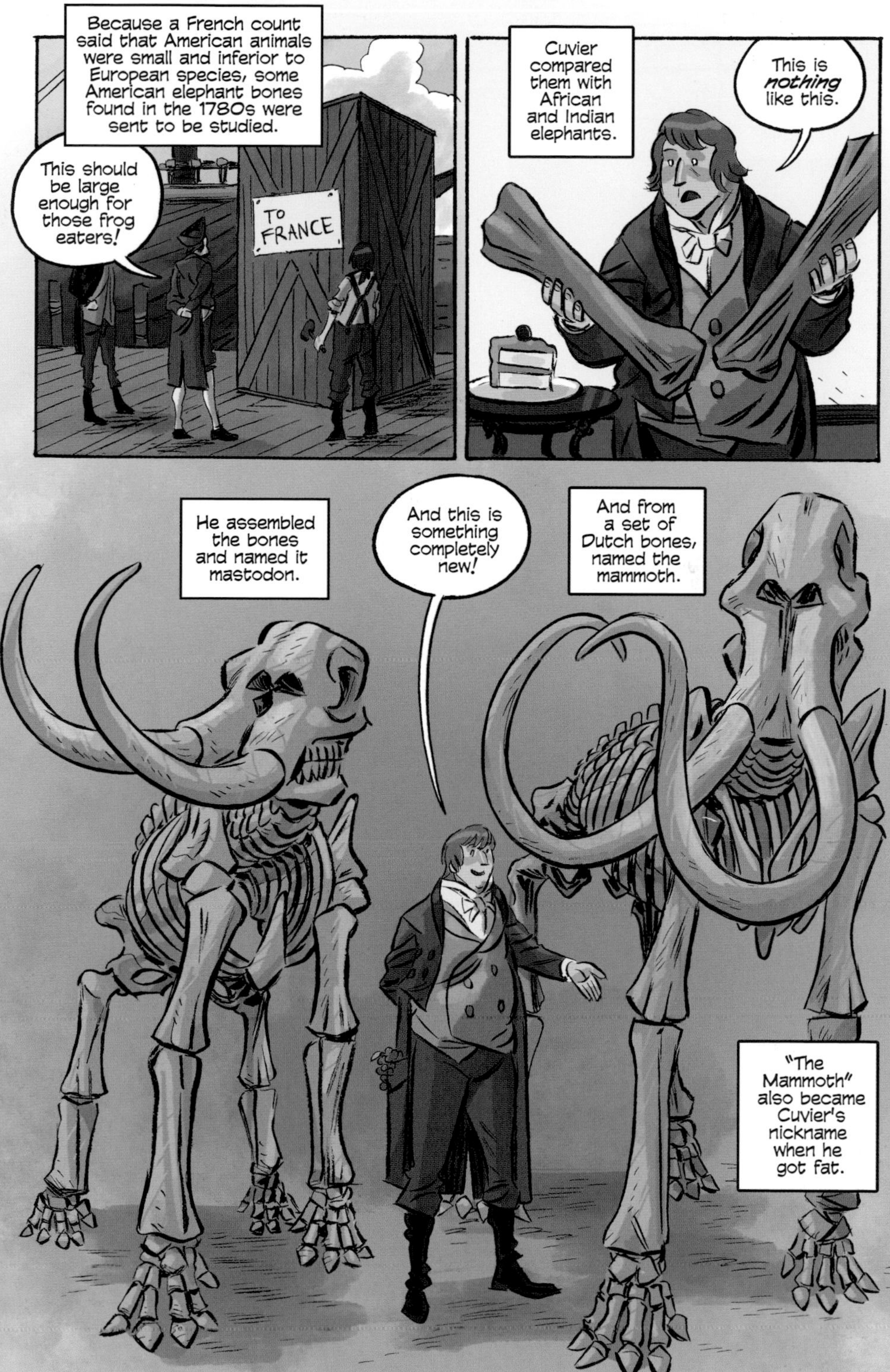

Because a French count said that American animals were small and inferior to European species, some American elephant bones found in the 1780s were sent to be studied.
This should be large enough for those frog eaters!
TO FRANCE
Cuvier compared them with African and Indian elephants.
This is *nothing* like this.
He assembled the bones and named it mastodon.
And this is something completely new!
And from a set of Dutch bones, named the mammoth.
"The Mammoth" also became Cuvier's nickname when he got fat.

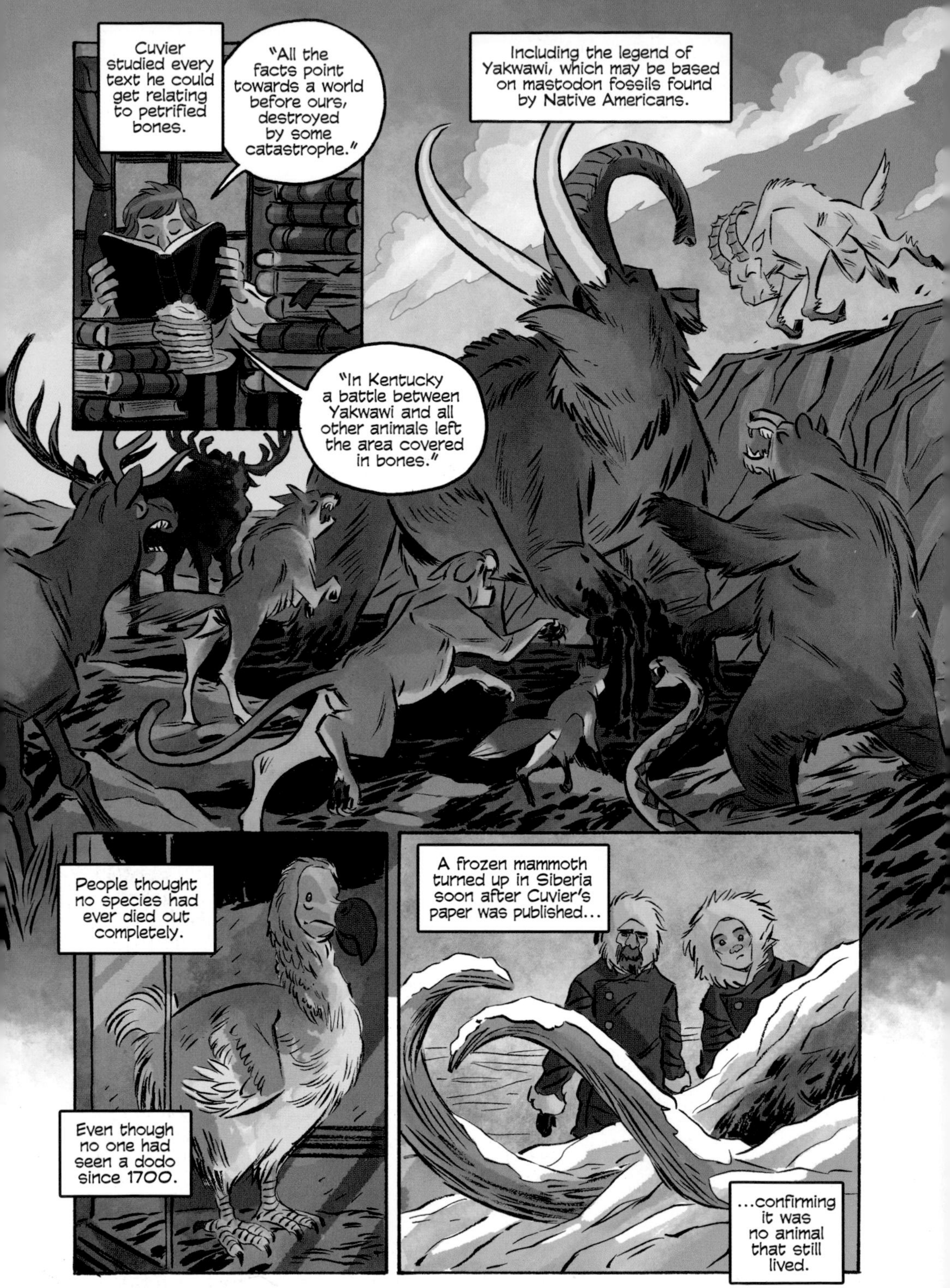
Cuvier studied every text he could get relating to petrified bones.
"All the facts point towards a world before ours, destroyed by some catastrophe."
Including the legend of Yakwawi, which may be based on mastodon fossils found by Native Americans.
"In Kentucky a battle between Yakwawi and all other animals left the area covered in bones."
People thought no species had ever died out completely.
Even though no one had seen a dodo since 1700.
A frozen mammoth turned up in Siberia soon after Cuvier's paper was published...
...confirming it was no animal that still lived.

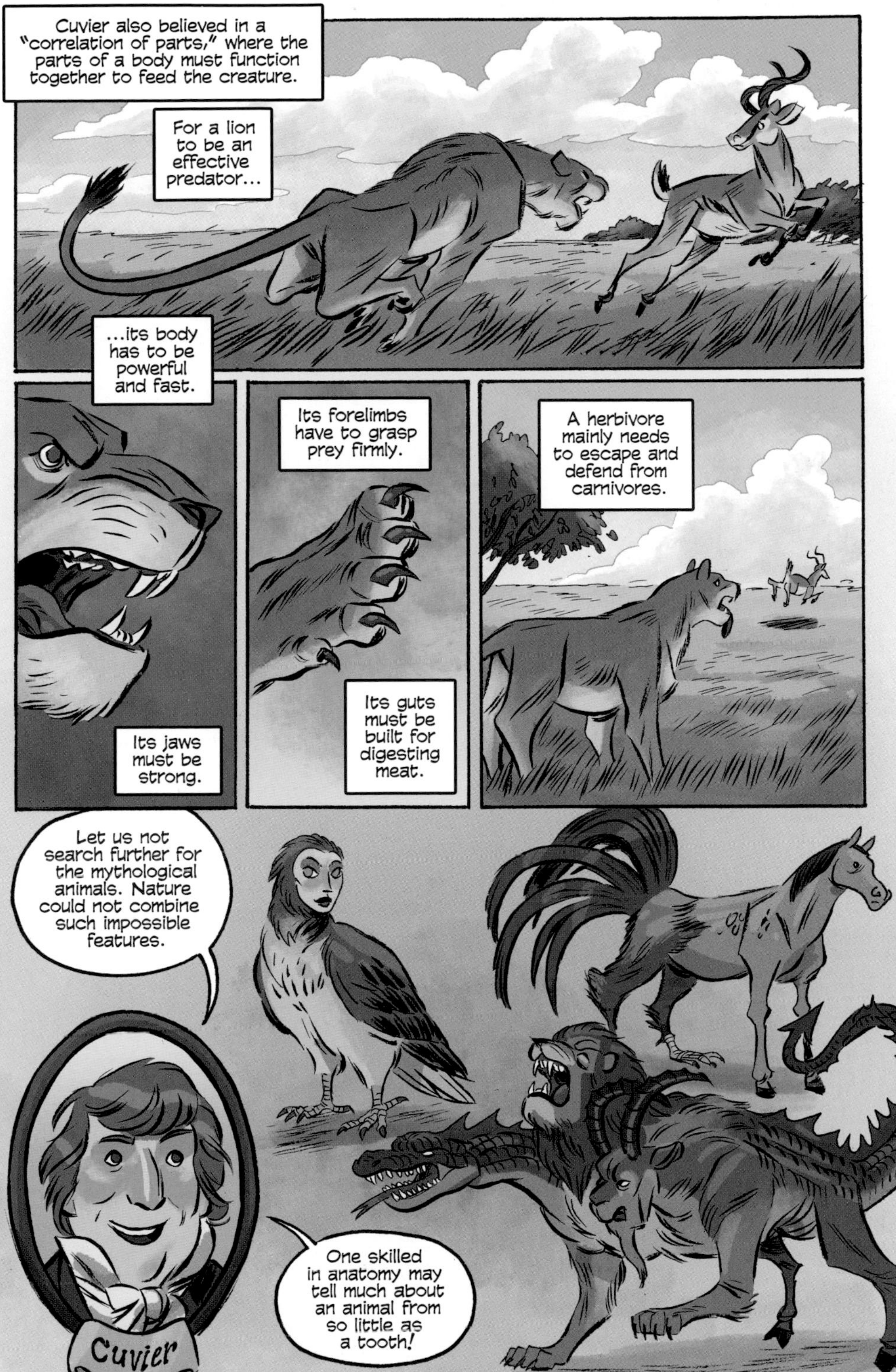
Cuvier also believed in a "correlation of parts," where the parts of a body must function together to feed the creature.
For a lion to be an effective predator...
...its body has to be powerful and fast.
Its jaws must be strong.
Its forelimbs have to grasp prey firmly.
Its guts must be built for digesting meat.
A herbivore mainly needs to escape and defend from carnivores.
Let us not search further for the mythological animals. Nature could not combine such impossible features.
Cuvier
One skilled in anatomy may tell much about an animal from so little as a tooth!

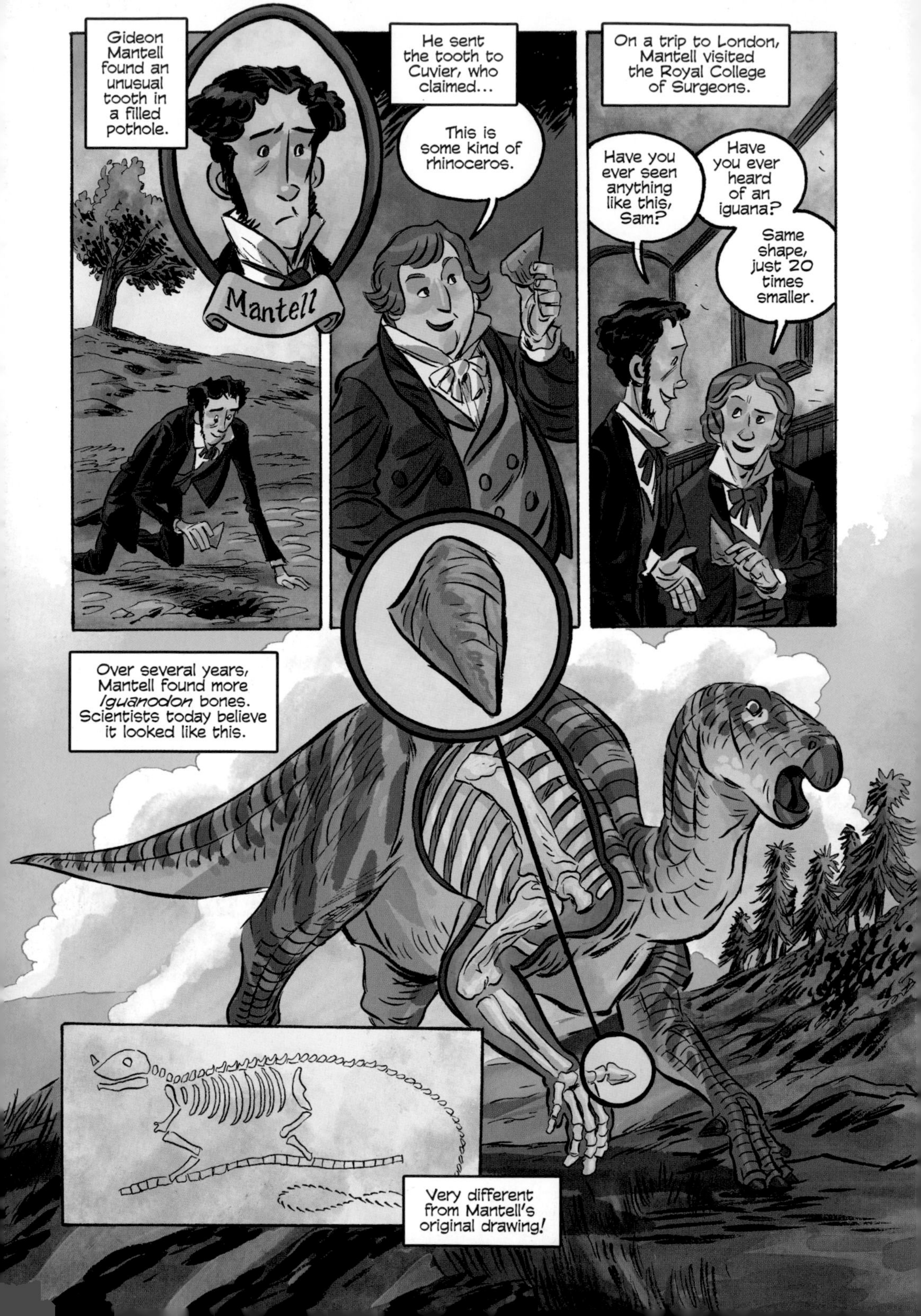
Gideon Mantell found an unusual tooth in a filled pothole.
Mantell
He sent the tooth to Cuvier, who claimed...
This is some kind of rhinoceros.
On a trip to London, Mantell visited the Royal College of Surgeons.
Have you ever seen anything like this, Sam?
Have you ever heard of an iguana?
Same shape, just 20 times smaller.
Over several years, Mantell found more *Iguanodon* bones. Scientists today believe it looked like this.
Very different from Mantell's original drawing!

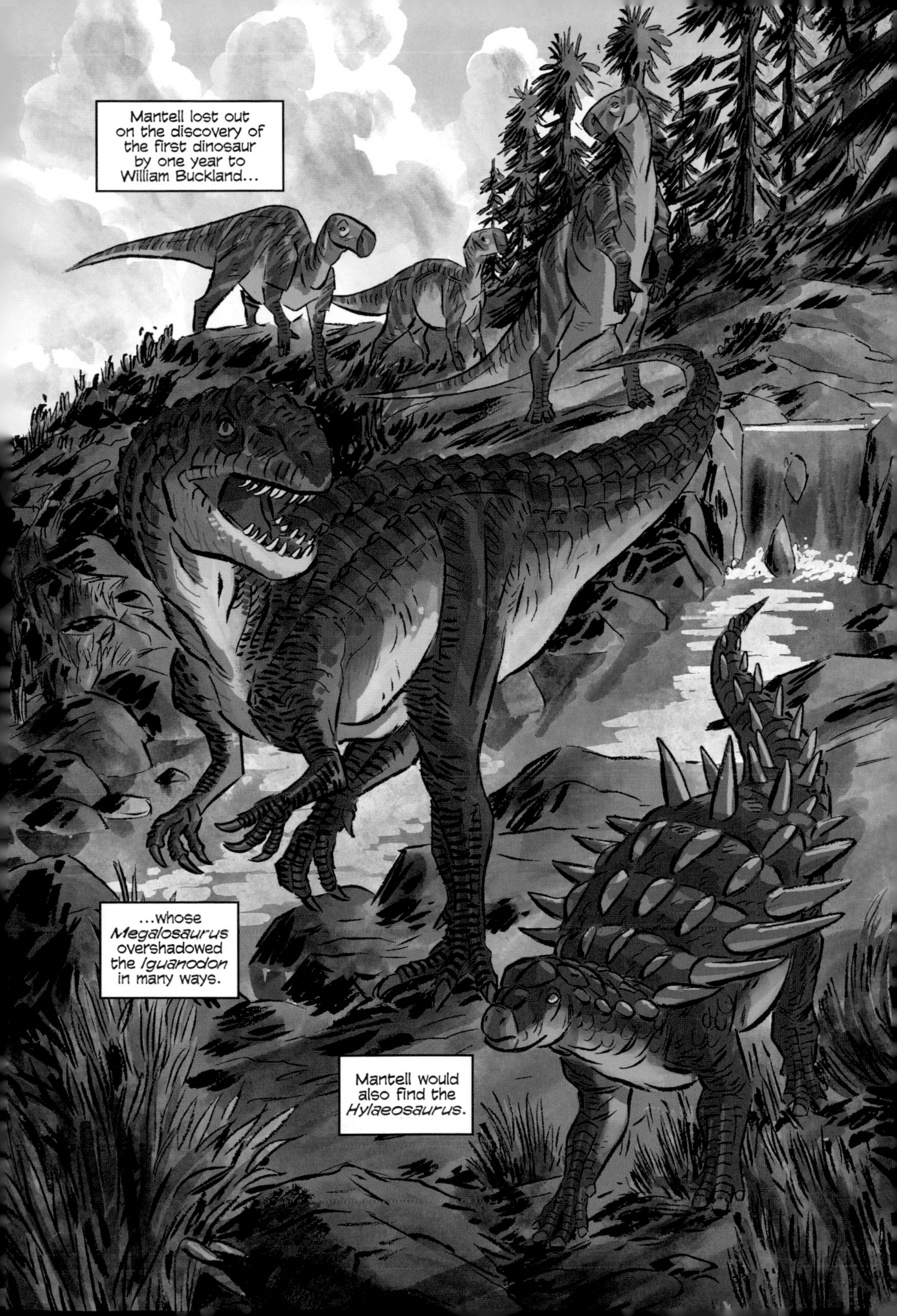

Mantell lost out on the discovery of the first dinosaur by one year to William Buckland...
...whose *Megalosaurus* overshadowed the *Iguanodon* in many ways.
Mantell would also find the *Hylaeosaurus*.

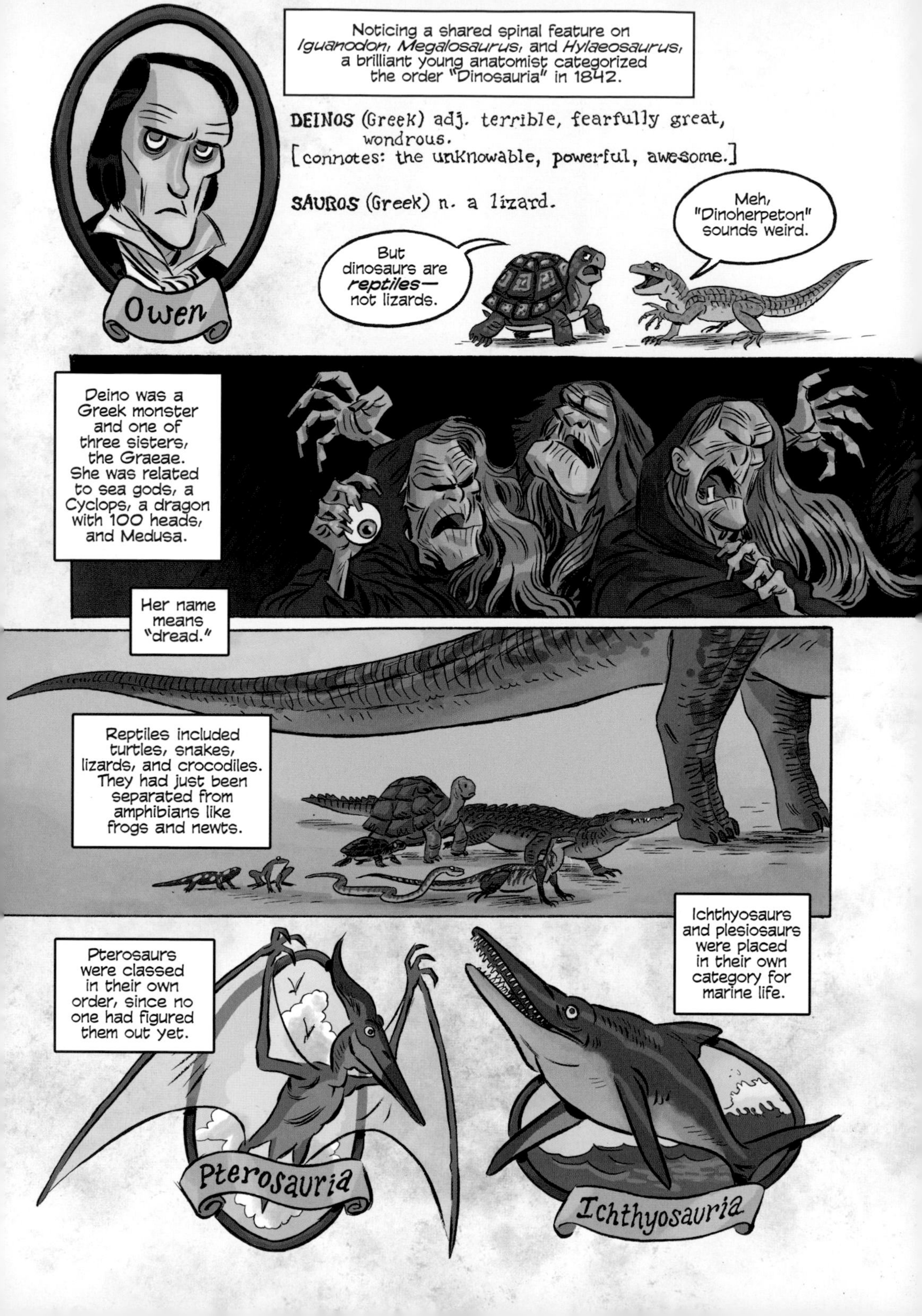
Noticing a shared spinal feature on *Iguanodon*, *Megalosaurus*, and *Hylaeosaurus*, a brilliant young anatomist categorized the order "Dinosauria" in 1842.
DEINOS (Greek) adj. terrible, fearfully great, wondrous.
[connotes: the unknowable, powerful, awesome.]
SAUROS (Greek) n. a lizard.
Owen
But dinosaurs are *reptiles*—not lizards.
Meh, "Dinoherpeton" sounds weird.
Deino was a Greek monster and one of three sisters, the Graeae. She was related to sea gods, a Cyclops, a dragon with 100 heads, and Medusa.
Her name means "dread."
Reptiles included turtles, snakes, lizards, and crocodiles. They had just been separated from amphibians like frogs and newts.
Pterosaurs were classed in their own order, since no one had figured them out yet.
Ichthyosaurs and plesiosaurs were placed in their own category for marine life.
Pterosauria
Ichthyosauria

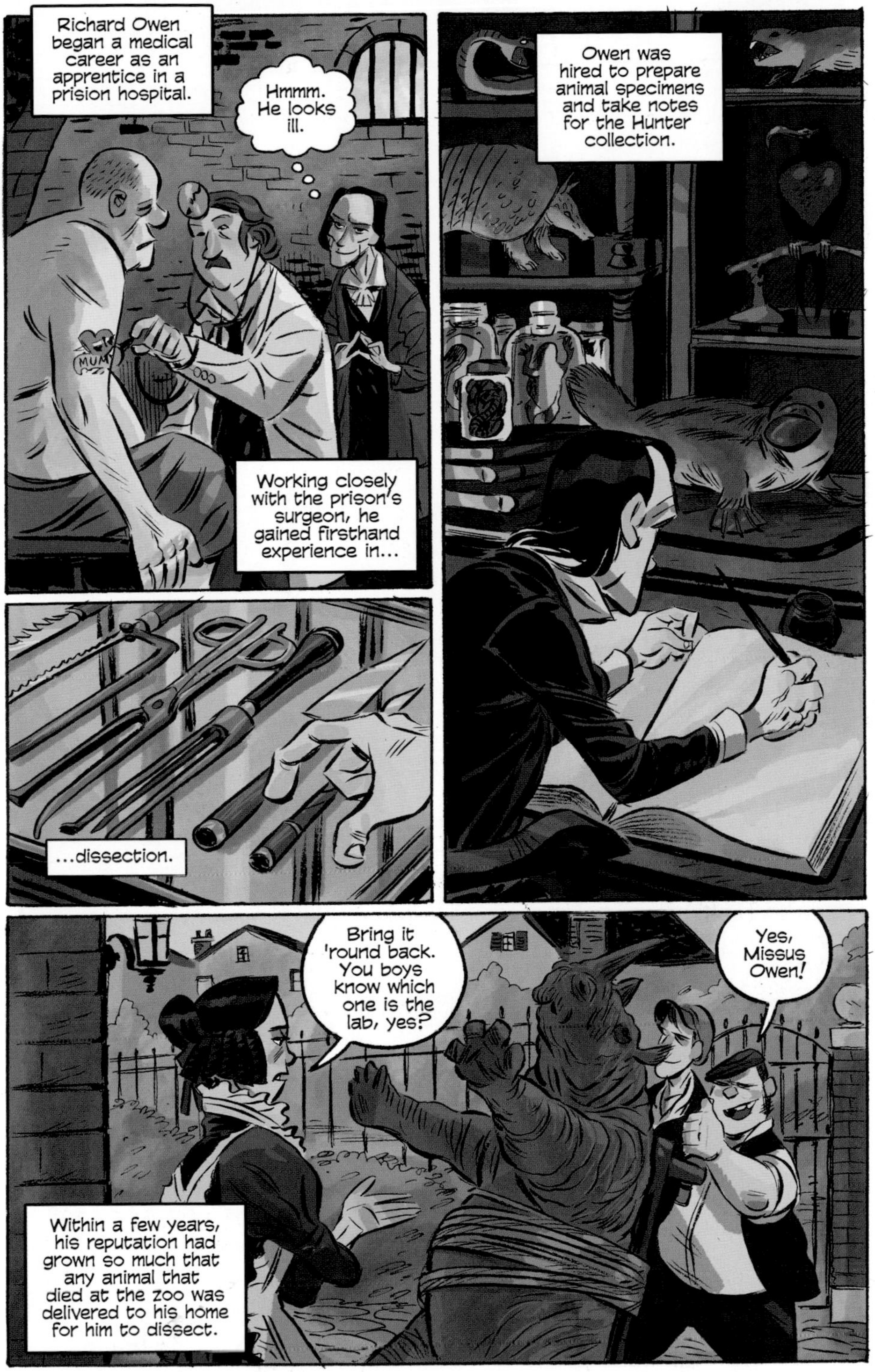
Richard Owen began a medical career as an apprentice in a prision hospital.
Hmmm. He looks ill.
MUM
Working closely with the prison's surgeon, he gained firsthand experience in...
...dissection.
Owen was hired to prepare animal specimens and take notes for the Hunter collection.
Bring it 'round back. You boys know which one is the lab, yes?
Yes, Missus Owen!
Within a few years, his reputation had grown so much that any animal that died at the zoo was delivered to his home for him to dissect.

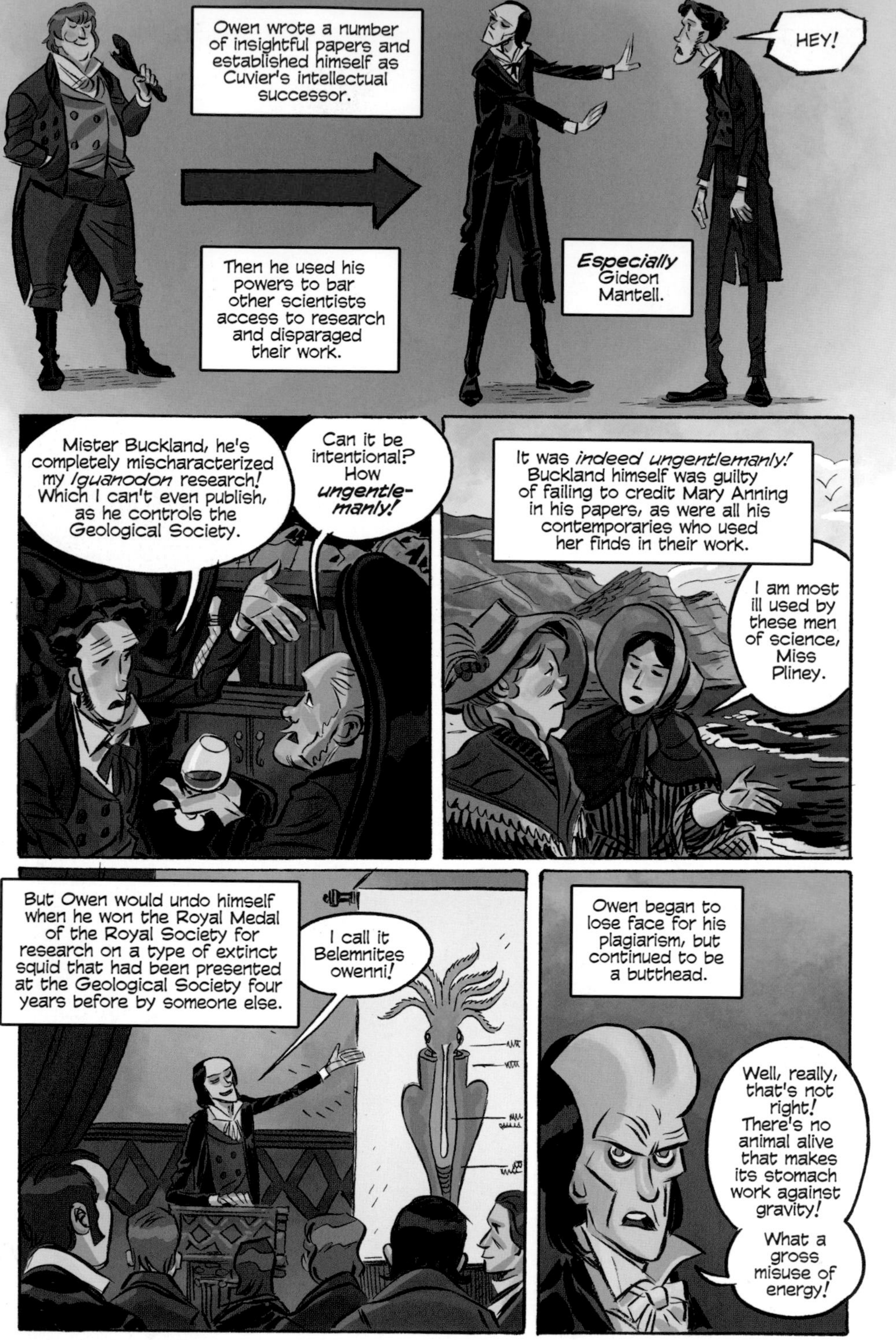
Owen wrote a number of insightful papers and established himself as Cuvier's intellectual successor.
HEY!
Then he used his powers to bar other scientists access to research and disparaged their work.
Especially Gideon Mantell.
Mister Buckland, he's completely mischaracterized my *Iguanodon* research! Which I can't even publish, as he controls the Geological Society.
Can it be intentional? How *ungentlemanly!*
It was *indeed ungentlemanly!* Buckland himself was guilty of failing to credit Mary Anning in his papers, as were all his contemporaries who used her finds in their work.
I am most ill used by these men of science, Miss Pliney.
But Owen would undo himself when he won the Royal Medal of the Royal Society for research on a type of extinct squid that had been presented at the Geological Society four years before by someone else.
I call it Belemnites owenni!
Owen began to lose face for his plagiarism, but continued to be a butthead.
Well, really, that's not right! There's no animal alive that makes its stomach work against gravity!
What a gross misuse of energy!

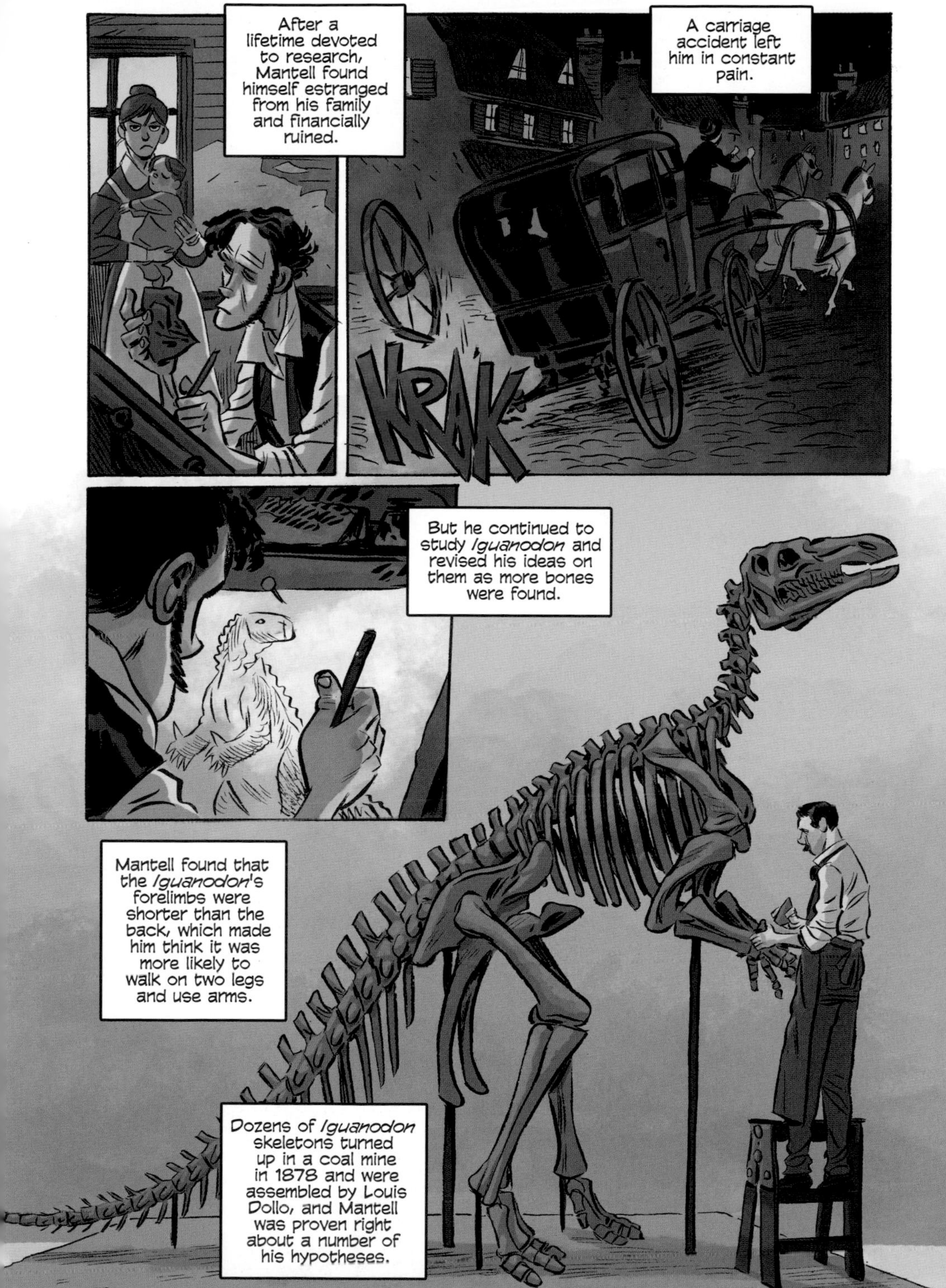
After a lifetime devoted to research, Mantell found himself estranged from his family and financially ruined.
A carriage accident left him in constant pain.
KRAK
But he continued to study *Iguanodon* and revised his ideas on them as more bones were found.
Mantell found that the *Iguanodon*'s forelimbs were shorter than the back, which made him think it was more likely to walk on two legs and use arms.
Dozens of *Iguanodon* skeletons turned up in a coal mine in 1878 and were assembled by Louis Dollo, and Mantell was proven right about a number of his hypotheses.

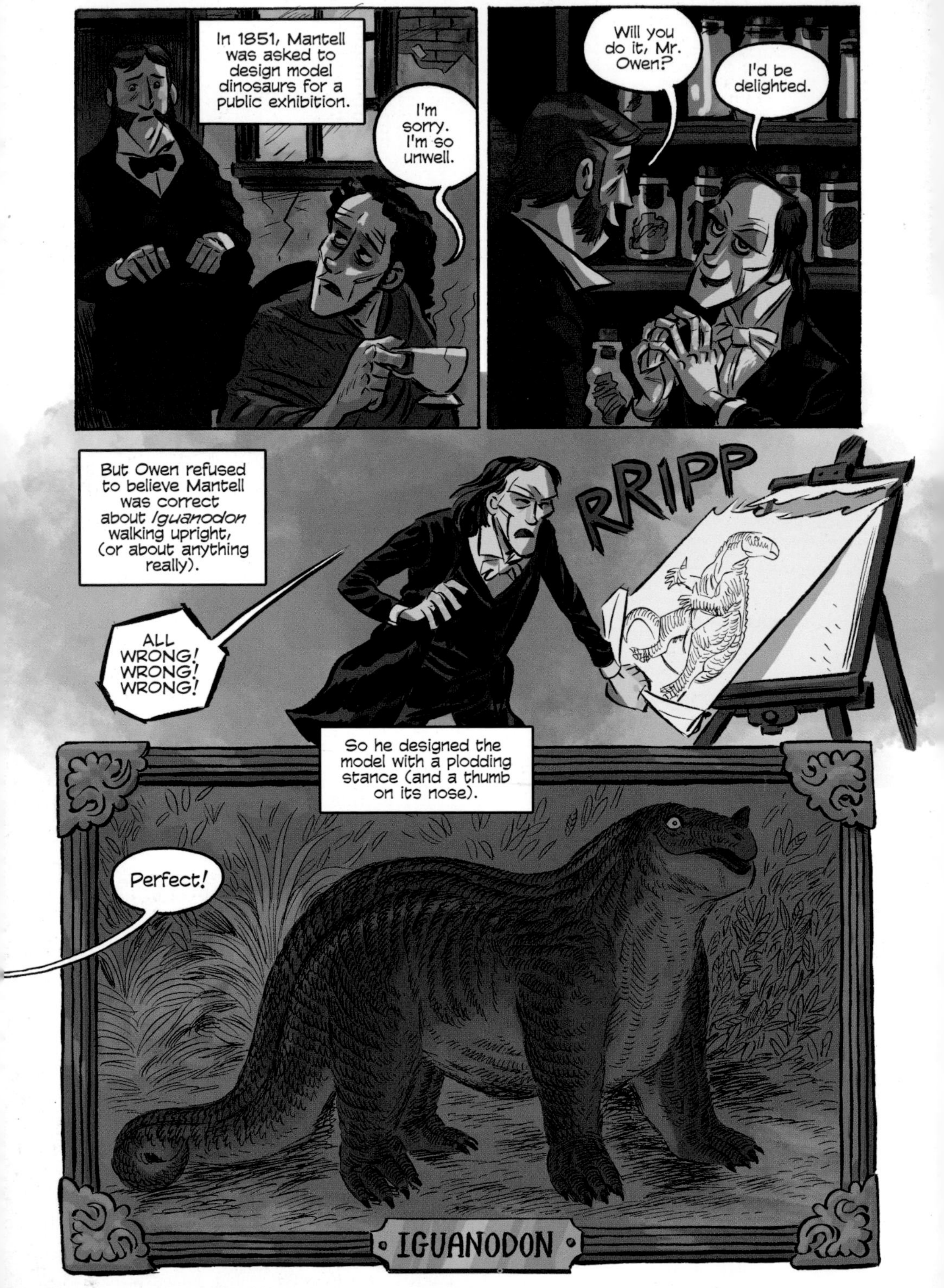

In 1851, Mantell was asked to design model dinosaurs for a public exhibition.
I'm sorry. I'm so unwell.
Will you do it, Mr. Owen?
I'd be delighted.
But Owen refused to believe Mantell was correct about *Iguanodon* walking upright, (or about anything really).
RRIPP
ALL WRONG! WRONG! WRONG!
So he designed the model with a plodding stance (and a thumb on its nose).
Perfect!
IGUANODON

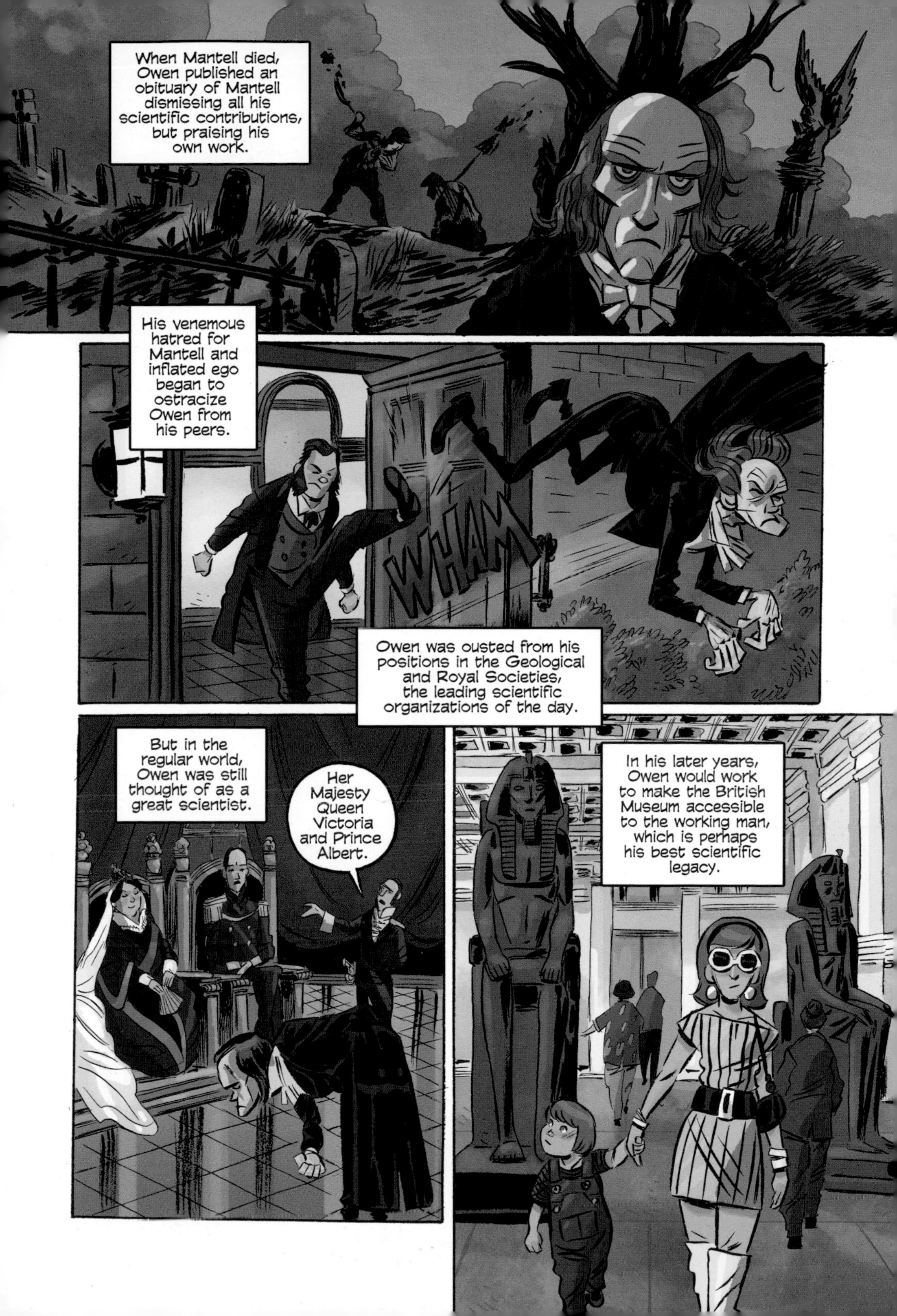
When Mantell died, Owen published an obituary of Mantell dismissing all his scientific contributions, but praising his own work.
His venemous hatred for Mantell and inflated ego began to ostracize Owen from his peers.
WHAM
Owen was ousted from his positions in the Geological and Royal Societies, the leading scientific organizations of the day.
But in the regular world, Owen was still thought of as a great scientist.
Her Majesty Queen Victoria and Prince Albert.
In his later years, Owen would work to make the British Museum accessible to the working man, which is perhaps his best scientific legacy.

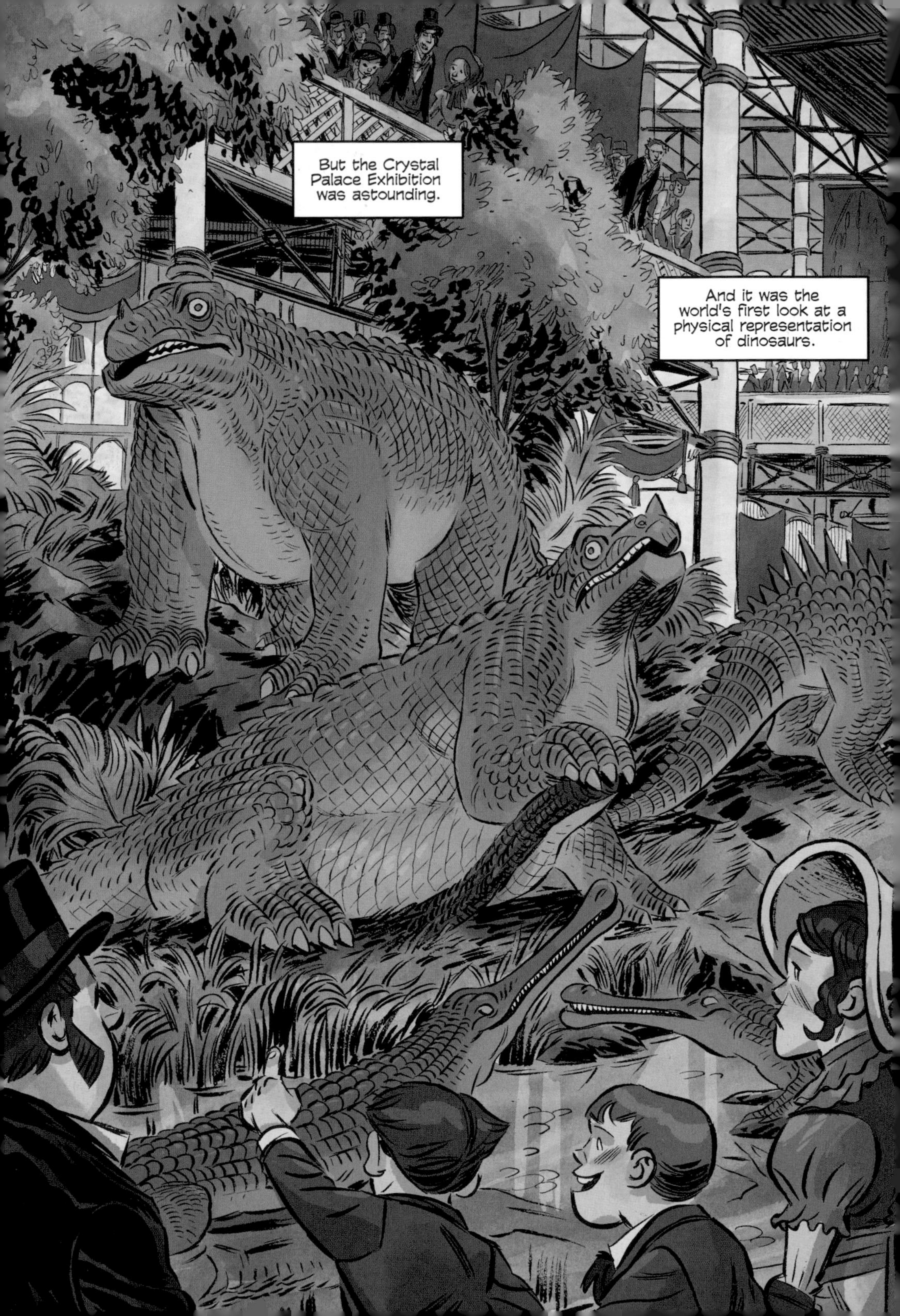
But the Crystal Palace Exhibition was astounding.
And it was the world's first look at a physical representation of dinosaurs.

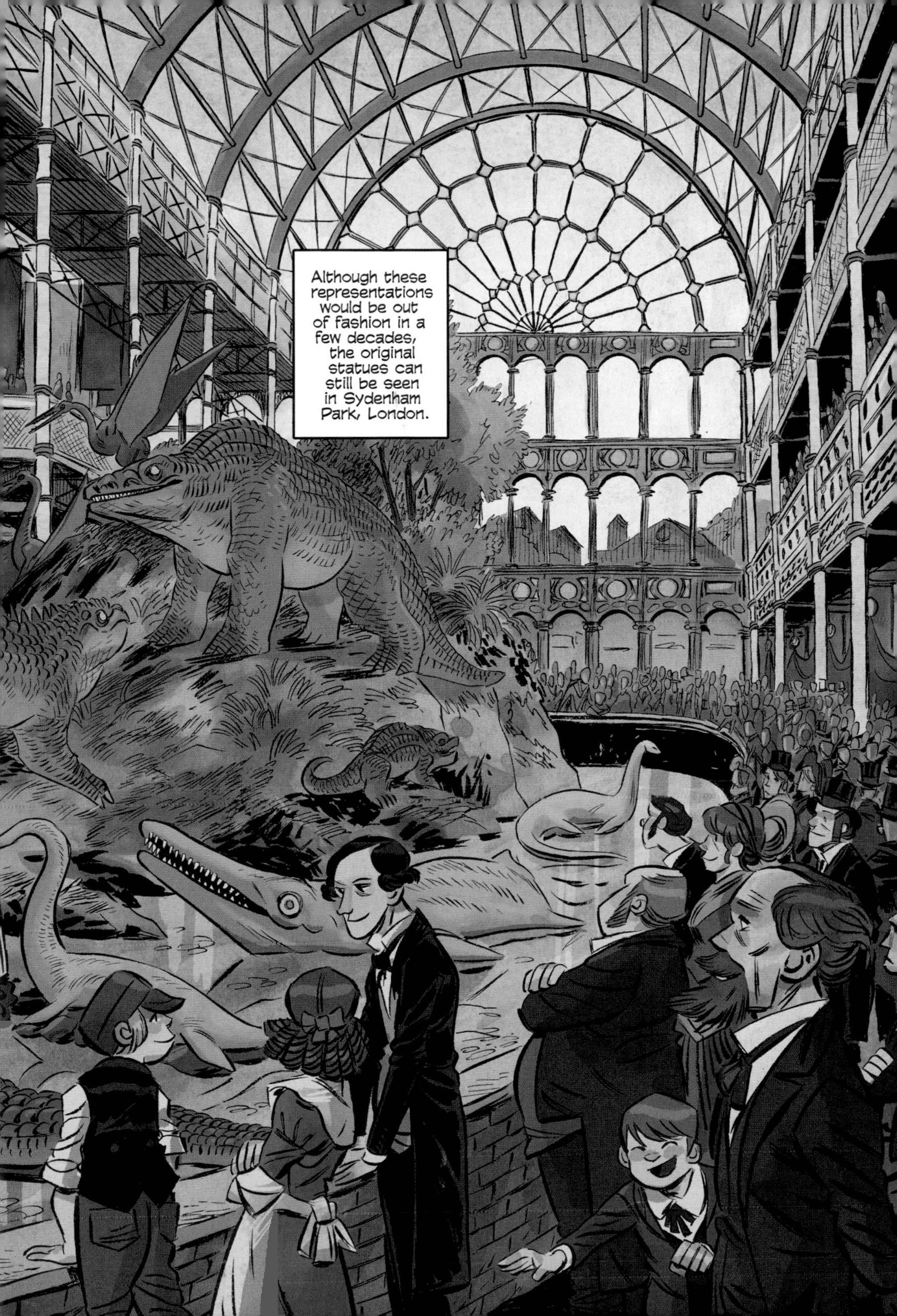
Although these representations would be out of fashion in a few decades, the original statues can still be seen in Sydenham Park, London.

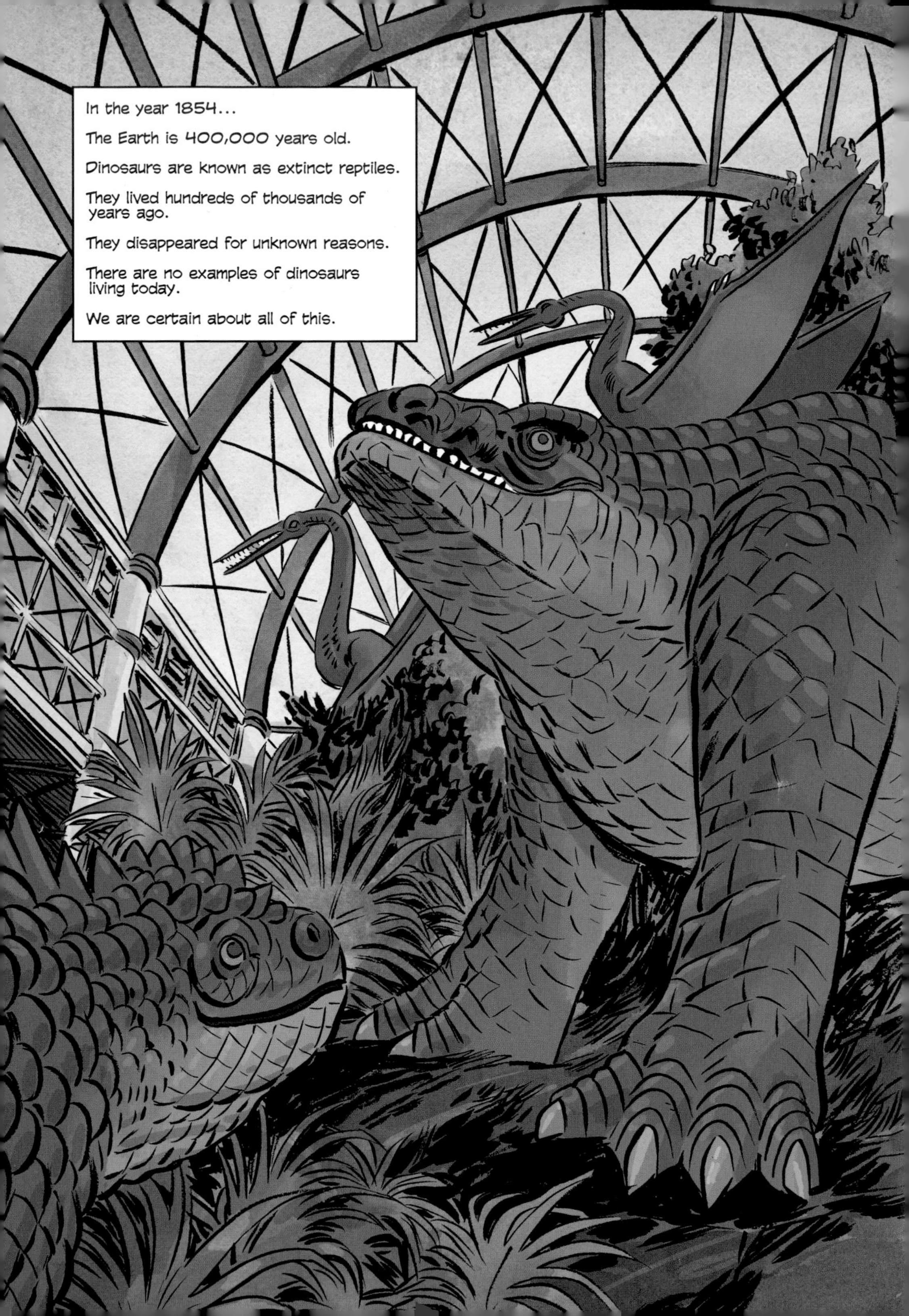
In the year 1854...
The Earth is 400,000 years old.
Dinosaurs are known as extinct reptiles.
They lived hundreds of thousands of years ago.
They disappeared for unknown reasons.
There are no examples of dinosaurs living today.
We are certain about all of this.

HOW DO DINOSAURS GET NAMED?

They're often named with a descriptive phrase in Greek or Latin, though lately Chinese and Mongolian descriptions have been used as well.

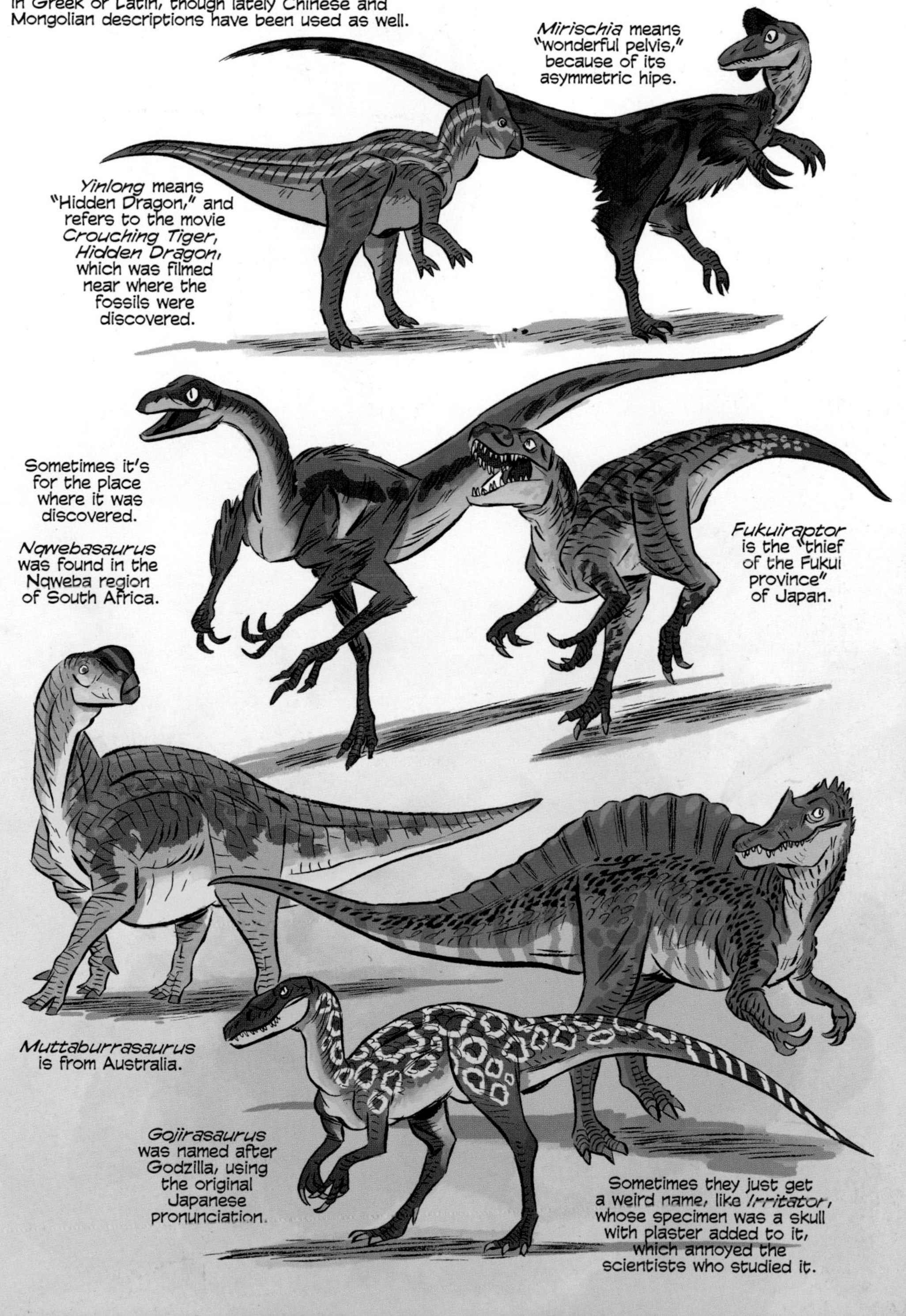

Mirischia means "wonderful pelvis," because of its asymmetric hips.
Yinlong means "Hidden Dragon," and refers to the movie *Crouching Tiger, Hidden Dragon*, which was filmed near where the fossils were discovered.
Sometimes it's for the place where it was discovered.
Nqwebasaurus was found in the Nqweba region of South Africa.
Fukuiraptor is the "thief of the Fukui province" of Japan.
Muttaburrasaurus is from Australia.
Gojirasaurus was named after Godzilla, using the original Japanese pronunciation.
Sometimes they just get a weird name, like *Irritator*, whose specimen was a skull with plaster added to it, which annoyed the scientists who studied it.

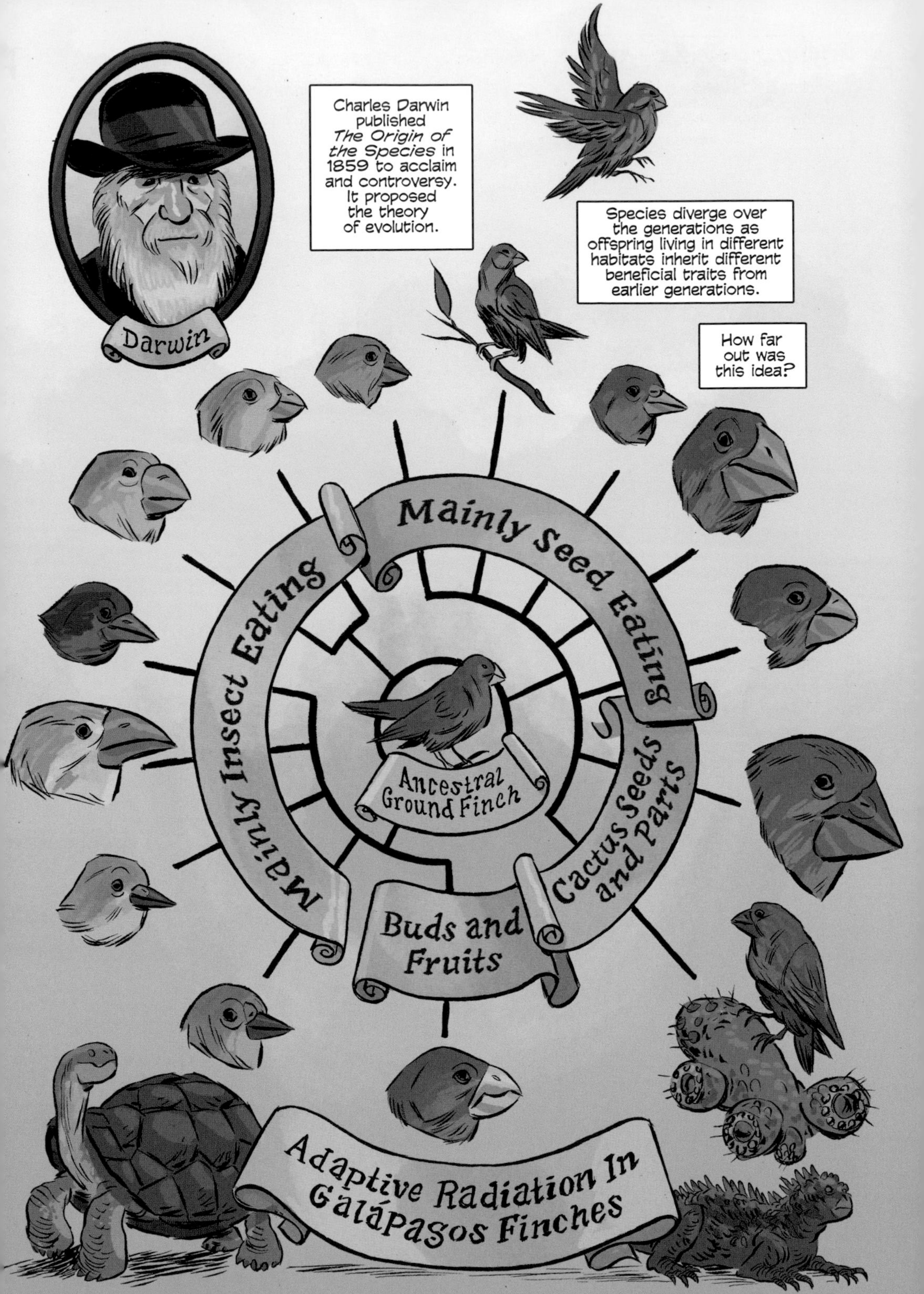
Darwin
Charles Darwin published *The Origin of the Species* in 1859 to acclaim and controversy. It proposed the theory of evolution.
Species diverge over the generations as offspring living in different habitats inherit different beneficial traits from earlier generations.
How far out was this idea?
Mainly Insect Eating
Mainly Seed Eating
Ancestral Ground Finch
Cactus Seeds and Parts
Buds and Fruits
Adaptive Radiation In Galápagos Finches

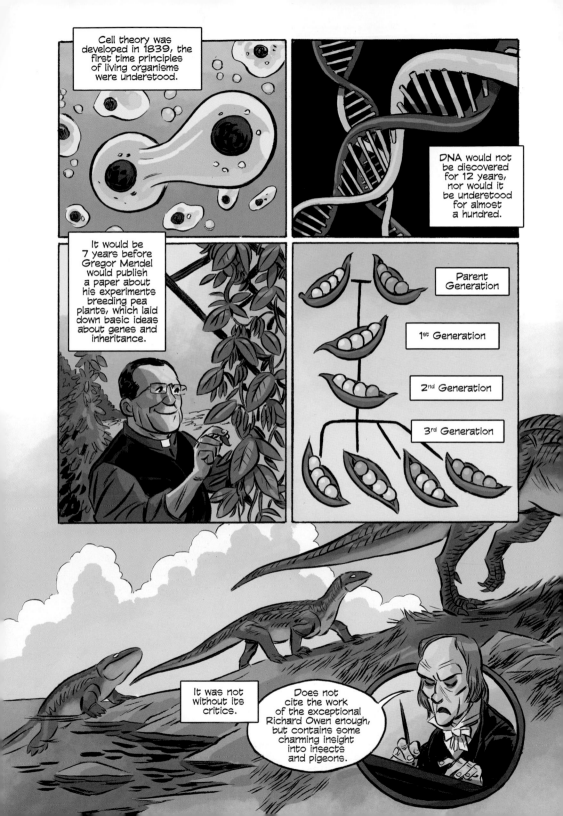

Cell theory was developed in 1839, the first time principles of living organisms were understood.

DNA would not be discovered for 12 years, nor would it be understood for almost a hundred.

It would be 7 years before Gregor Mendel would publish a paper about his experiments breeding pea plants, which laid down basic ideas about genes and inheritance.

Parent Generation

1ˢᵗ Generation

2ⁿᵈ Generation

3ʳᵈ Generation

It was not without its critics.

Does not cite the work of the exceptional Richard Owen enough, but contains some charming insight into insects and pigeons.

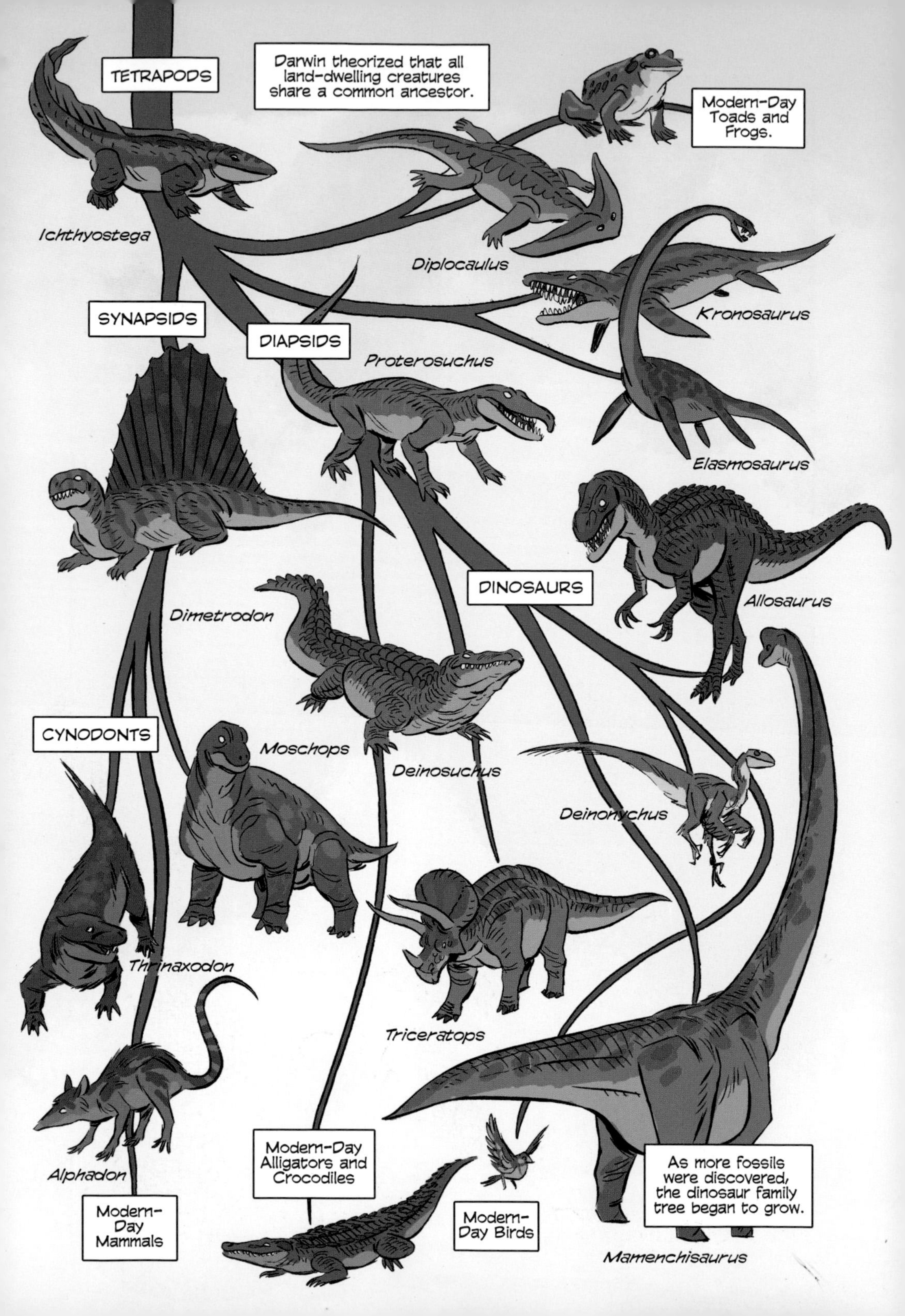

Darwin theorized that all land-dwelling creatures share a common ancestor.
TETRAPODS
Ichthyostega
Modern-Day Toads and Frogs.
Diplocaulus
Kronosaurus
SYNAPSIDS
DIAPSIDS
Proterosuchus
Elasmosaurus
Dimetrodon
DINOSAURS
Allosaurus
CYNODONTS
Moschops
Deinosuchus
Deinonychus
Thrinaxodon
Triceratops
Alphadon
Modern-Day Mammals
Modern-Day Alligators and Crocodiles
Modern-Day Birds
As more fossils were discovered, the dinosaur family tree began to grow.
Mamenchisaurus

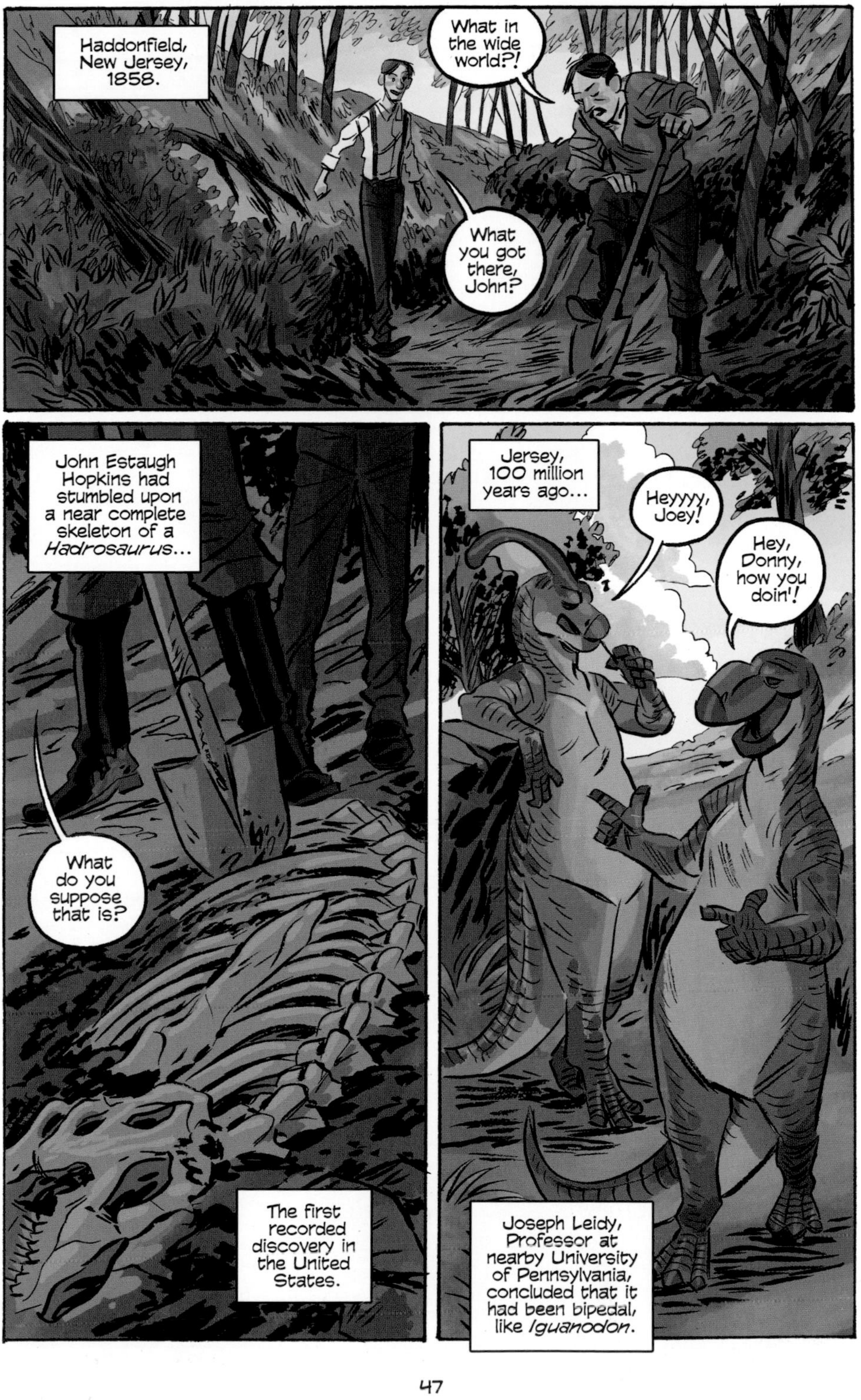
Haddonfield, New Jersey, 1858.
What in the wide world?!
What you got there, John?
John Estaugh Hopkins had stumbled upon a near complete skeleton of a *Hadrosaurus*...
What do you suppose that is?
The first recorded discovery in the United States.
Jersey, 100 million years ago...
Heyyyy, Joey!
Hey, Donny, how you doin'!
Joseph Leidy, Professor at nearby University of Pennsylvania, concluded that it had been bipedal, like *Iguanodon*.

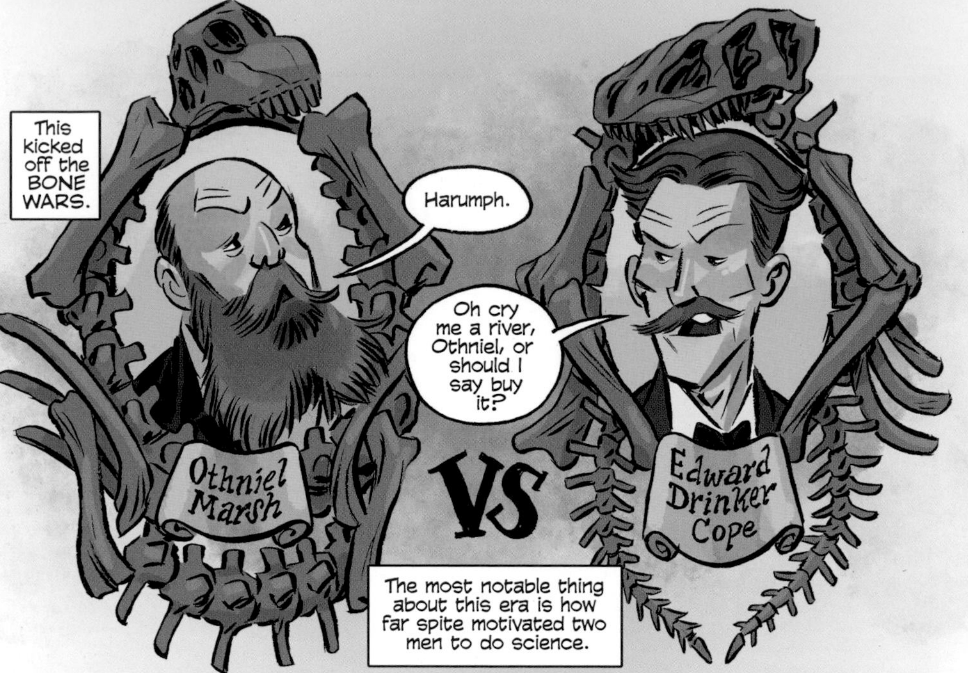
This kicked off the BONE WARS.
Harumph.
Oh cry me a river, Othniel, or should I say buy it?
Othniel Marsh
VS
Edward Drinker Cope
The most notable thing about this era is how far spite motivated two men to do science.

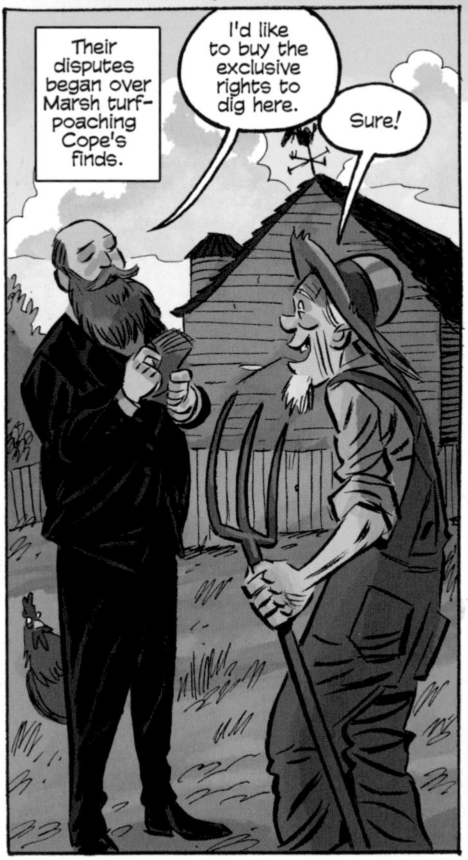
Their disputes began over Marsh turf-poaching Cope's finds.
I'd like to buy the exclusive rights to dig here.
Sure!

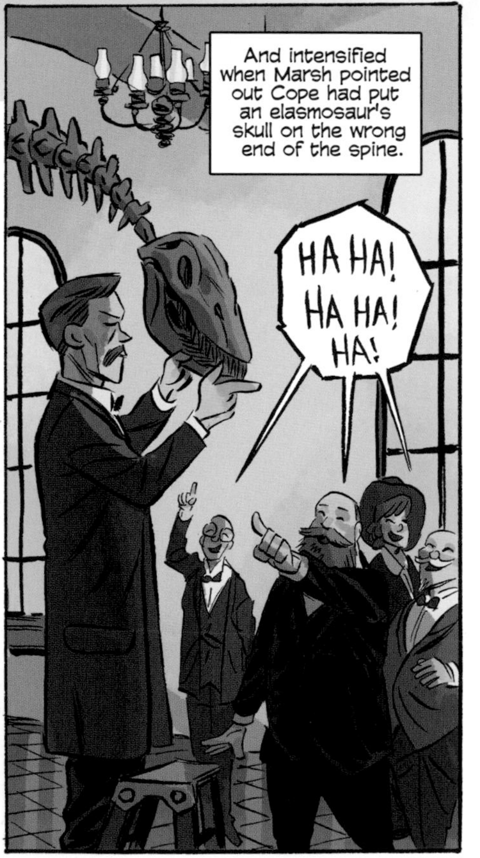
And intensified when Marsh pointed out Cope had put an elasmosaur's skull on the wrong end of the spine.
HA HA! HA HA! HA!

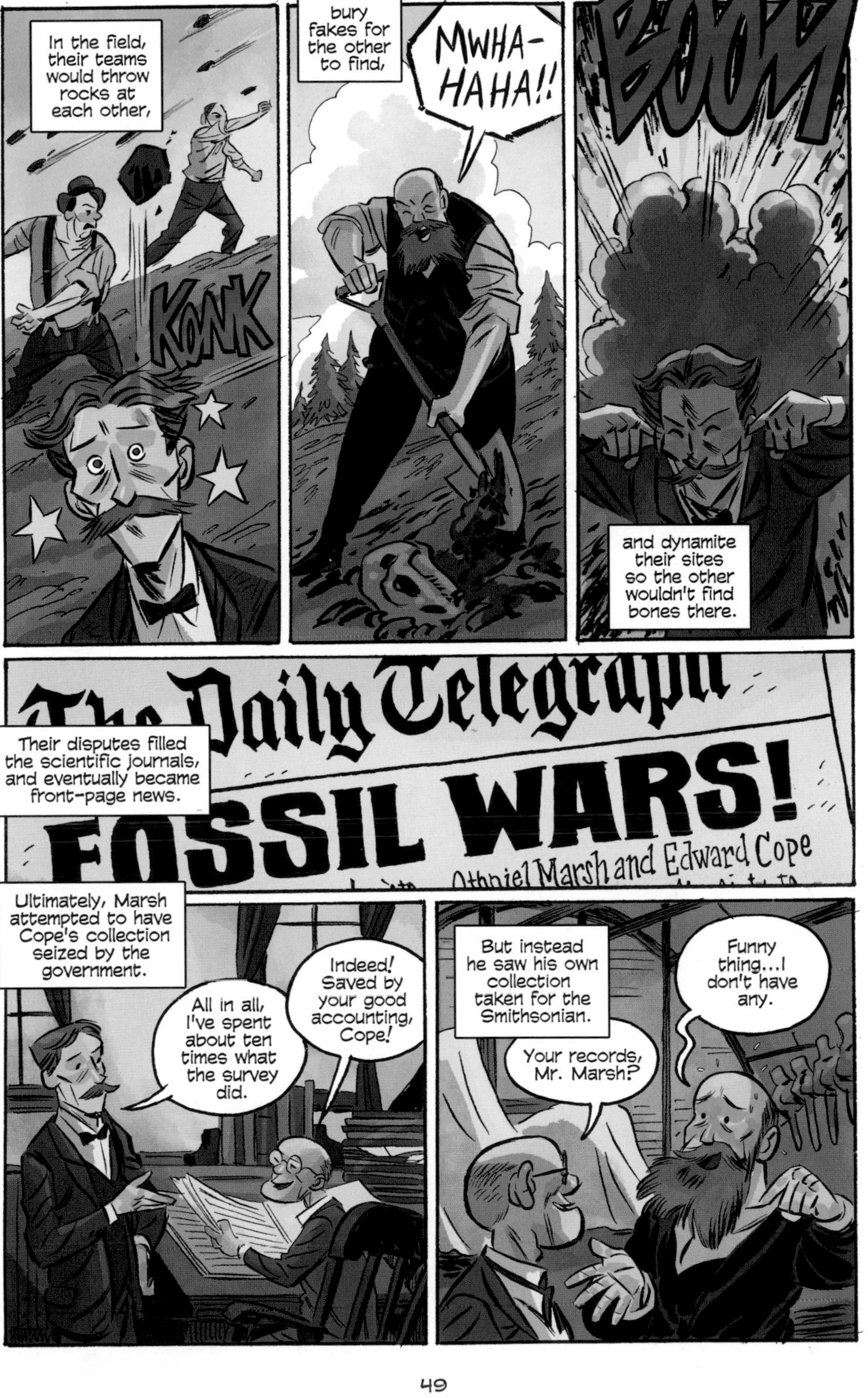
In the field, their teams would throw rocks at each other,
KONK
bury fakes for the other to find,
MWHA-HAHA!!
BOOM
and dynamite their sites so the other wouldn't find bones there.
The Daily Telegraph
Their disputes filled the scientific journals, and eventually became front-page news.
FOSSIL WARS!
Othniel Marsh and Edward Cope
Ultimately, Marsh attempted to have Cope's collection seized by the government.
All in all, I've spent about ten times what the survey did.
Indeed! Saved by your good accounting, Cope!
But instead he saw his own collection taken for the Smithsonian.
Funny thing...I don't have any.
Your records, Mr. Marsh?

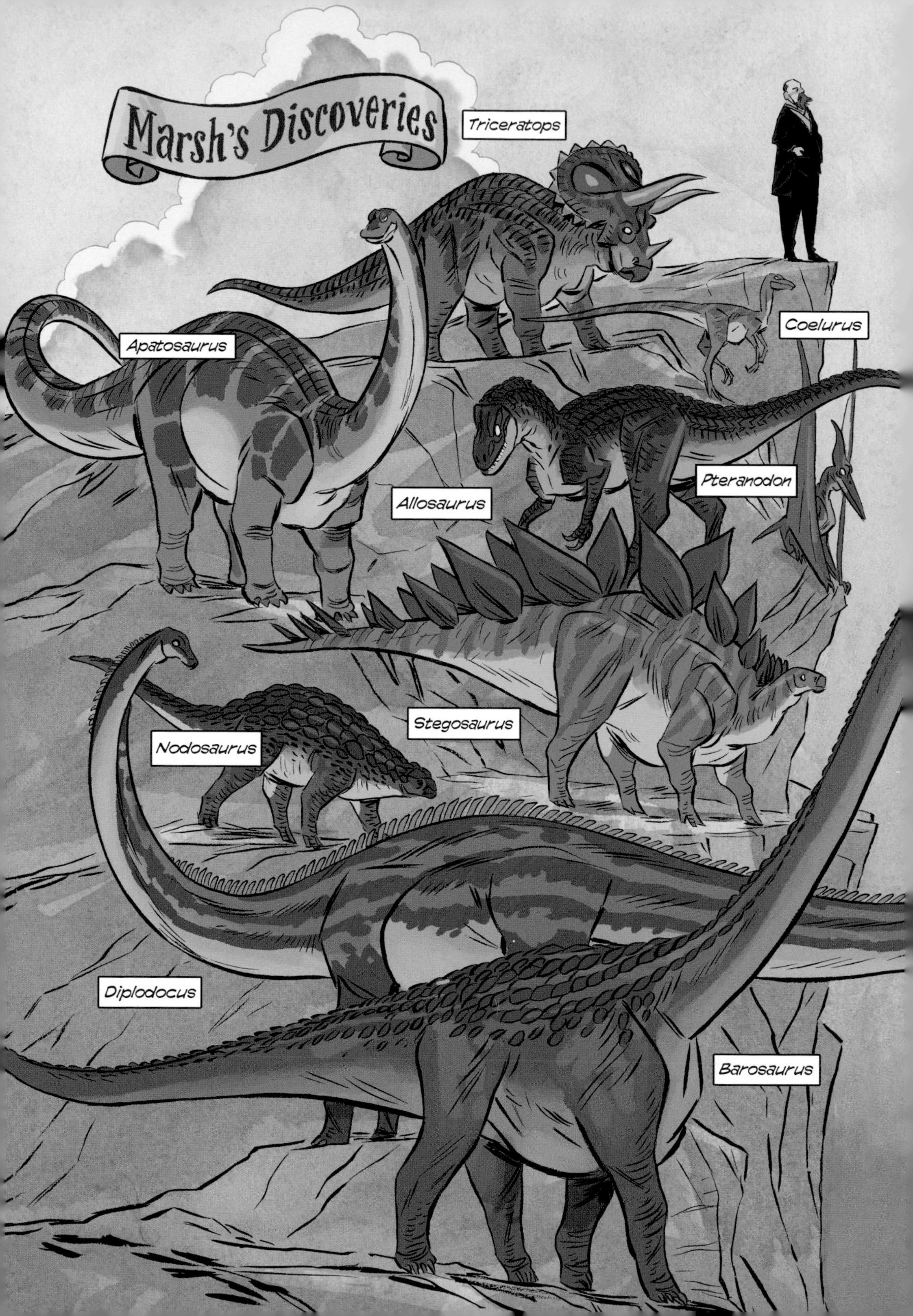
Marsh's Discoveries
Triceratops
Apatosaurus
Coelurus
Allosaurus
Pteranodon
Stegosaurus
Nodosaurus
Diplodocus
Barosaurus

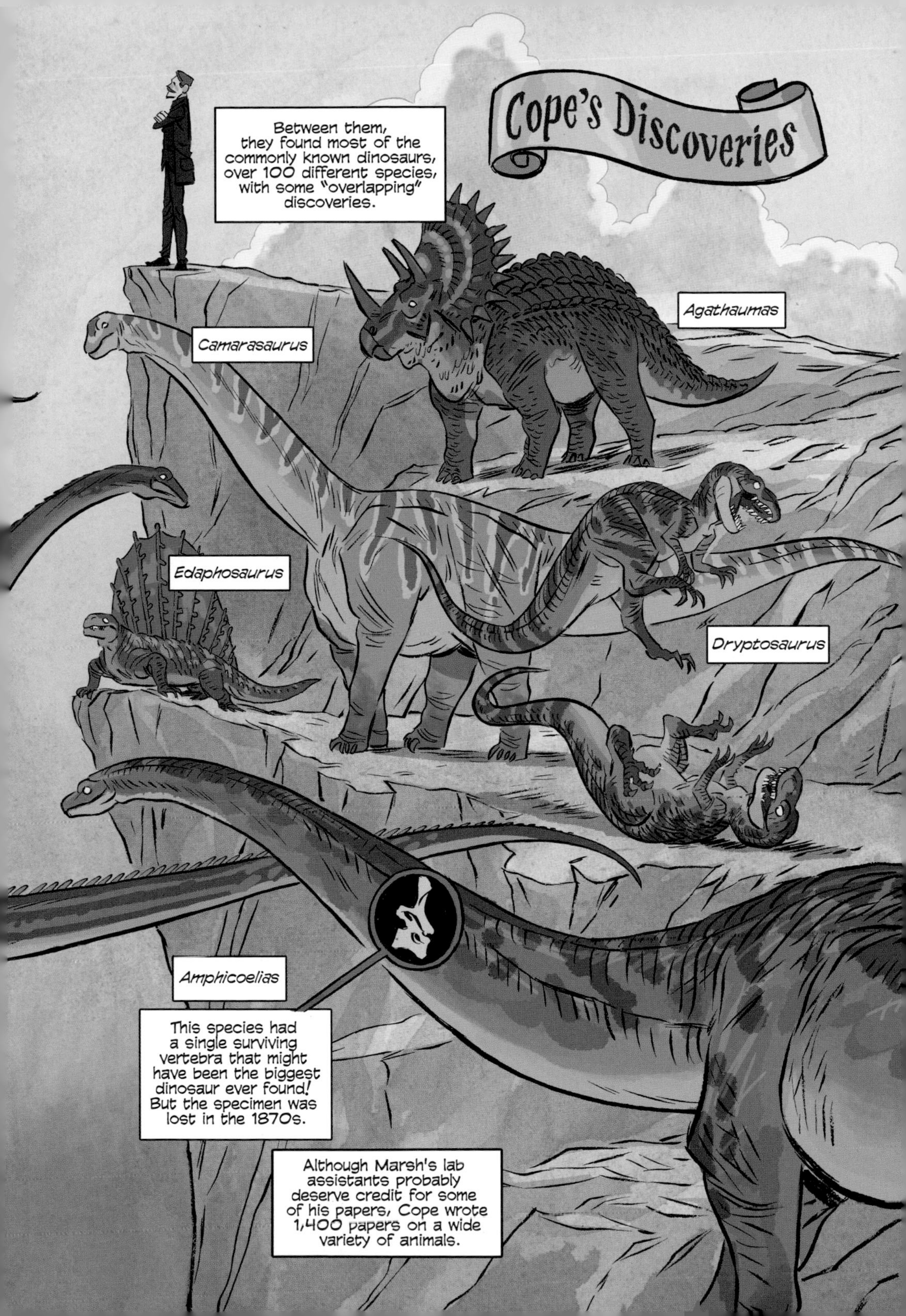

Cope's Discoveries
Between them, they found most of the commonly known dinosaurs, over 100 different species, with some "overlapping" discoveries.
Agathaumas
Camarasaurus
Edaphosaurus
Dryptosaurus
Amphicoelias
This species had a single surviving vertebra that might have been the biggest dinosaur ever found! But the specimen was lost in the 1870s.
Although Marsh's lab assistants probably deserve credit for some of his papers, Cope wrote 1,400 papers on a wide variety of animals.

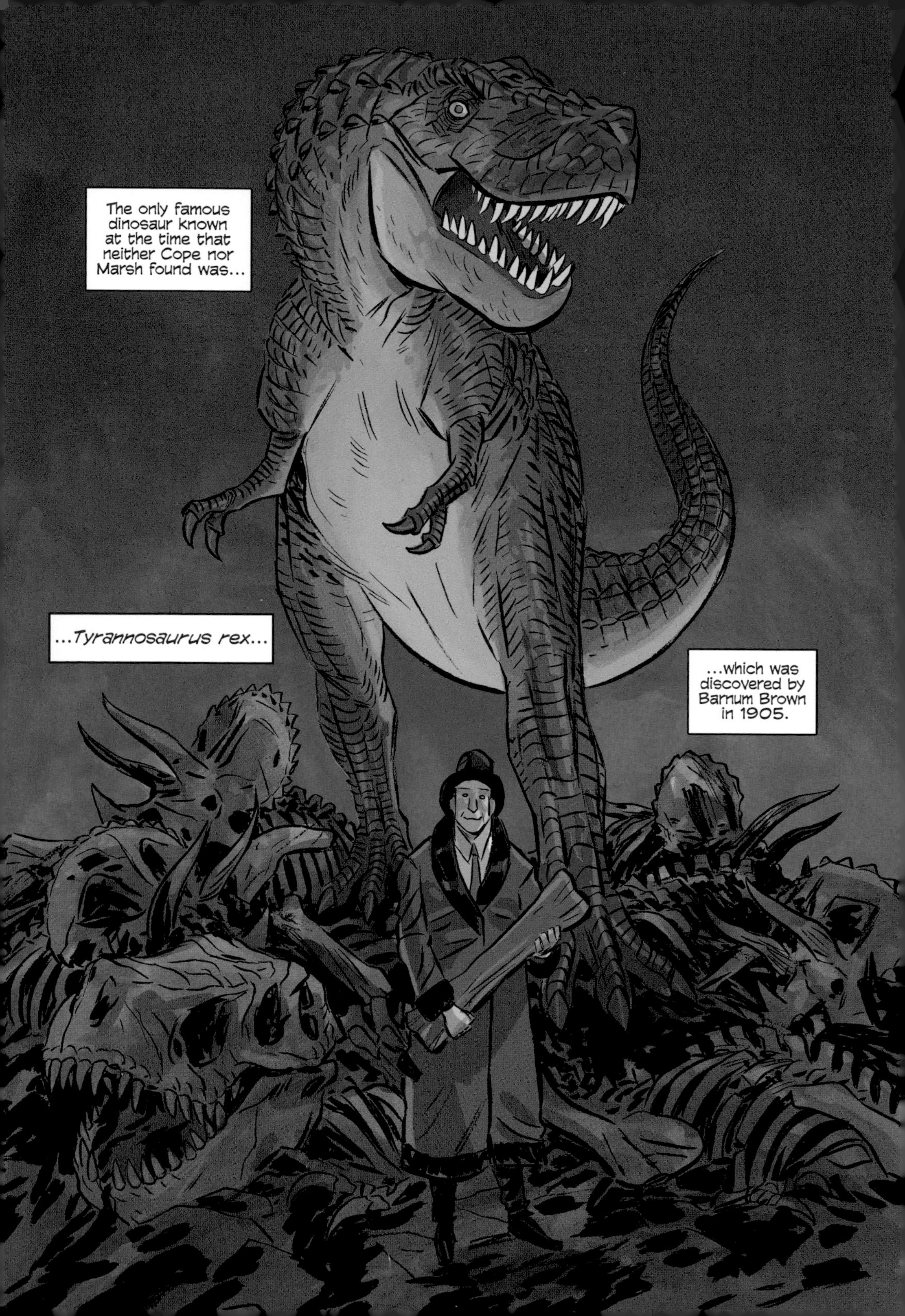

The only famous dinosaur known at the time that neither Cope nor Marsh found was...
...*Tyrannosaurus rex*...
...which was discovered by Barnum Brown in 1905.

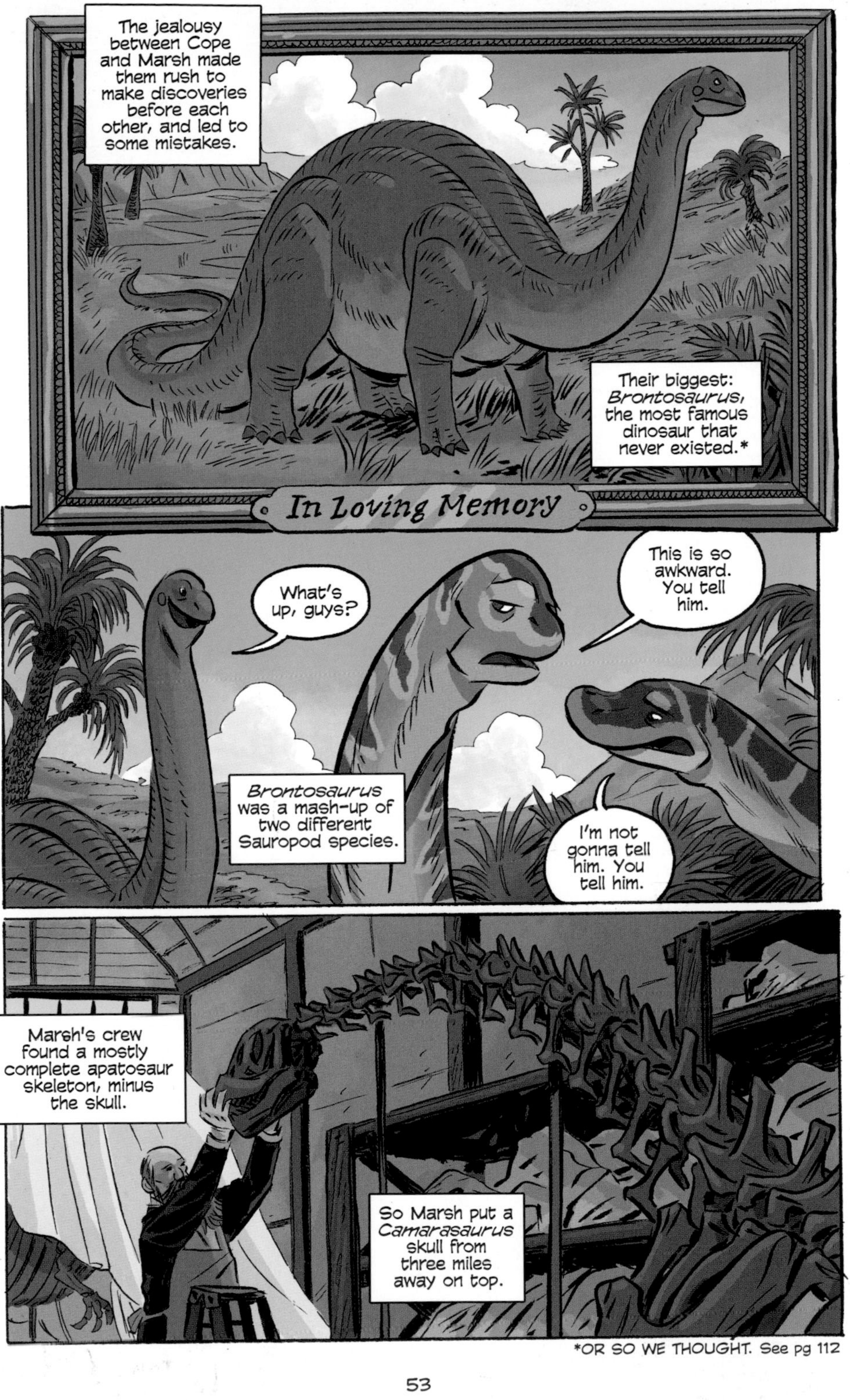
The jealousy between Cope and Marsh made them rush to make discoveries before each other, and led to some mistakes.
Their biggest: *Brontosaurus*, the most famous dinosaur that never existed.*
In Loving Memory
What's up, guys?
This is so awkward. You tell him.
Brontosaurus was a mash-up of two different Sauropod species.
I'm not gonna tell him. You tell him.
Marsh's crew found a mostly complete apatosaur skeleton, minus the skull.
So Marsh put a *Camarasaurus* skull from three miles away on top.

*OR SO WE THOUGHT. See pg 112

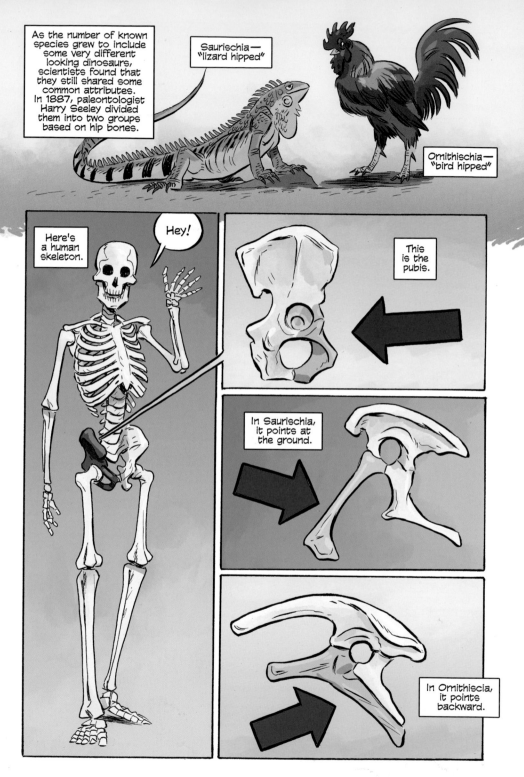

As the number of known species grew to include some very different looking dinosaurs, scientists found that they still shared some common attributes. In 1887, paleontologist Harry Seeley divided them into two groups based on hip bones.

Saurischia— "lizard hipped"

Ornithischia— "bird hipped"

Here's a human skeleton.

Hey!

This is the pubis.

In Saurischia, it points at the ground.

In Ornithiscia, it points backward.

54

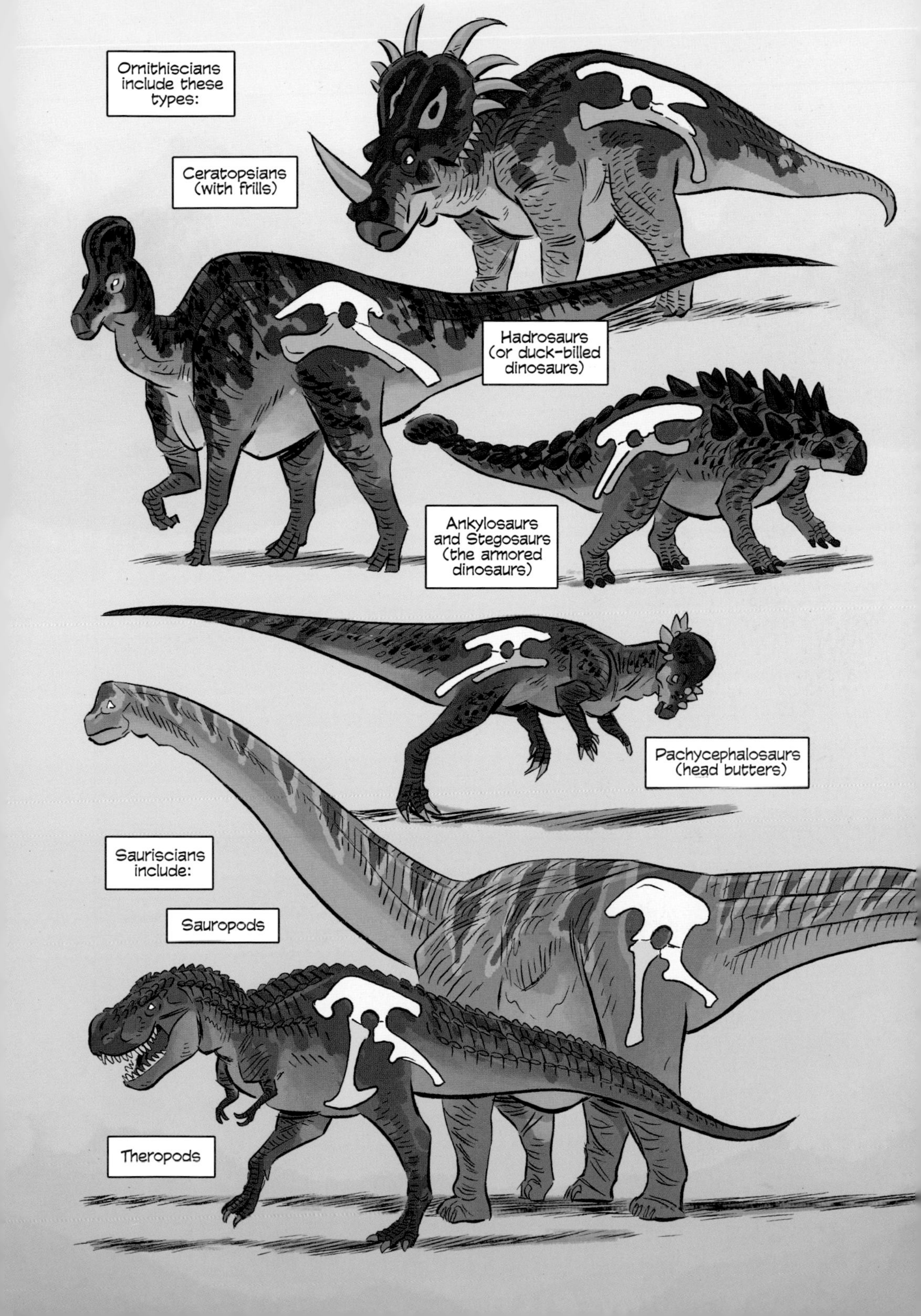
Ornithiscians include these types:
Ceratopsians (with frills)
Hadrosaurs (or duck-billed dinosaurs)
Ankylosaurs and Stegosaurs (the armored dinosaurs)
Pachycephalosaurs (head butters)
Sauriscians include:
Sauropods
Theropods

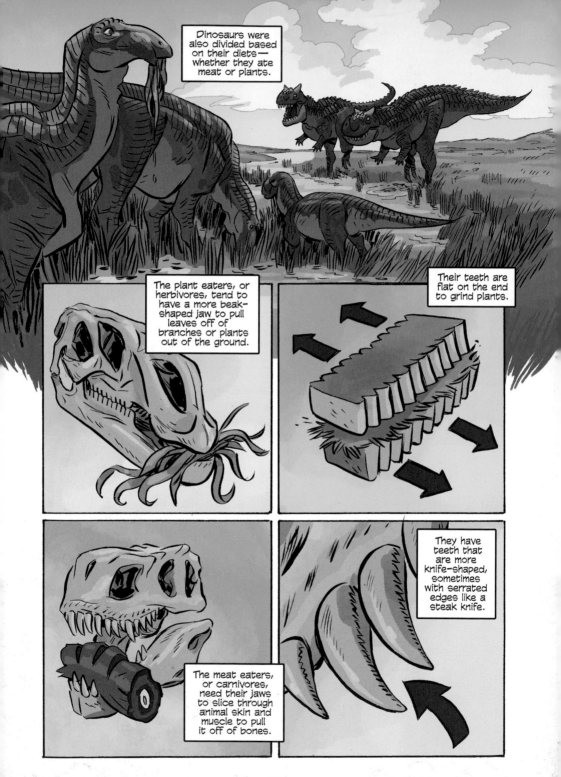

Dinosaurs were also divided based on their diets— whether they ate meat or plants.

The plant eaters, or herbivores, tend to have a more beak-shaped jaw to pull leaves off of branches or plants out of the ground.

Their teeth are flat on the end to grind plants.

The meat eaters, or carnivores, need their jaws to slice through animal skin and muscle to pull it off of bones.

They have teeth that are more knife-shaped, sometimes with serrated edges like a steak knife.

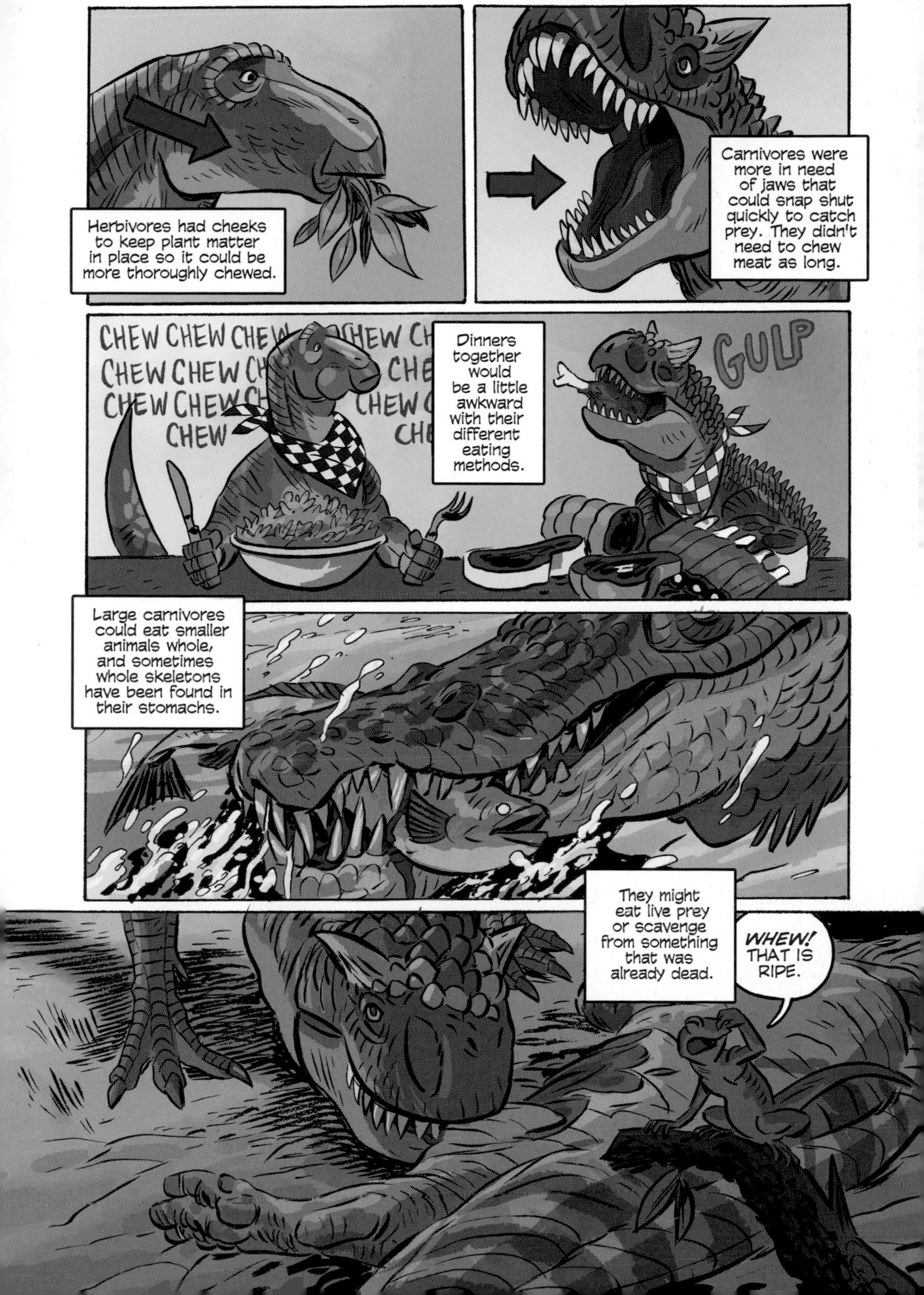

Herbivores had cheeks to keep plant matter in place so it could be more thoroughly chewed.
Carnivores were more in need of jaws that could snap shut quickly to catch prey. They didn't need to chew meat as long.
CHEW CHEW CHEW CHEW CHEW CHEW CHEW CHEW CHEW CHEW
Dinners together would be a little awkward with their different eating methods.
GULP
Large carnivores could eat smaller animals whole, and sometimes whole skeletons have been found in their stomachs.
They might eat live prey or scavenge from something that was already dead.
WHEW! THAT IS RIPE.

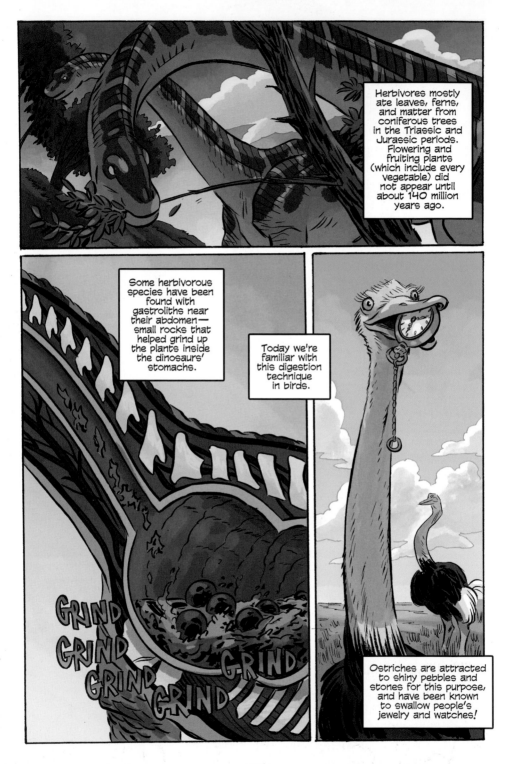

Herbivores mostly ate leaves, ferns, and matter from coniferous trees in the Triassic and Jurassic periods. Flowering and fruiting plants (which include every vegetable) did not appear until about 140 million years ago.

Some herbivorous species have been found with gastroliths near their abdomen — small rocks that helped grind up the plants inside the dinosaurs' stomachs.

Today we're familiar with this digestion technique in birds.

GRIND
GRIND
GRIND
GRIND
GRIND
GRIND

Ostriches are attracted to shiny pebbles and stones for this purpose, and have been known to swallow people's jewelry and watches!

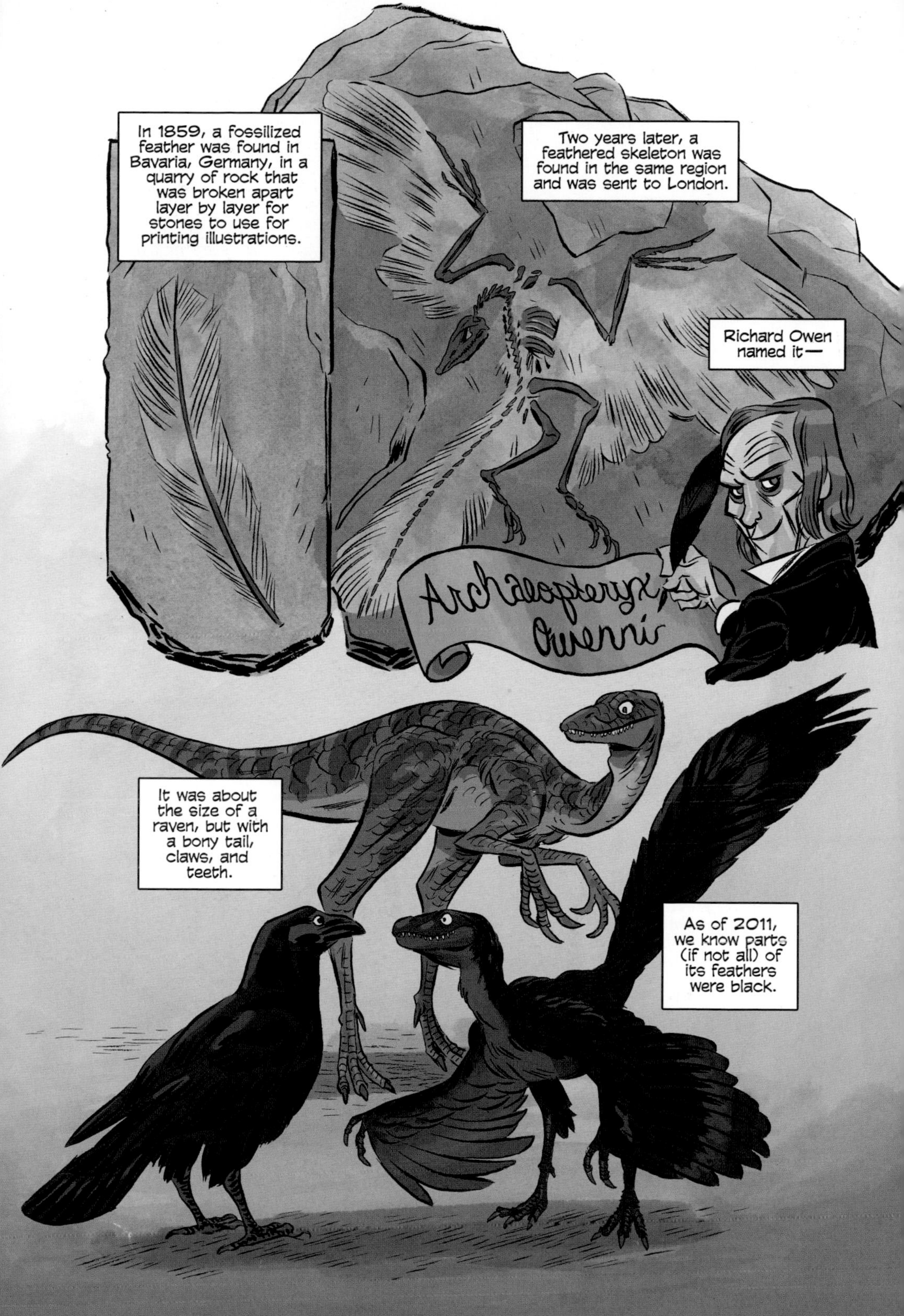
In 1859, a fossilized feather was found in Bavaria, Germany, in a quarry of rock that was broken apart layer by layer for stones to use for printing illustrations.
Two years later, a feathered skeleton was found in the same region and was sent to London.
Richard Owen named it—
Archaeopteryx Owenni
It was about the size of a raven, but with a bony tail, claws, and teeth.
As of 2011, we know parts (if not all) of its feathers were black.

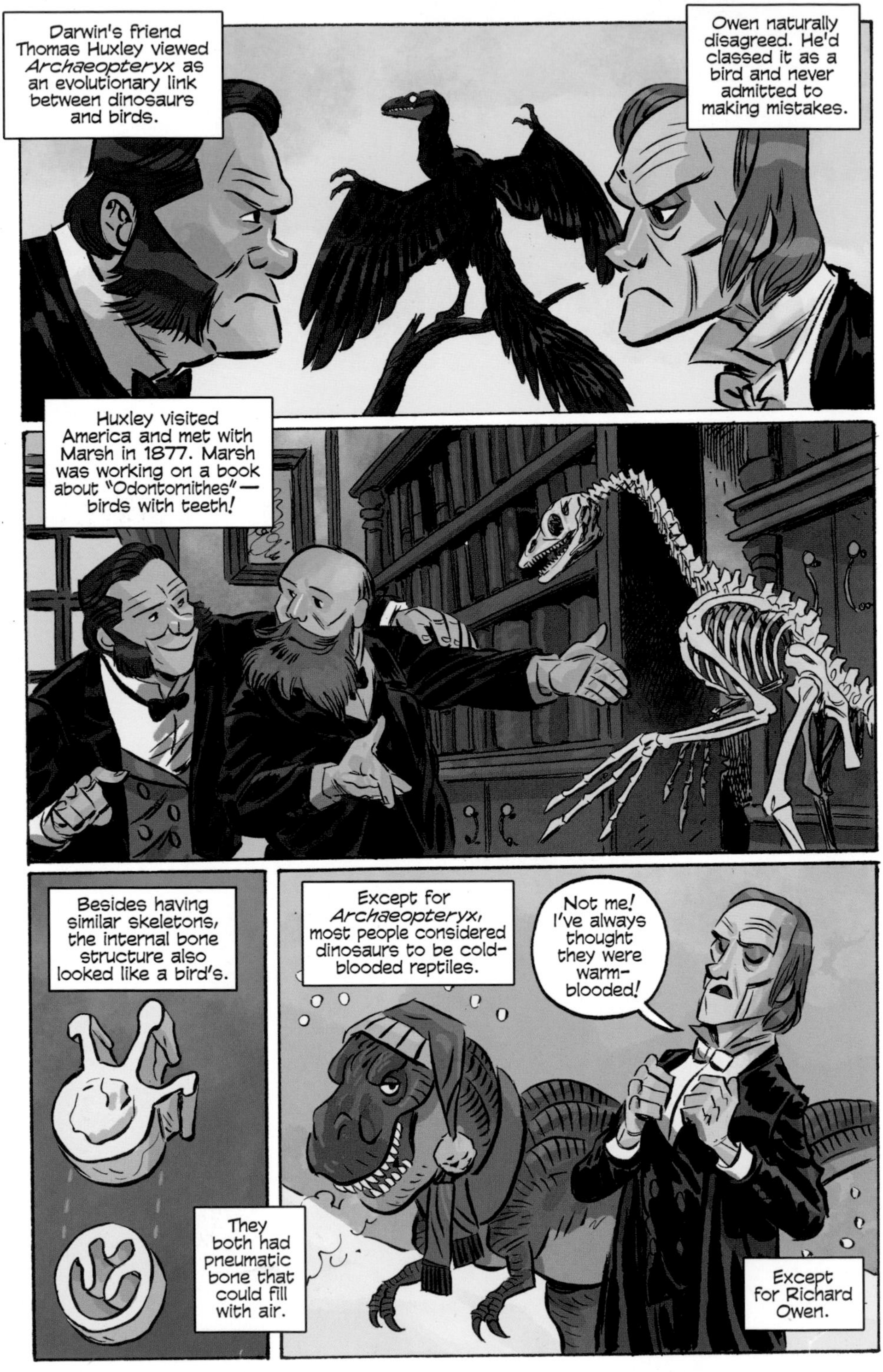
Darwin's friend Thomas Huxley viewed *Archaeopteryx* as an evolutionary link between dinosaurs and birds.
Owen naturally disagreed. He'd classed it as a bird and never admitted to making mistakes.
Huxley visited America and met with Marsh in 1877. Marsh was working on a book about "Odontornithes"—birds with teeth!
Besides having similar skeletons, the internal bone structure also looked like a bird's.
They both had pneumatic bone that could fill with air.
Except for *Archaeopteryx*, most people considered dinosaurs to be cold-blooded reptiles.
Not me! I've always thought they were warm-blooded!
Except for Richard Owen.

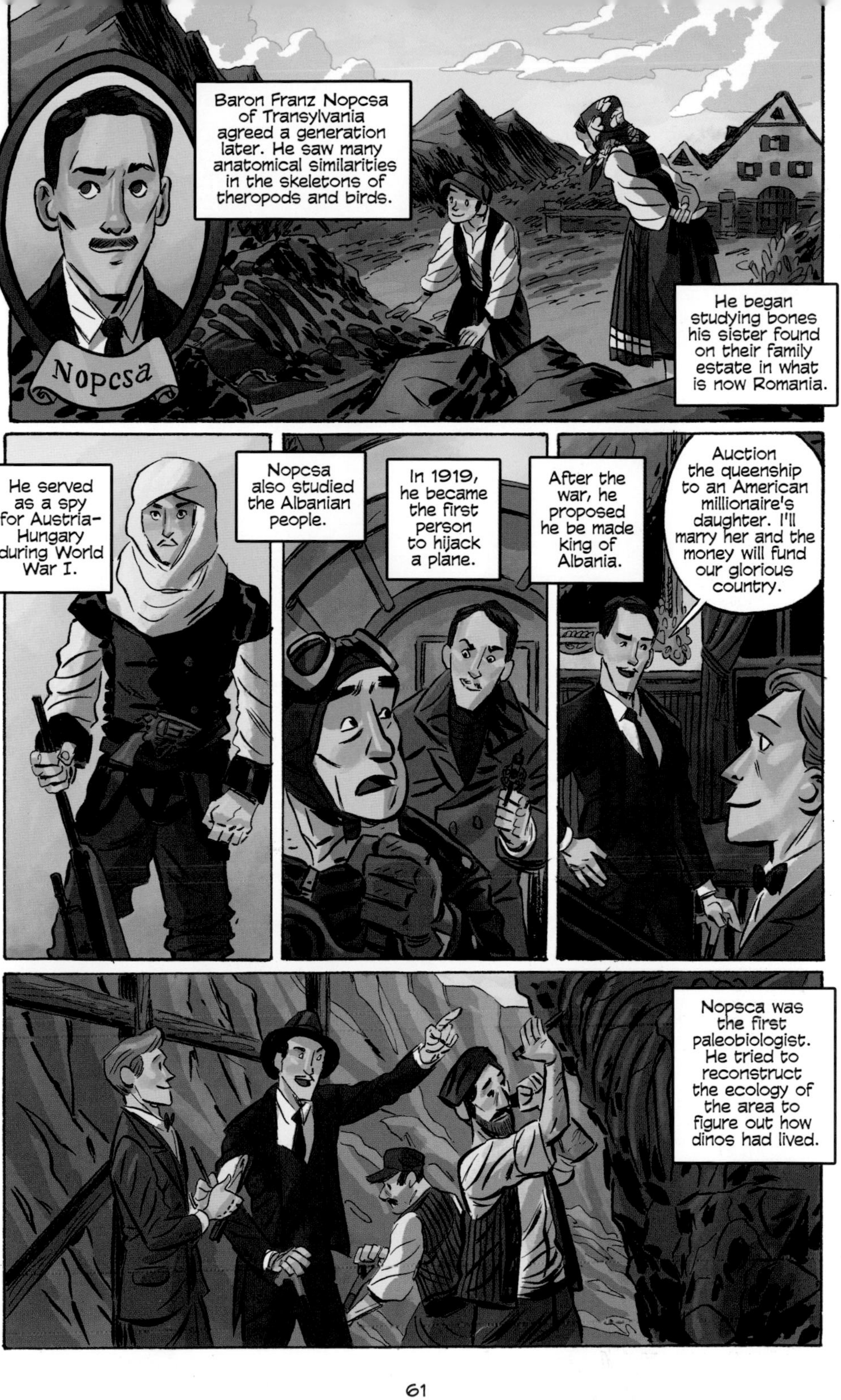
Baron Franz Nopcsa of Transylvania agreed a generation later. He saw many anatomical similarities in the skeletons of theropods and birds.
Nopcsa
He began studying bones his sister found on their family estate in what is now Romania.
He served as a spy for Austria-Hungary during World War I.
Nopcsa also studied the Albanian people.
In 1919, he became the first person to hijack a plane.
After the war, he proposed he be made king of Albania.
Auction the queenship to an American millionaire's daughter. I'll marry her and the money will fund our glorious country.
Nopsca was the first paleobiologist. He tried to reconstruct the ecology of the area to figure out how dinos had lived.

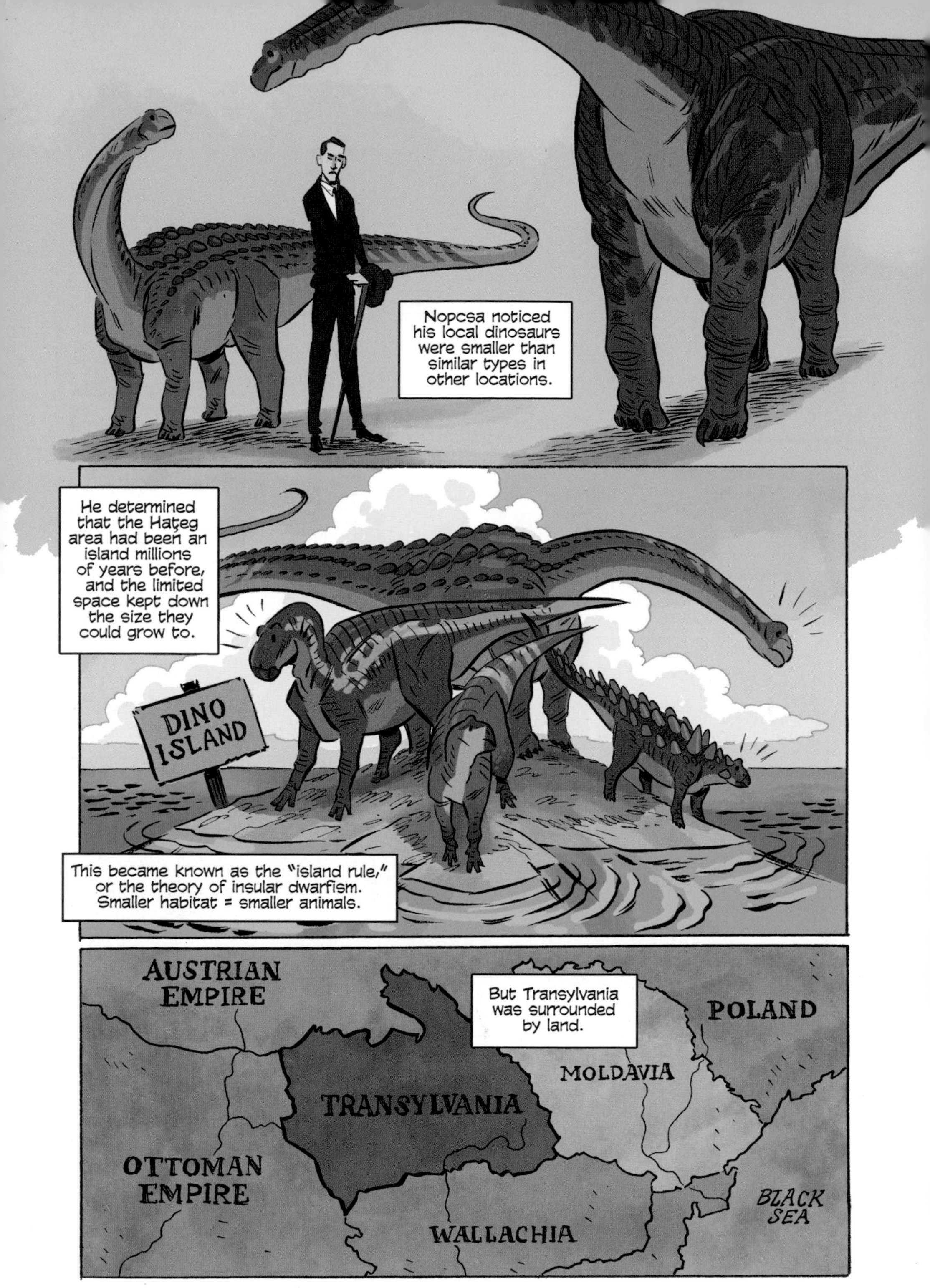

Nopcsa noticed his local dinosaurs were smaller than similar types in other locations.
He determined that the Haţeg area had been an island millions of years before, and the limited space kept down the size they could grow to.
DINO ISLAND
This became known as the "island rule," or the theory of insular dwarfism. Smaller habitat = smaller animals.
But Transylvania was surrounded by land.
AUSTRIAN EMPIRE
POLAND
MOLDAVIA
TRANSYLVANIA
OTTOMAN EMPIRE
BLACK SEA
WALLACHIA

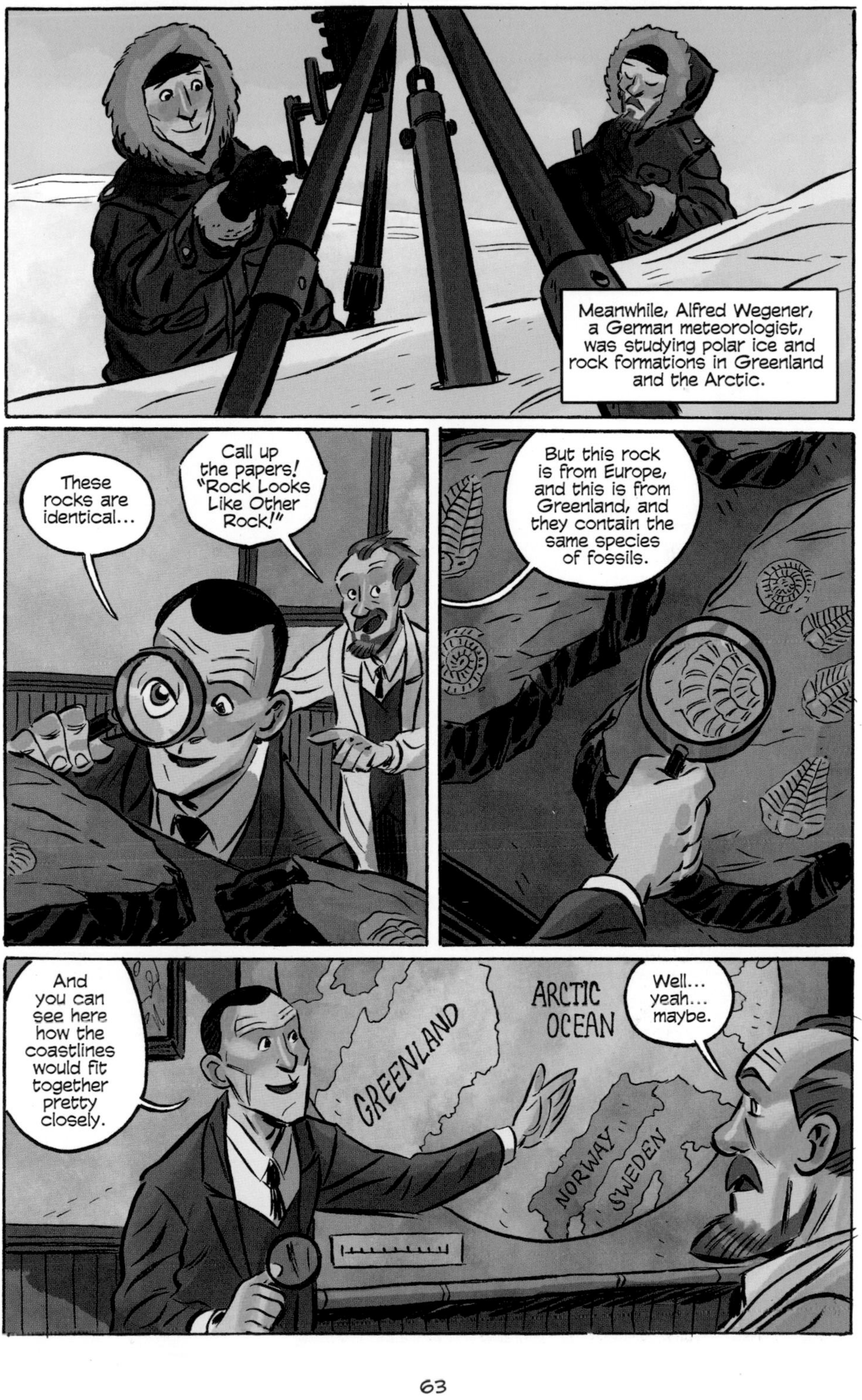

Meanwhile, Alfred Wegener, a German meteorologist, was studying polar ice and rock formations in Greenland and the Arctic.
These rocks are identical...
Call up the papers! "Rock Looks Like Other Rock!"
But this rock is from Europe, and this is from Greenland, and they contain the same species of fossils.
And you can see here how the coastlines would fit together pretty closely.
ARCTIC OCEAN
GREENLAND
NORWAY
SWEDEN
Well... yeah... maybe.

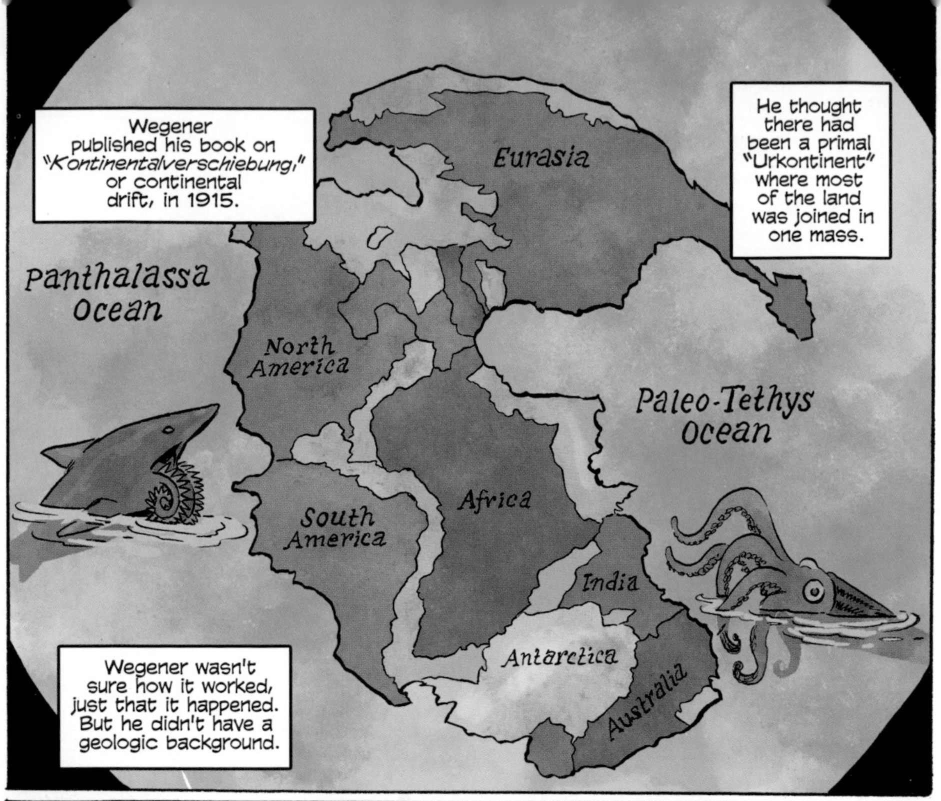
Wegener published his book on "Kontinentalverschiebung," or continental drift, in 1915.
He thought there had been a primal "Urkontinent" where most of the land was joined in one mass.
Eurasia
Panthalassa Ocean
North America
Paleo-Tethys Ocean
Africa
South America
India
Antarctica
Australia
Wegener wasn't sure how it worked, just that it happened. But he didn't have a geologic background.

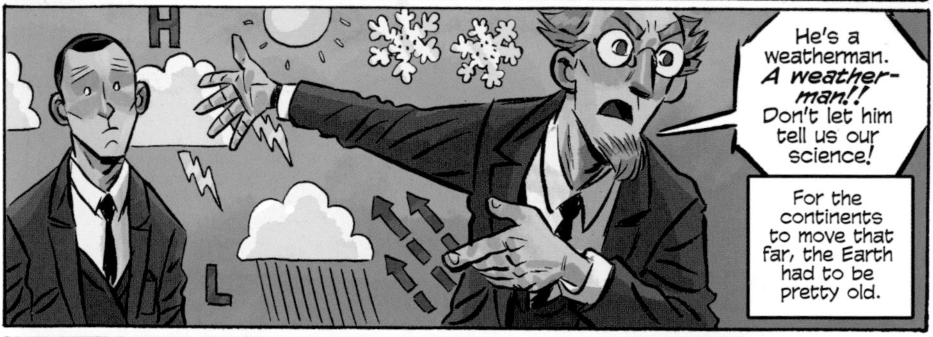
H
L
He's a weatherman. ***A weather-man!!*** Don't let him tell us our science!
For the continents to move that far, the Earth had to be pretty old.

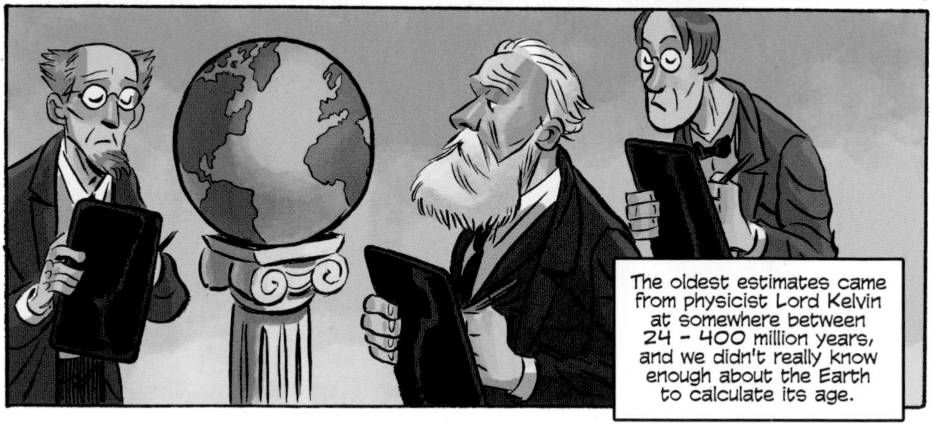
The oldest estimates came from physicist Lord Kelvin at somewhere between 24 - 400 million years, and we didn't really know enough about the Earth to calculate its age.

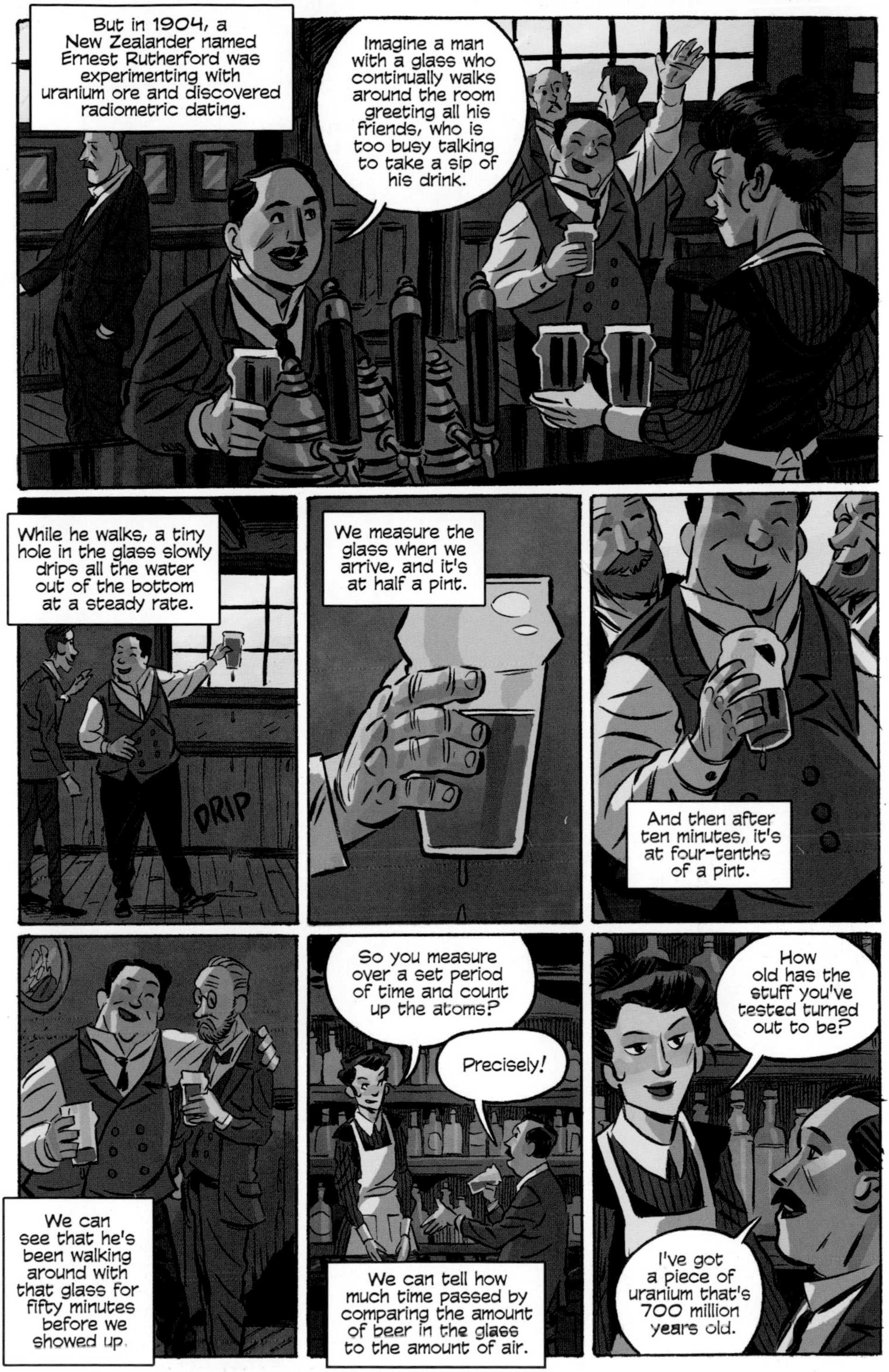
But in 1904, a New Zealander named Ernest Rutherford was experimenting with uranium ore and discovered radiometric dating.
Imagine a man with a glass who continually walks around the room greeting all his friends, who is too busy talking to take a sip of his drink.
While he walks, a tiny hole in the glass slowly drips all the water out of the bottom at a steady rate.
DRIP
We measure the glass when we arrive, and it's at half a pint.
And then after ten minutes, it's at four-tenths of a pint.
We can see that he's been walking around with that glass for fifty minutes before we showed up.
So you measure over a set period of time and count up the atoms?
Precisely!
We can tell how much time passed by comparing the amount of beer in the glass to the amount of air.
How old has the stuff you've tested turned out to be?
I've got a piece of uranium that's 700 million years old.

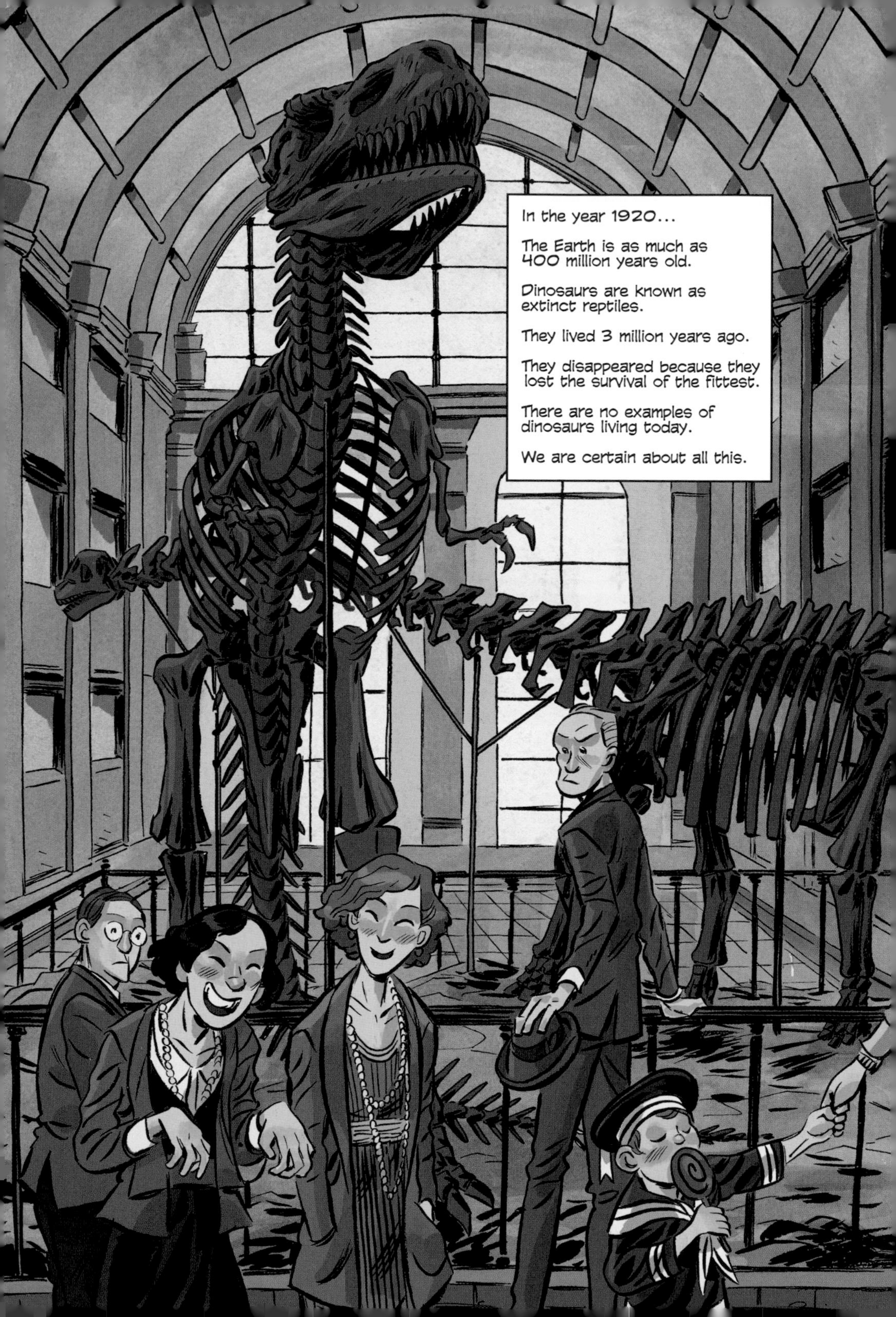
In the year 1920...
The Earth is as much as 400 million years old.
Dinosaurs are known as extinct reptiles.
They lived 3 million years ago.
They disappeared because they lost the survival of the fittest.
There are no examples of dinosaurs living today.
We are certain about all this.

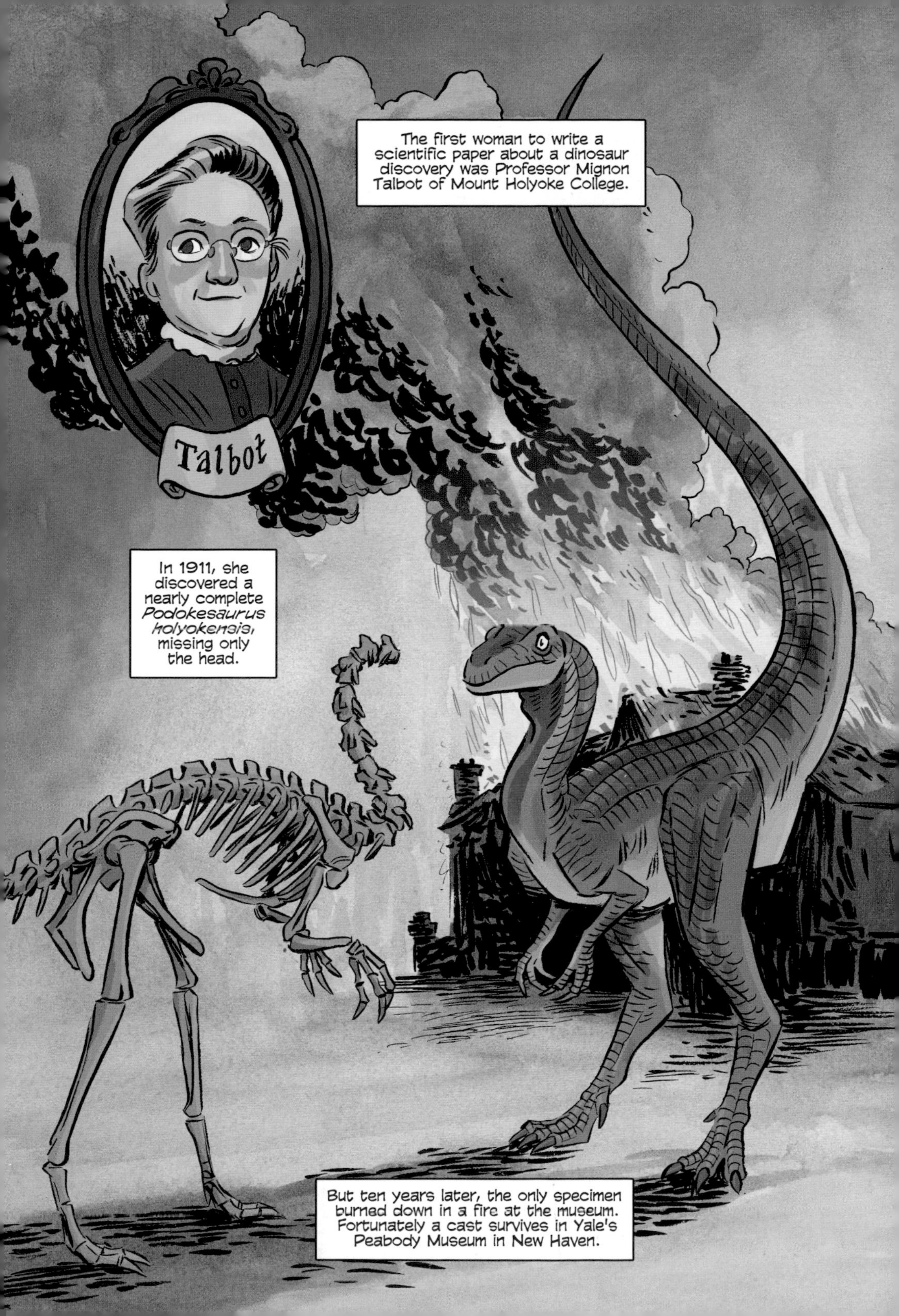

The first woman to write a scientific paper about a dinosaur discovery was Professor Mignon Talbot of Mount Holyoke College.
Talbot
In 1911, she discovered a nearly complete *Podokesaurus holyokensis*, missing only the head.
But ten years later, the only specimen burned down in a fire at the museum. Fortunately a cast survives in Yale's Peabody Museum in New Haven.

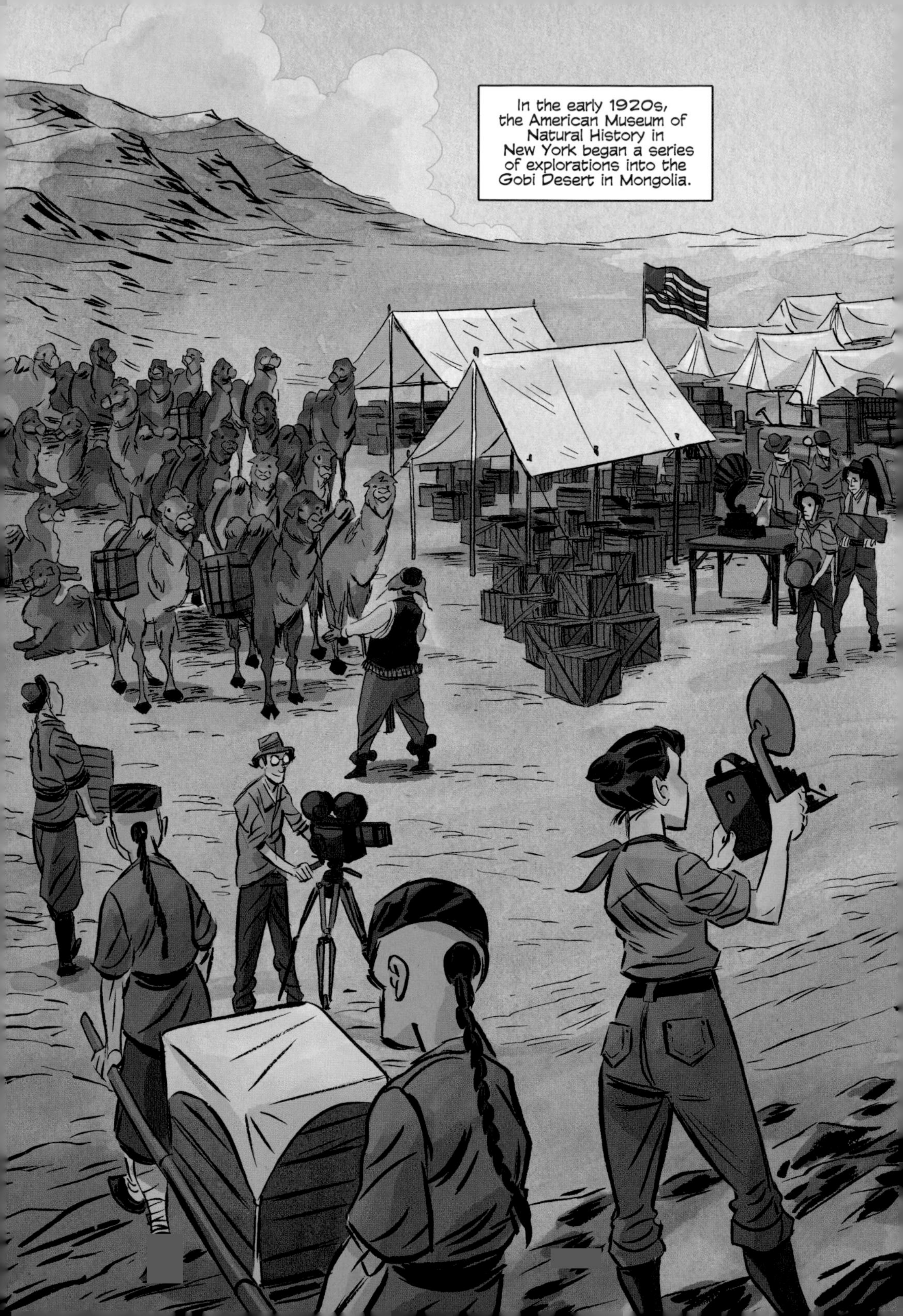
In the early 1920s, the American Museum of Natural History in New York began a series of explorations into the Gobi Desert in Mongolia.

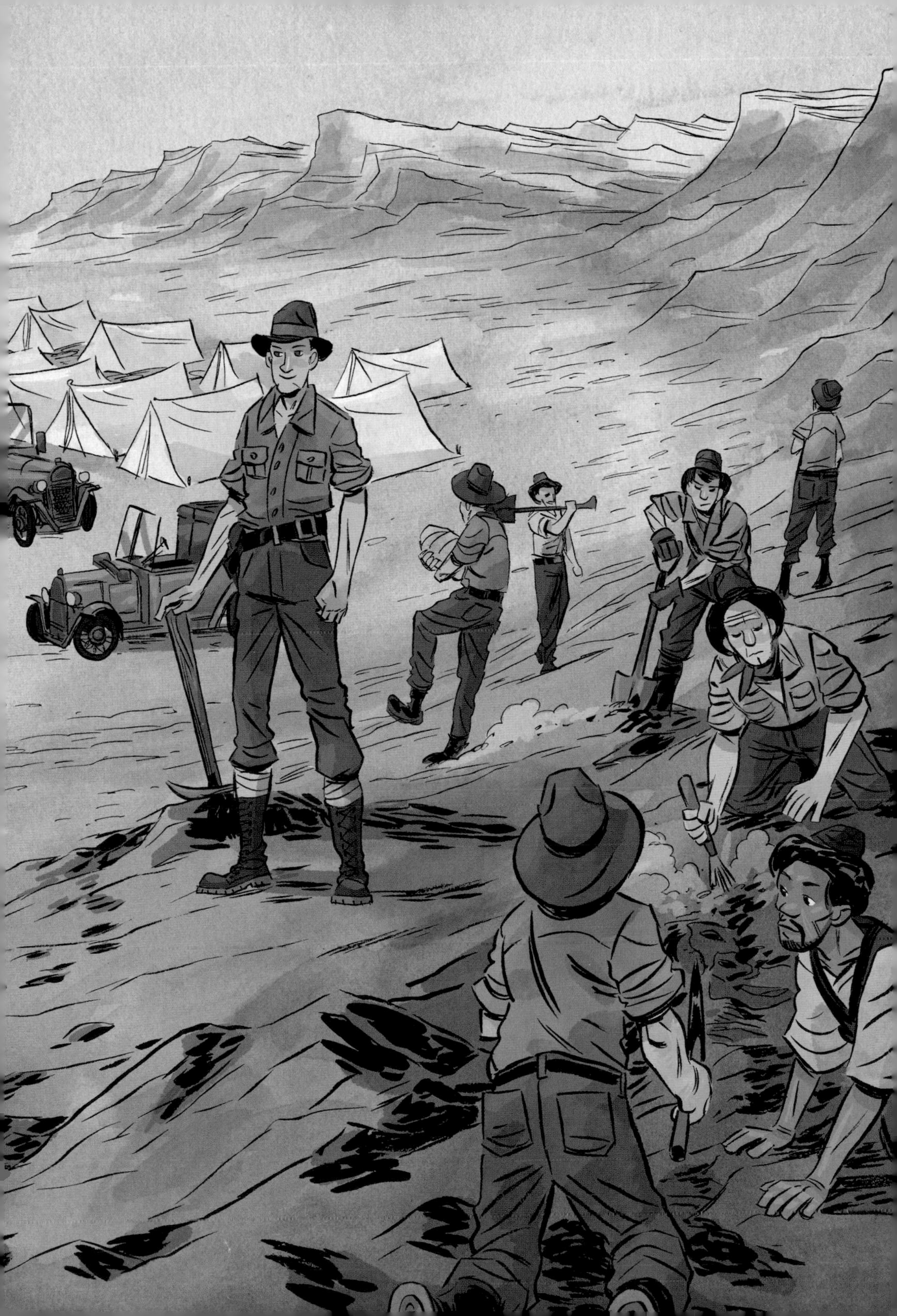

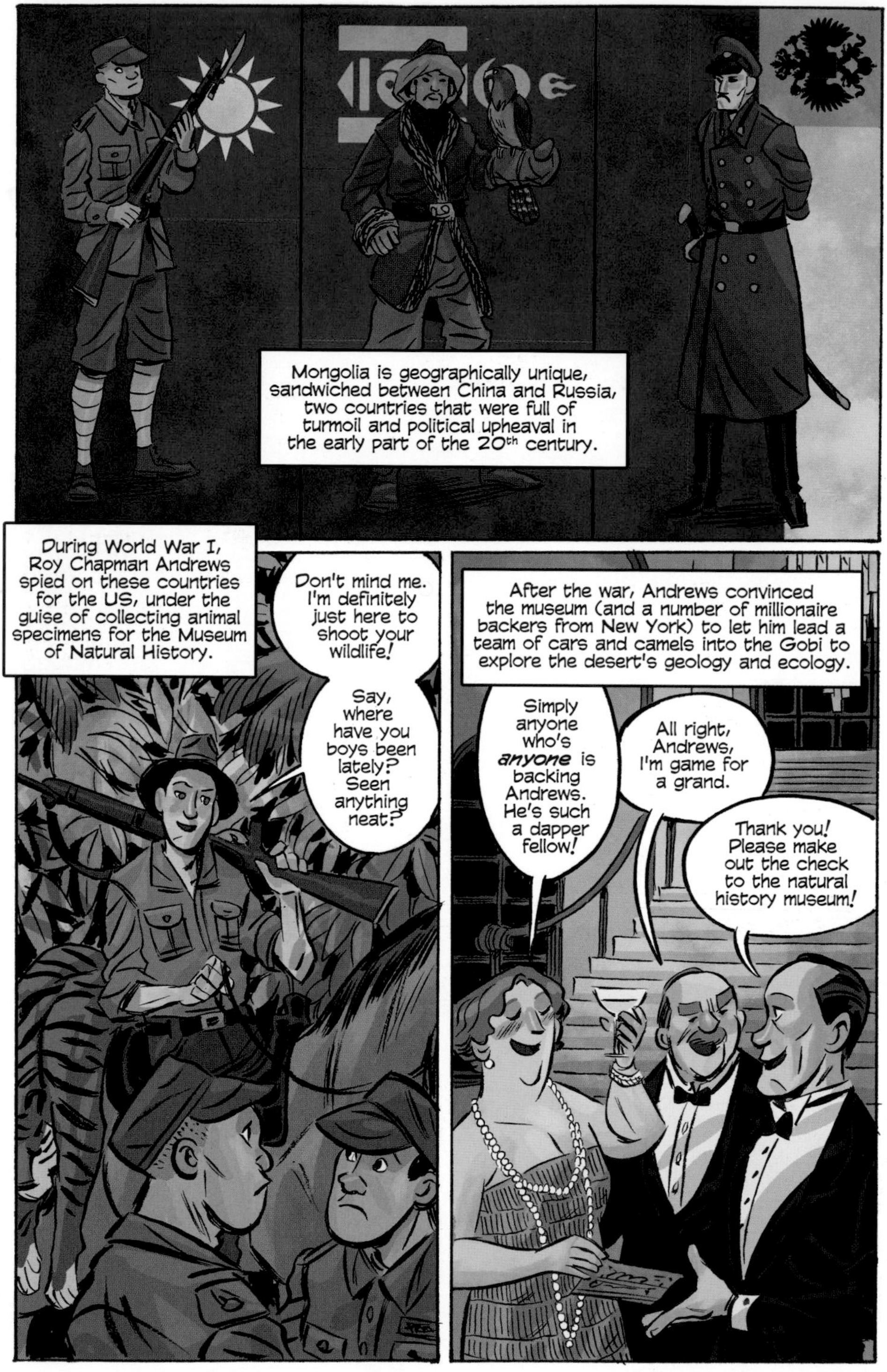

Mongolia is geographically unique, sandwiched between China and Russia, two countries that were full of turmoil and political upheaval in the early part of the 20th century.
During World War I, Roy Chapman Andrews spied on these countries for the US, under the guise of collecting animal specimens for the Museum of Natural History.
Don't mind me. I'm definitely just here to shoot your wildlife!
Say, where have you boys been lately? Seen anything neat?
After the war, Andrews convinced the museum (and a number of millionaire backers from New York) to let him lead a team of cars and camels into the Gobi to explore the desert's geology and ecology.
Simply anyone who's *anyone* is backing Andrews. He's such a dapper fellow!
All right, Andrews, I'm game for a grand.
Thank you! Please make out the check to the natural history museum!

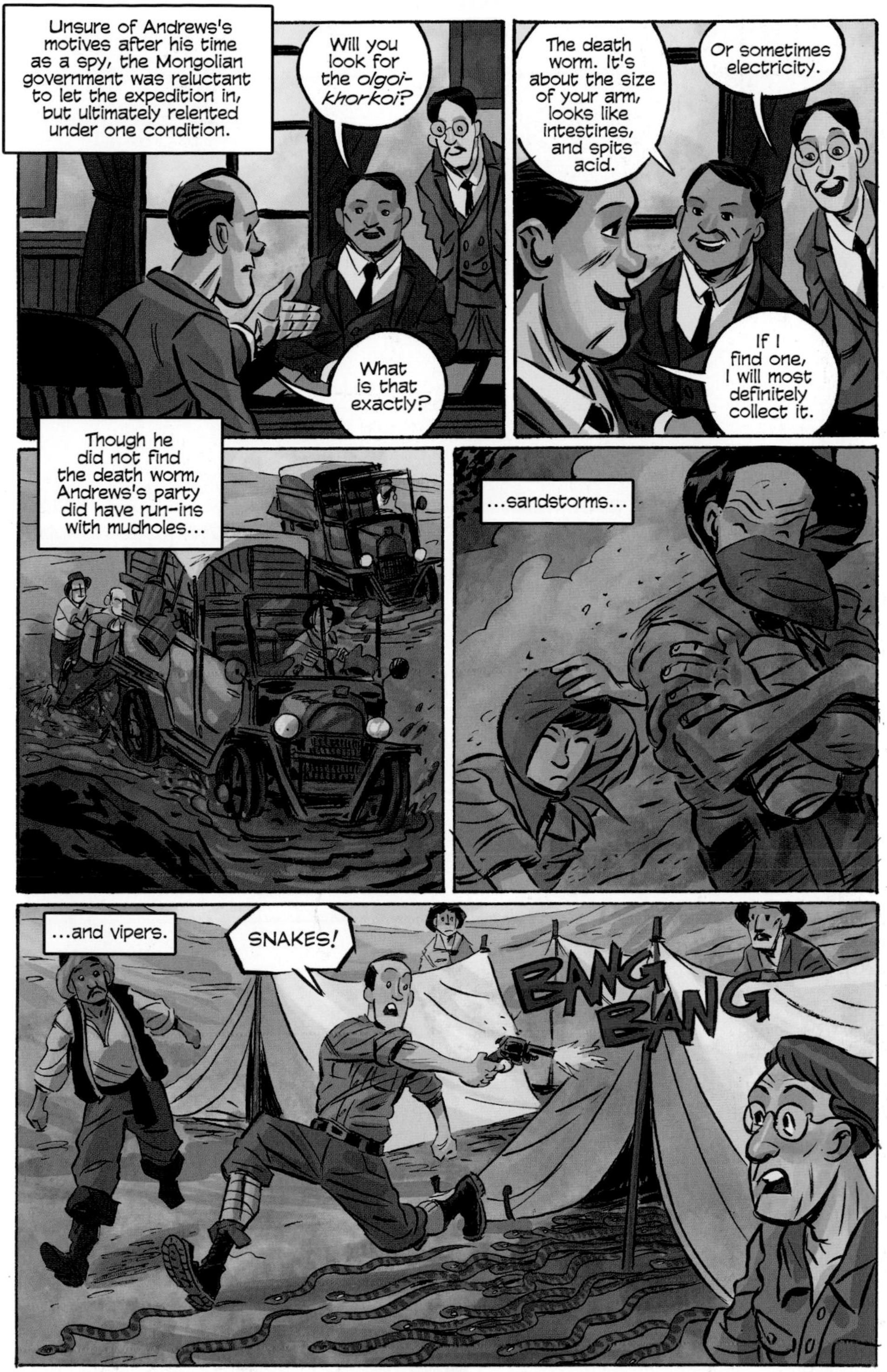
Unsure of Andrews's motives after his time as a spy, the Mongolian government was reluctant to let the expedition in, but ultimately relented under one condition.
Will you look for the *olgoi-khorkoi*?
What is that exactly?
The death worm. It's about the size of your arm, looks like intestines, and spits acid.
Or sometimes electricity.
If I find one, I will most definitely collect it.
Though he did not find the death worm, Andrews's party did have run-ins with mudholes...
...sandstorms...
...and vipers.
SNAKES!
BANG BANG

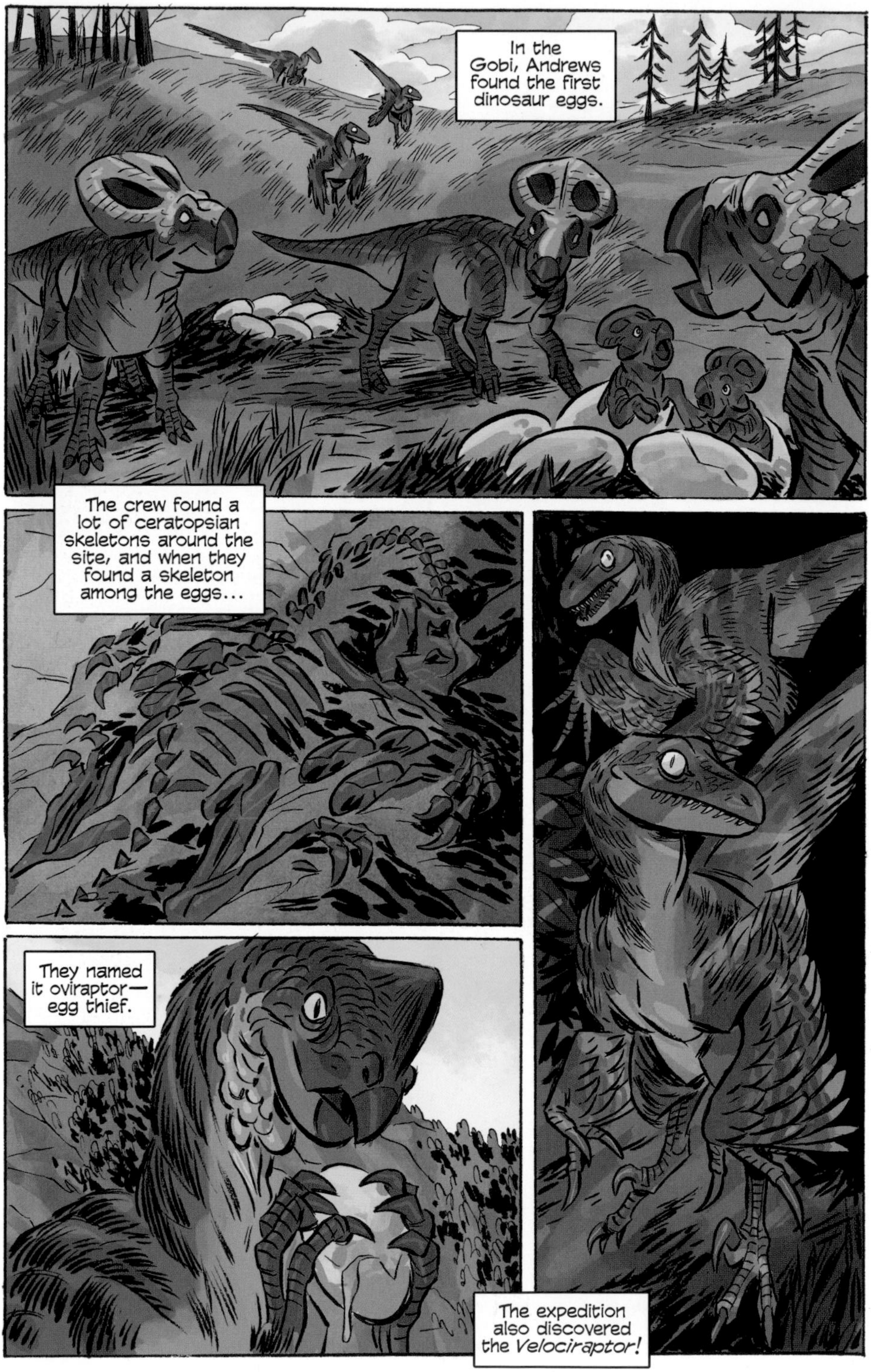
In the Gobi, Andrews found the first dinosaur eggs.
The crew found a lot of ceratopsian skeletons around the site, and when they found a skeleton among the eggs...
They named it oviraptor—egg thief.
The expedition also discovered the *Velociraptor*!

The museum made about 5 trips to the Gobi during 1923-30, but encountered increasing problems. Political unrest from revolutions happening in each country also complicated the trips.

We need to avoid the soldiers if we want to keep our supplies.

Mongolia was taken over by Russia, and an expedition there became far too bureaucratic and expensive for the museum to finance.

WE WANT WORK NOW!

UNEMPLOYED WILL TAKE ANY JOB

WILL TAKE ANY JOB

WANTED ANY JOB 2 YEARS

WANED JOB

GIVE MY DAD A JOB

The Great Depression and then World War II turned a lot of focus onto physics and nuclear research.

This rocky portion of history prevented much paleontology and geology from being done.

But some geology was squeezed in, thanks to Princeton mineralogist Harry Hess, who left the fathometer on his submarine running day and night through out the war.

Yes, sir!

Keep up the good work, Hess, the Nazis could be on us at any moment!

73

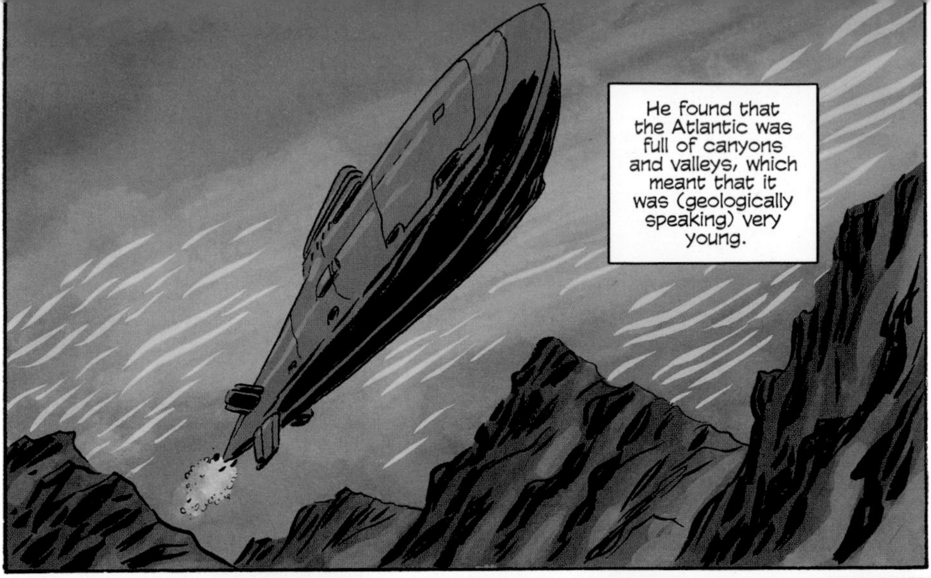
He found that the Atlantic was full of canyons and valleys, which meant that it was (geologically speaking) very young.

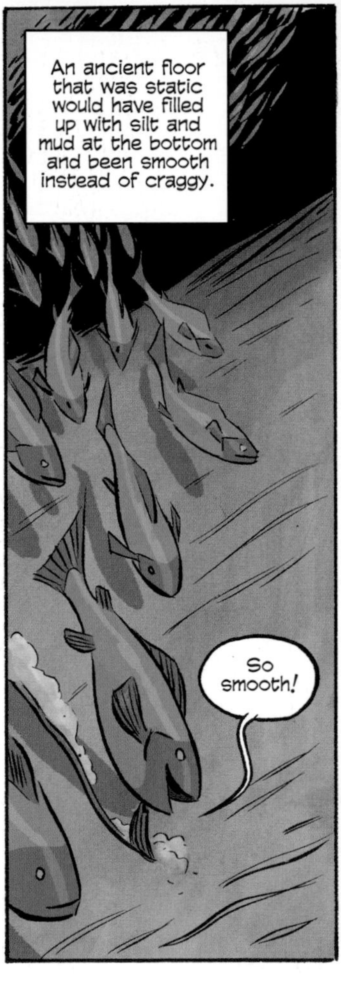
An ancient floor that was static would have filled up with silt and mud at the bottom and been smooth instead of craggy.
So smooth!

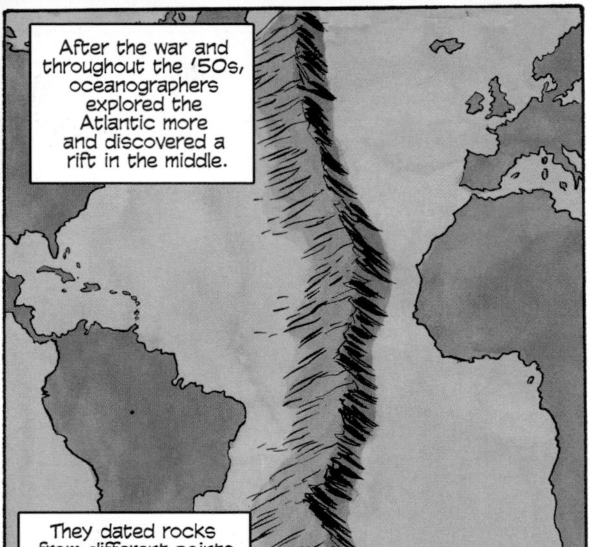
After the war and throughout the '50s, oceanographers explored the Atlantic more and discovered a rift in the middle.

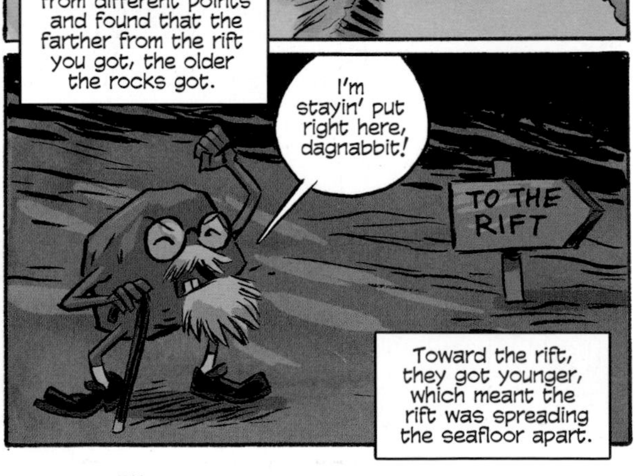
They dated rocks from different points and found that the farther from the rift you got, the older the rocks got.
I'm stayin' put right here, dagnabbit!
TO THE RIFT
Toward the rift, they got younger, which meant the rift was spreading the seafloor apart.

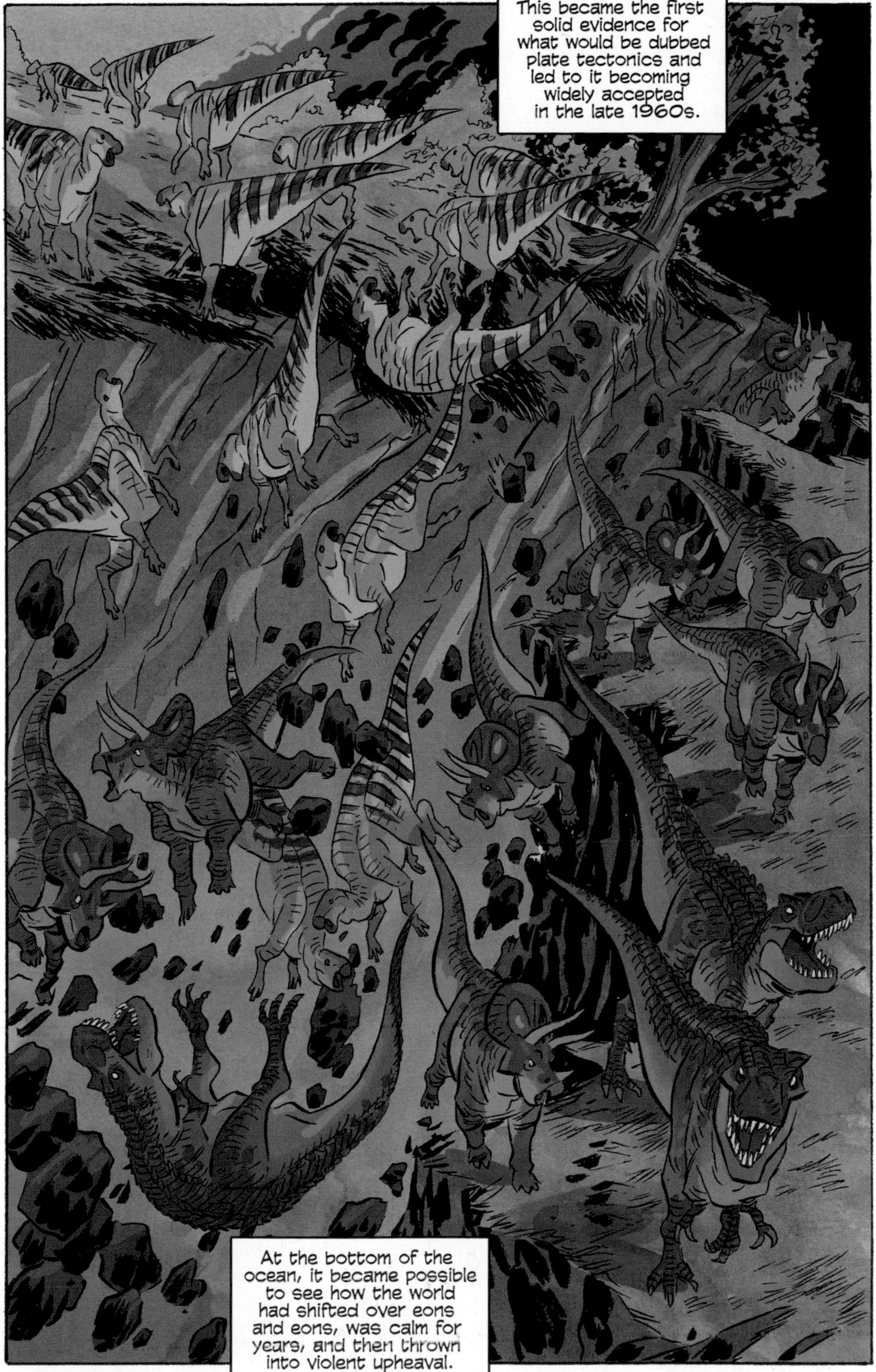
This became the first solid evidence for what would be dubbed plate tectonics and led to it becoming widely accepted in the late 1960s.
At the bottom of the ocean, it became possible to see how the world had shifted over eons and eons, was calm for years, and then thrown into violent upheaval.

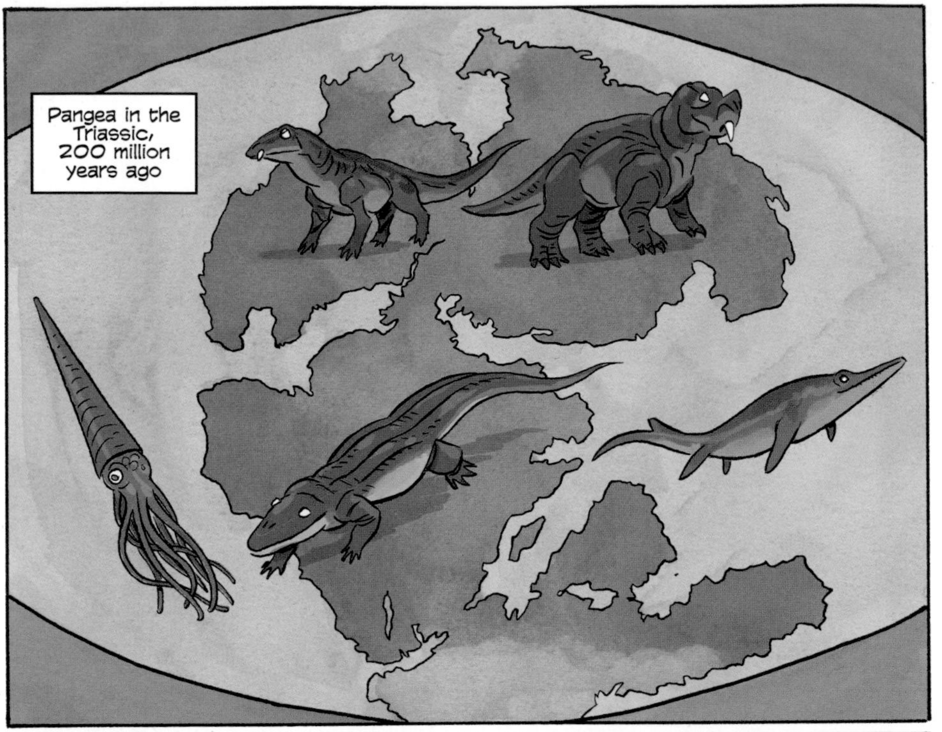
Pangea in the Triassic, 200 million years ago

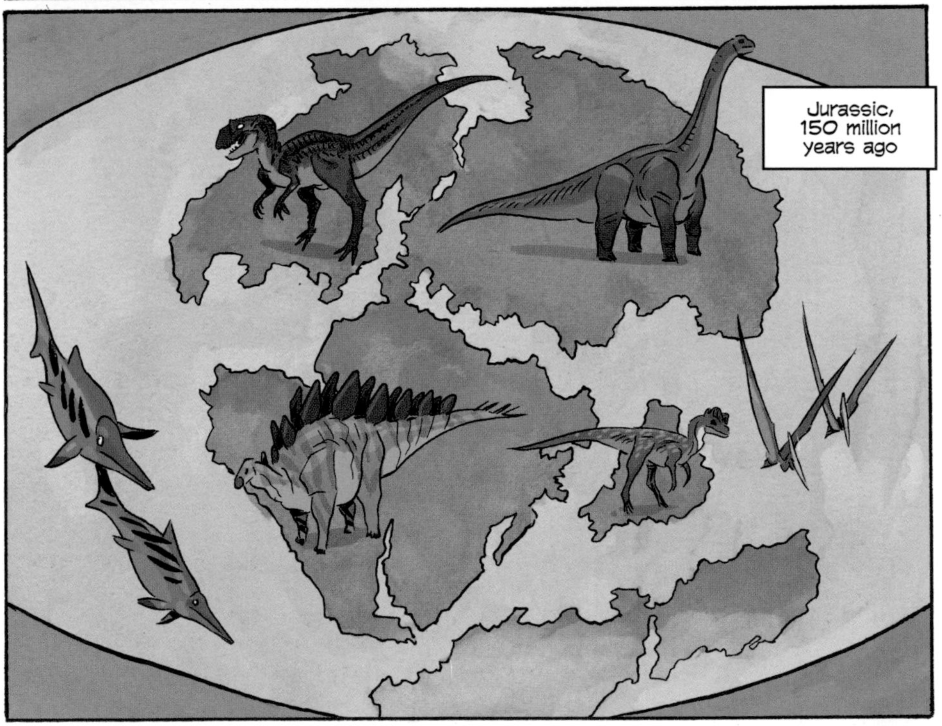
Jurassic, 150 million years ago

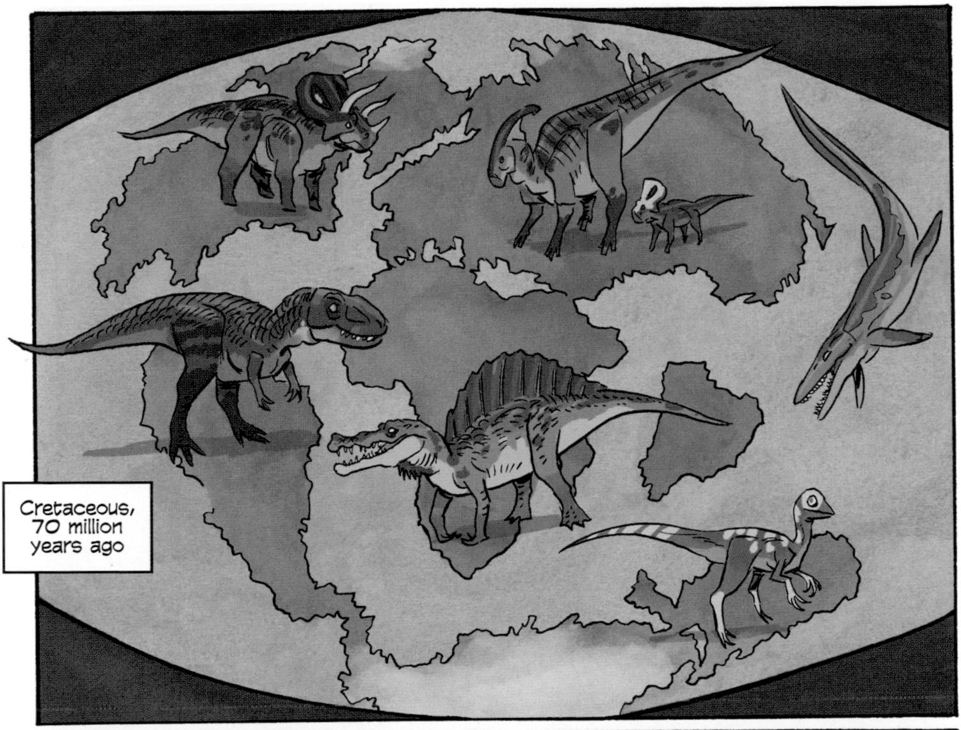
Cretaceous,
70 million
years ago

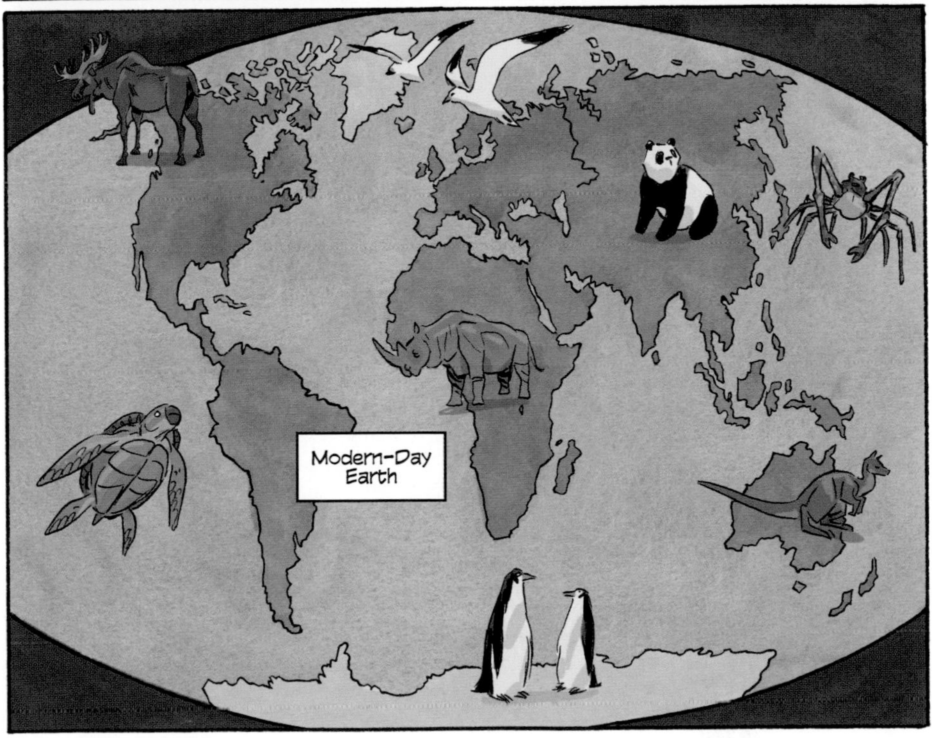
Modern-Day
Earth

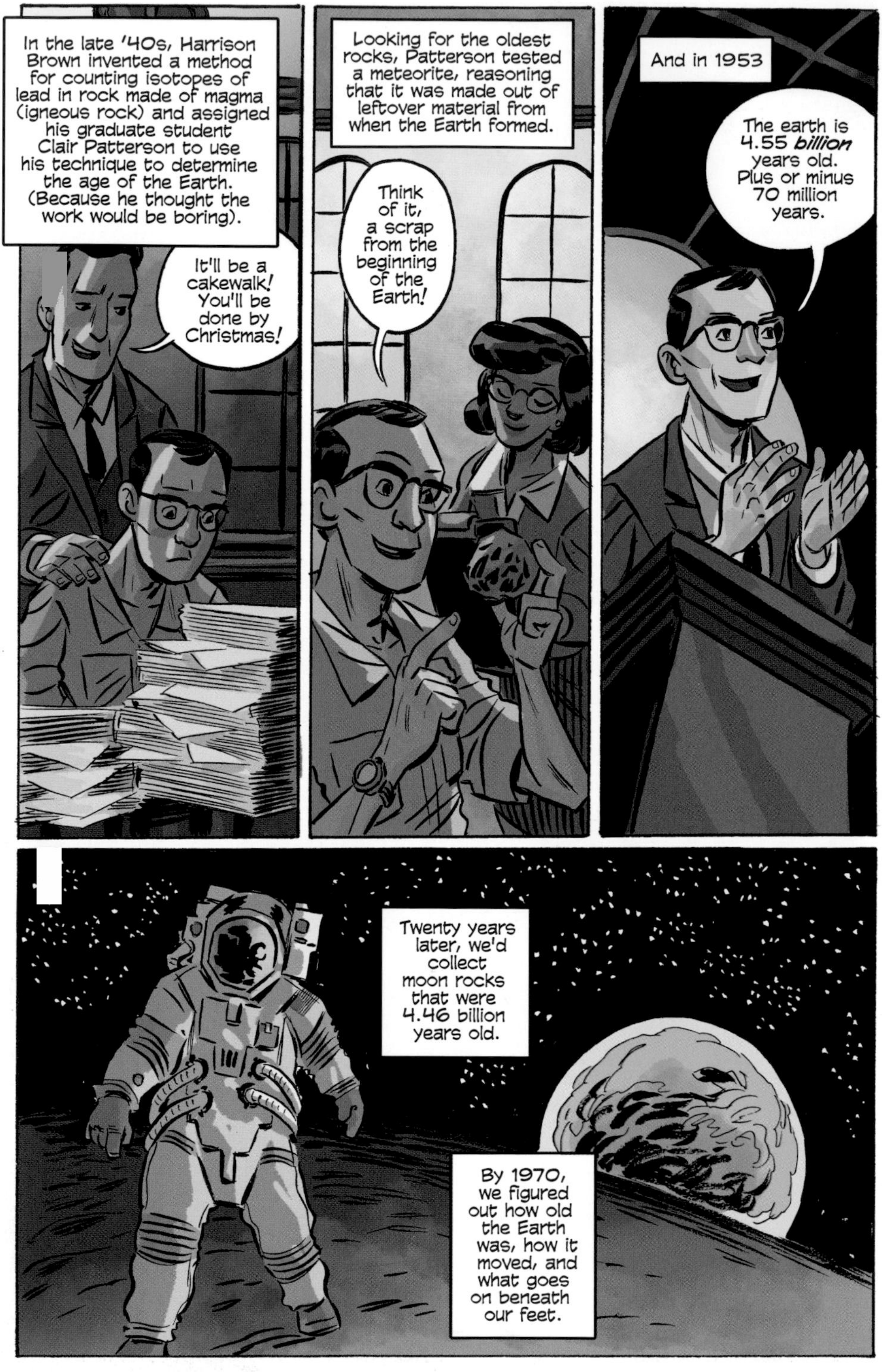

In the late '40s, Harrison Brown invented a method for counting isotopes of lead in rock made of magma (igneous rock) and assigned his graduate student Clair Patterson to use his technique to determine the age of the Earth. (Because he thought the work would be boring).
It'll be a cakewalk! You'll be done by Christmas!
Looking for the oldest rocks, Patterson tested a meteorite, reasoning that it was made out of leftover material from when the Earth formed.
Think of it, a scrap from the beginning of the Earth!
And in 1953
The earth is 4.55 *billion* years old. Plus or minus 70 million years.
Twenty years later, we'd collect moon rocks that were 4.46 billion years old.
By 1970, we figured out how old the Earth was, how it moved, and what goes on beneath our feet.

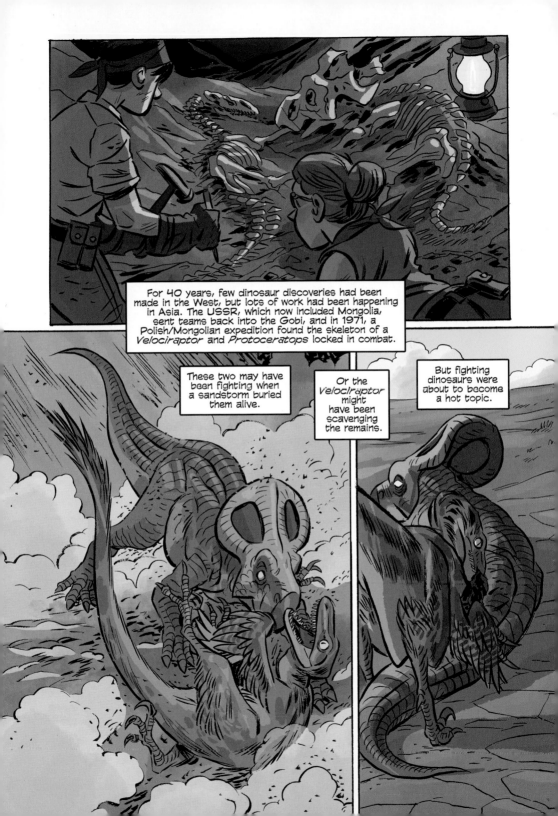

For 40 years, few dinosaur discoveries had been made in the West, but lots of work had been happening in Asia. The USSR, which now included Mongolia, sent teams back into the Gobi, and in 1971, a Polish/Mongolian expedition found the skeleton of a *Velociraptor* and *Protoceratops* locked in combat.

These two may have been fighting when a sandstorm buried them alive.

Or the *Velociraptor* might have been scavenging the remains.

But fighting dinosaurs were about to become a hot topic.

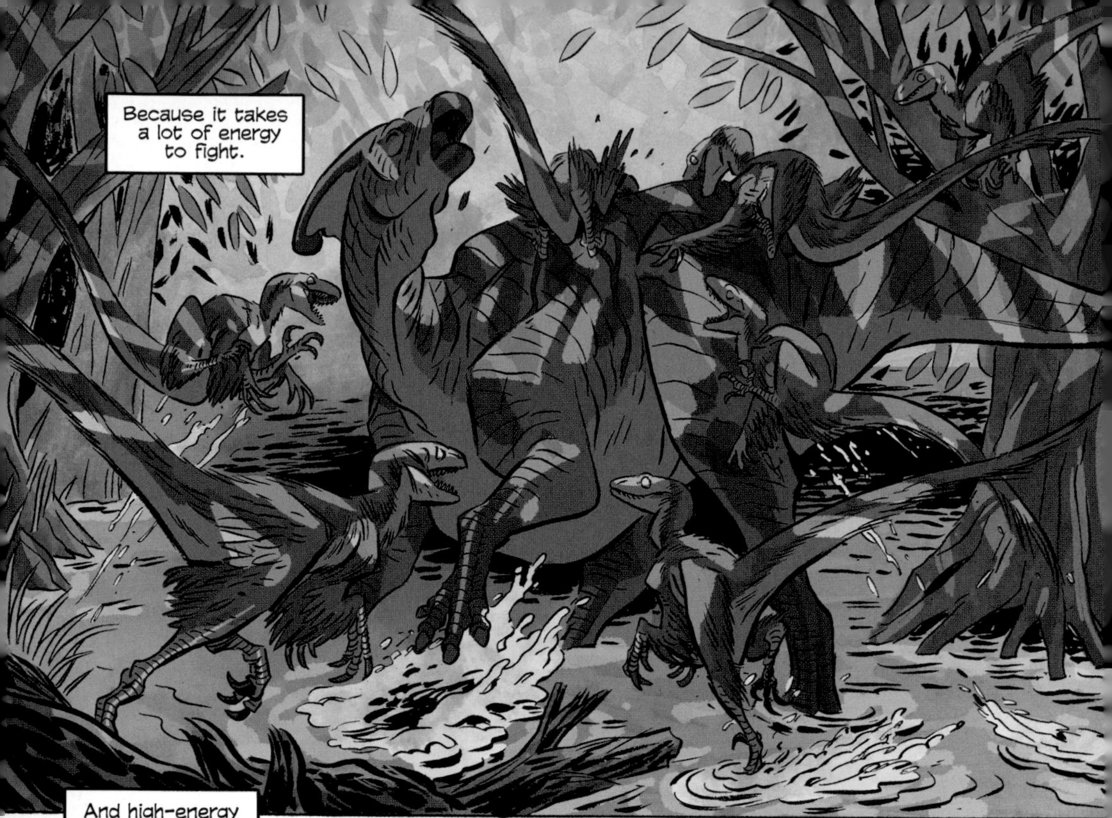
Because it takes a lot of energy to fight.

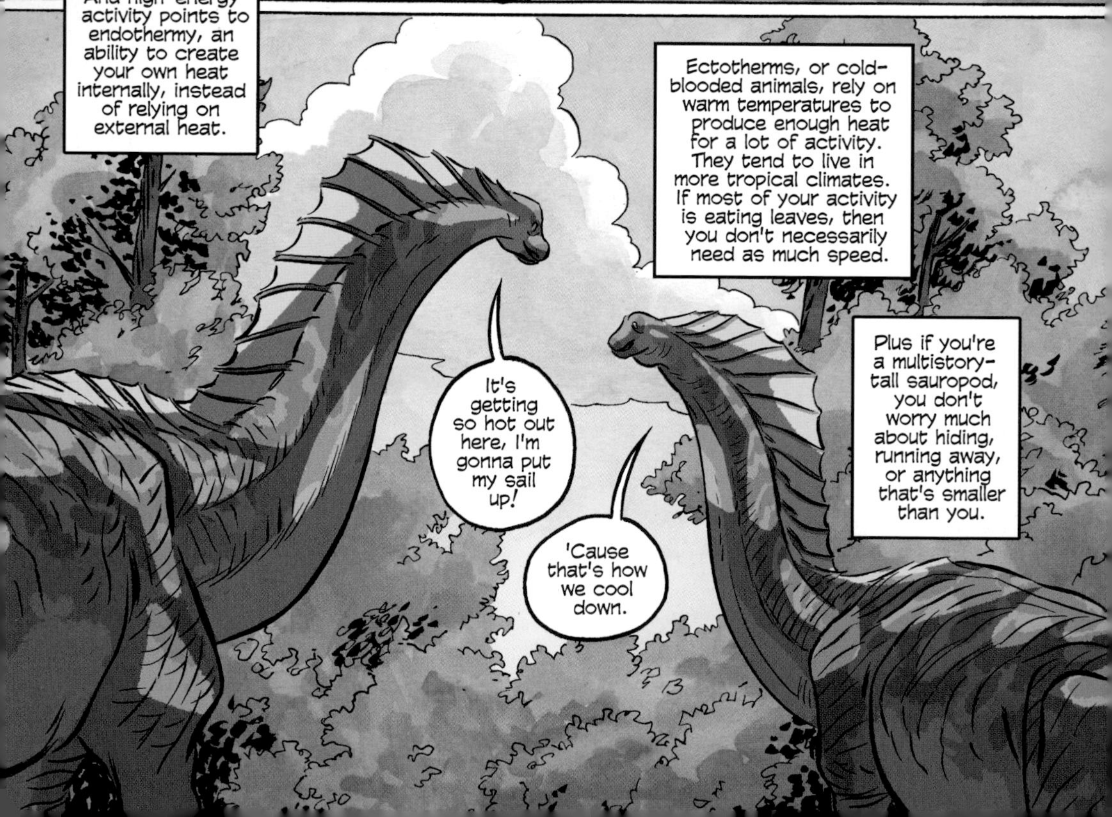
And high-energy activity points to endothermy, an ability to create your own heat internally, instead of relying on external heat.
Ectotherms, or cold-blooded animals, rely on warm temperatures to produce enough heat for a lot of activity. They tend to live in more tropical climates. If most of your activity is eating leaves, then you don't necessarily need as much speed.
It's getting so hot out here, I'm gonna put my sail up!
'Cause that's how we cool down.
Plus if you're a multistory-tall sauropod, you don't worry much about hiding, running away, or anything that's smaller than you.

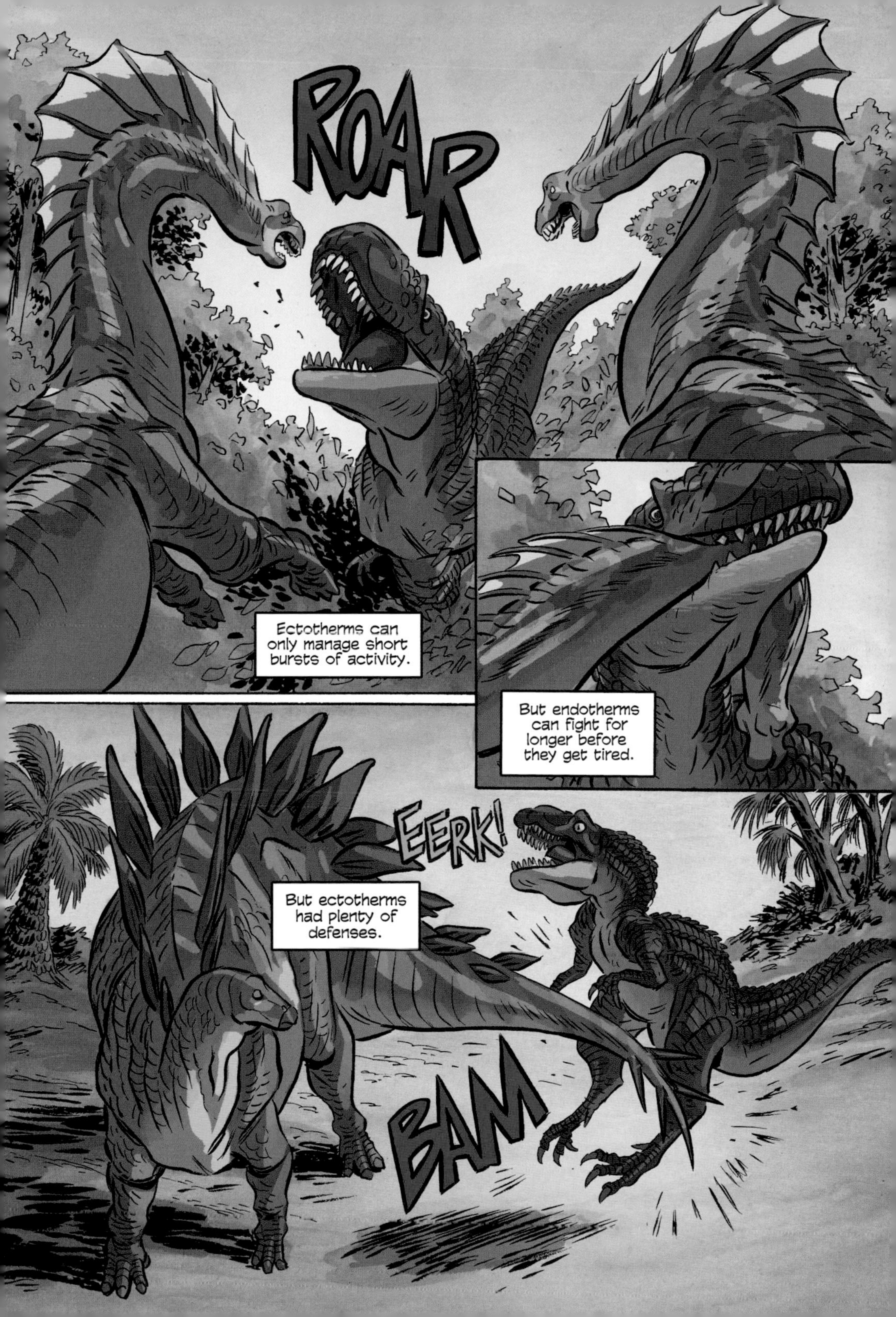
ROAR
Ectotherms can only manage short bursts of activity.
But endotherms can fight for longer before they get tired.
EERK!
But ectotherms had plenty of defenses.
BAM

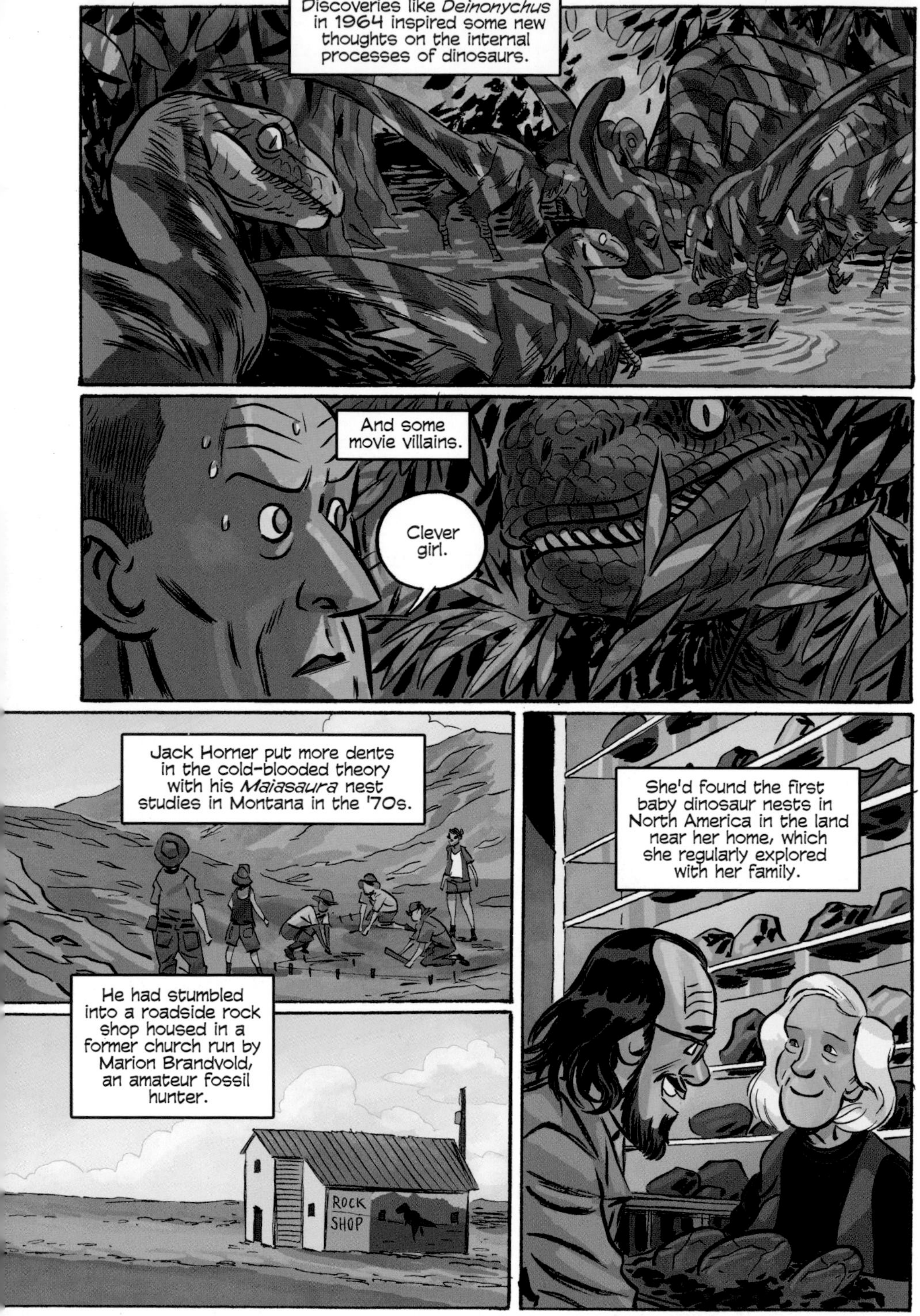
Discoveries like *Deinonychus* in 1964 inspired some new thoughts on the internal processes of dinosaurs.
And some movie villains.
Clever girl.
Jack Horner put more dents in the cold-blooded theory with his *Maiasaura* nest studies in Montana in the '70s.
He had stumbled into a roadside rock shop housed in a former church run by Marion Brandvold, an amateur fossil hunter.
ROCK SHOP
She'd found the first baby dinosaur nests in North America in the land near her home, which she regularly explored with her family.

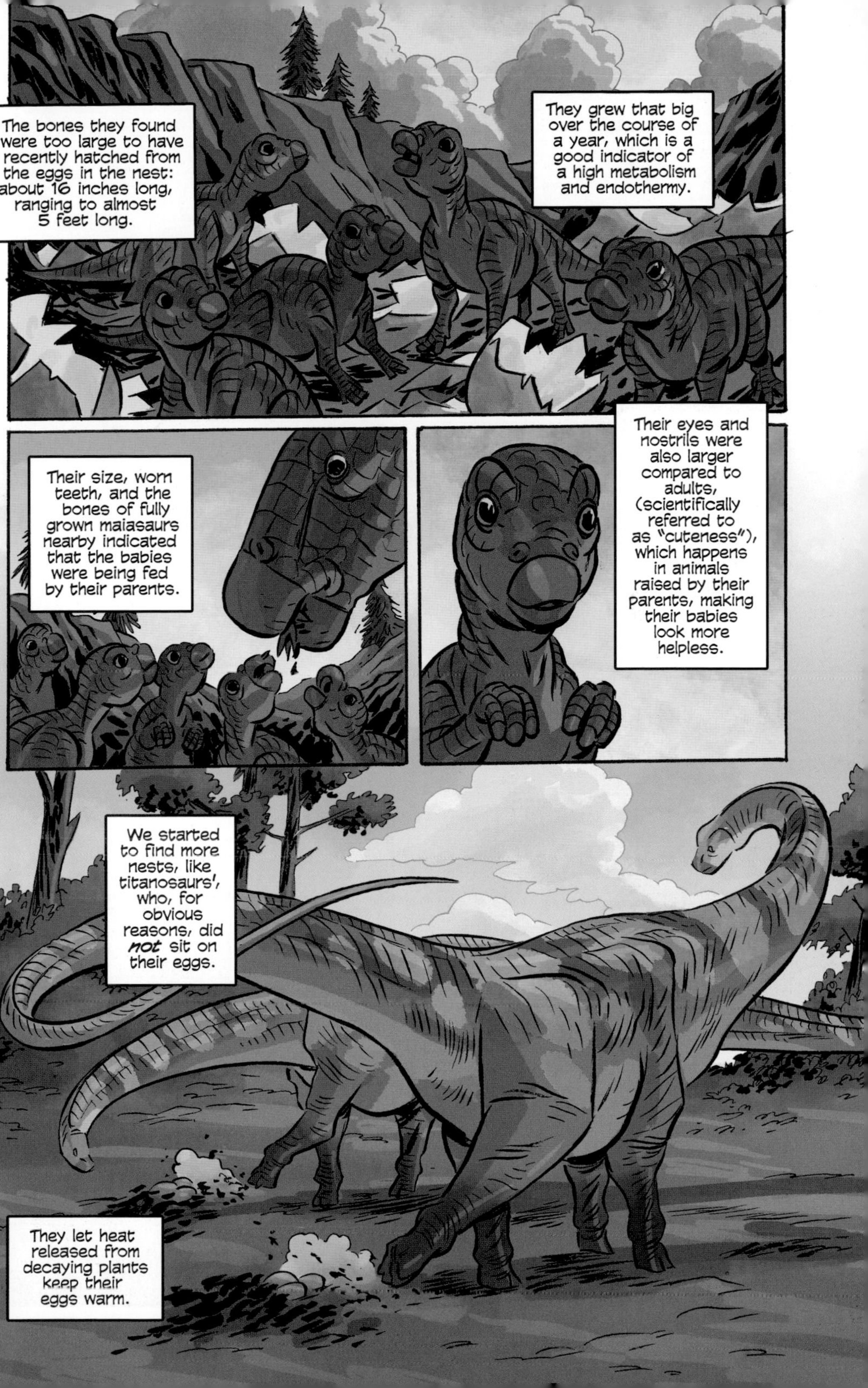

The bones they found were too large to have recently hatched from the eggs in the nest: about 16 inches long, ranging to almost 5 feet long.
They grew that big over the course of a year, which is a good indicator of a high metabolism and endothermy.
Their size, worn teeth, and the bones of fully grown maiasaurs nearby indicated that the babies were being fed by their parents.
Their eyes and nostrils were also larger compared to adults, (scientifically referred to as "cuteness"), which happens in animals raised by their parents, making their babies look more helpless.
We started to find more nests, like titanosaurs', who, for obvious reasons, did *not* sit on their eggs.
They let heat released from decaying plants keep their eggs warm.

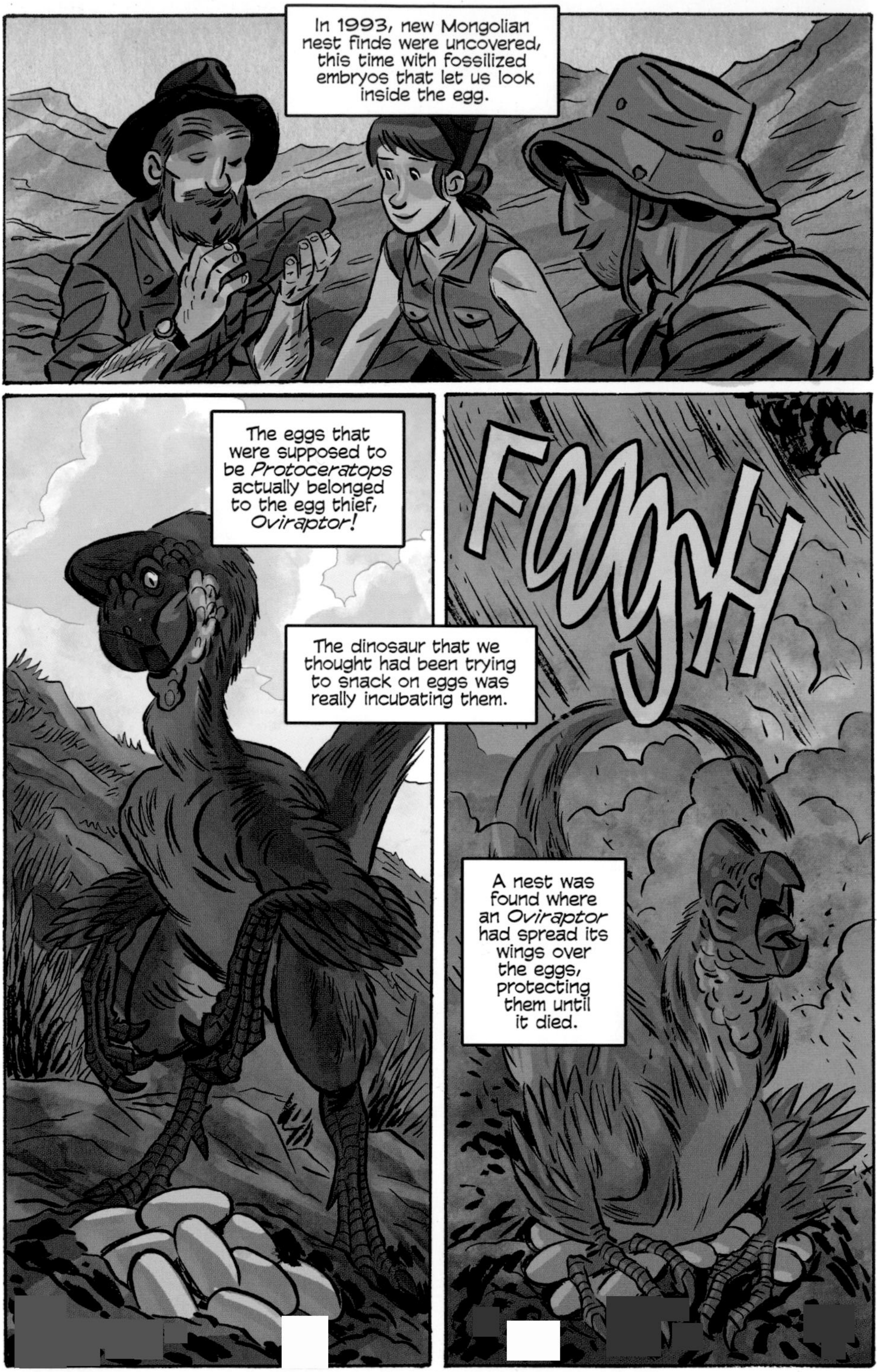
In 1993, new Mongolian nest finds were uncovered, this time with fossilized embryos that let us look inside the egg.
The eggs that were supposed to be *Protoceratops* actually belonged to the egg thief, *Oviraptor*!
The dinosaur that we thought had been trying to snack on eggs was really incubating them.
FOOGH
A nest was found where an *Oviraptor* had spread its wings over the eggs, protecting them until it died.

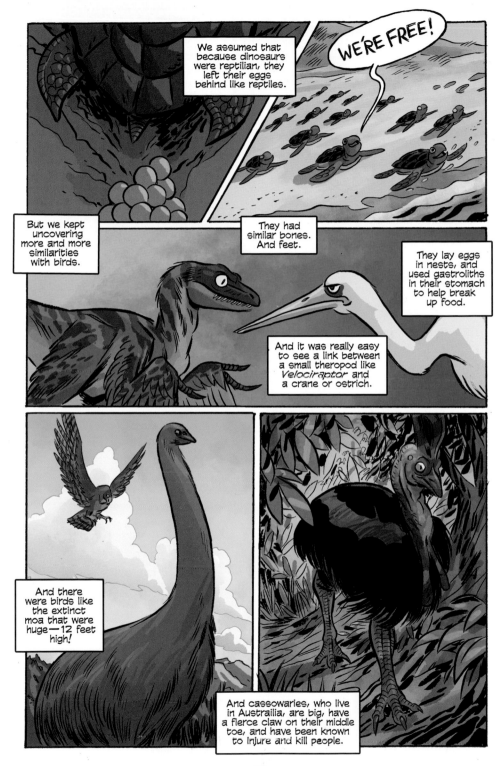

We assumed that because dinosaurs were reptilian, they left their eggs behind like reptiles.

WE'RE FREE!

But we kept uncovering more and more similarities with birds.

They had similar bones. And feet.

They lay eggs in nests, and used gastroliths in their stomach to help break up food.

And it was really easy to see a link between a small theropod like *Velociraptor* and a crane or ostrich.

And there were birds like the extinct moa that were huge—12 feet high!

And cassowaries, who live in Austrailia, are big, have a fierce claw on their middle toe, and have been known to injure and kill people.

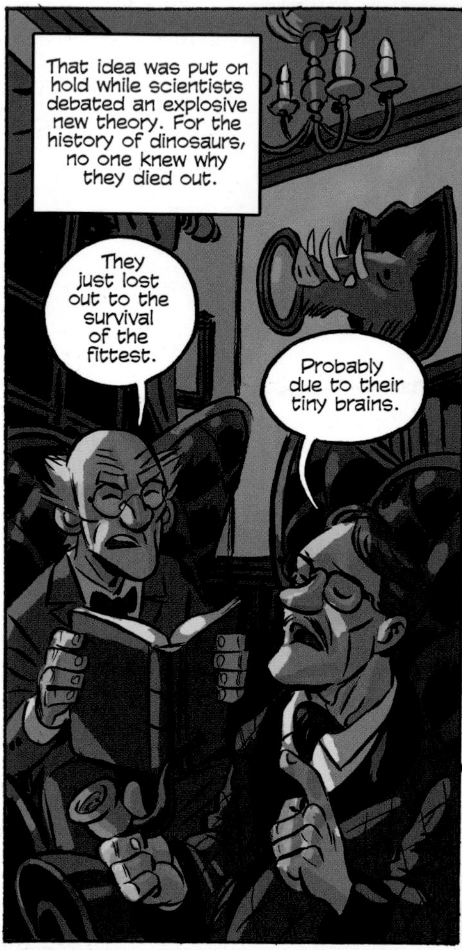
That idea was put on hold while scientists debated an explosive new theory. For the history of dinosaurs, no one knew why they died out.
They just lost out to the survival of the fittest.
Probably due to their tiny brains.

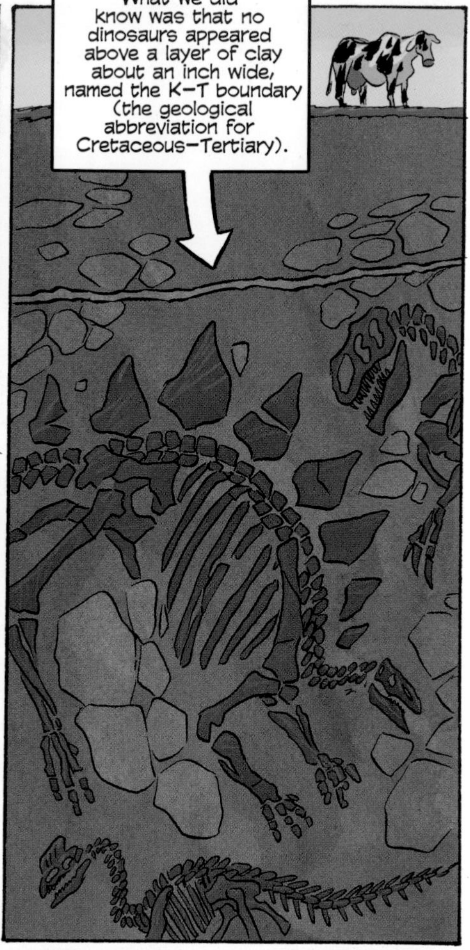
What we did know was that no dinosaurs appeared above a layer of clay about an inch wide, named the K–T boundary (the geological abbreviation for Cretaceous–Tertiary).

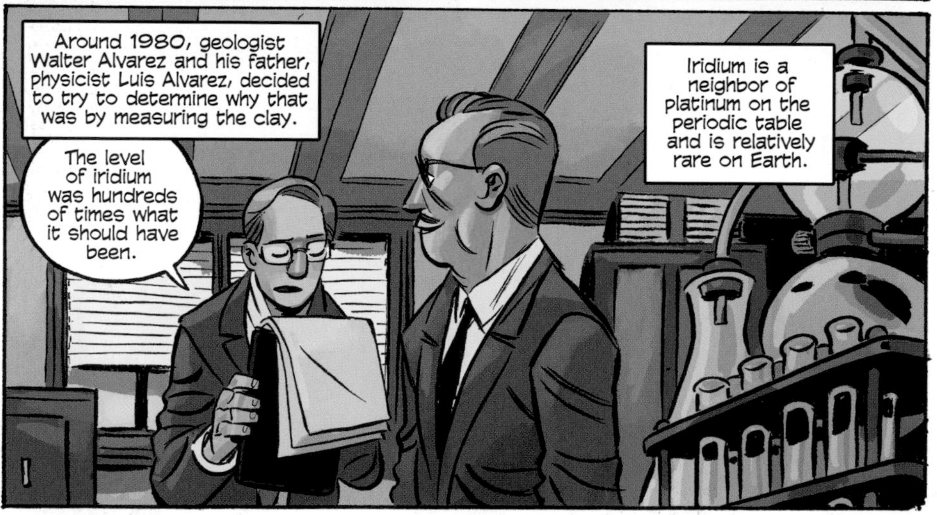
Around 1980, geologist Walter Alvarez and his father, physicist Luis Alvarez, decided to try to determine why that was by measuring the clay.
The level of iridium was hundreds of times what it should have been.
Iridium is a neighbor of platinum on the periodic table and is relatively rare on Earth.

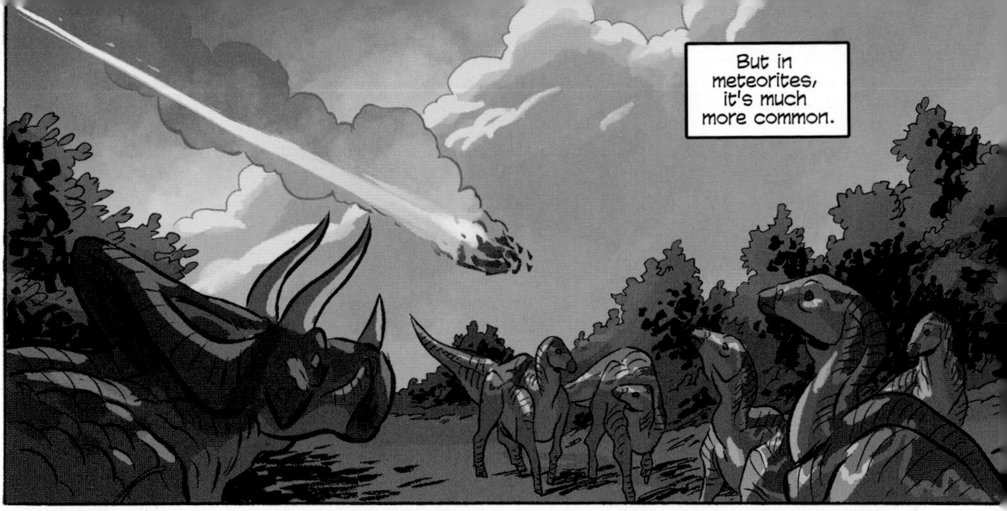
But in meteorites, it's much more common.

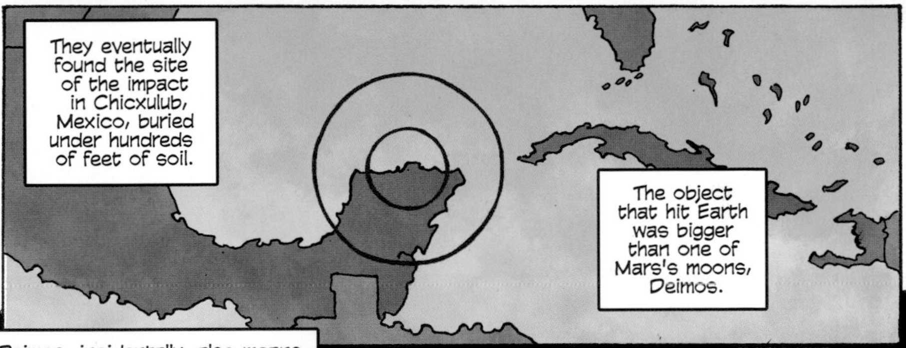
They eventually found the site of the impact in Chicxulub, Mexico, buried under hundreds of feet of soil.
The object that hit Earth was bigger than one of Mars's moons, Deimos.

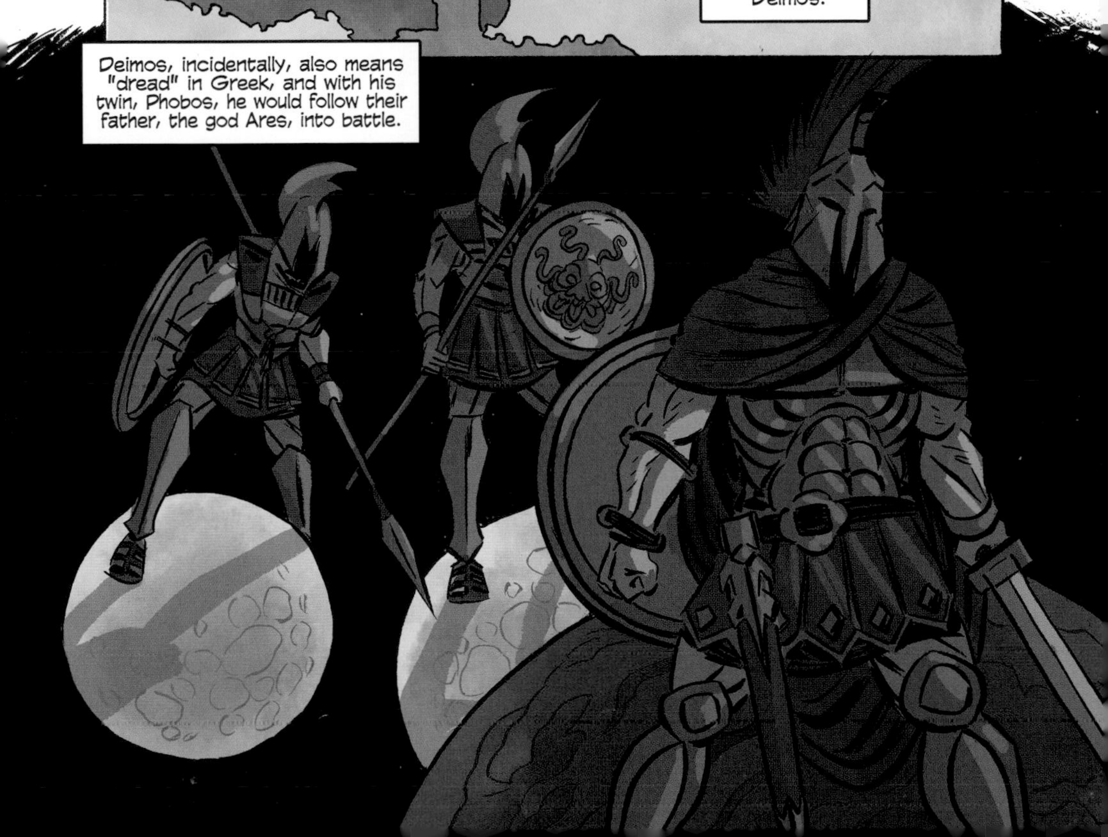
Deimos, incidentally, also means "dread" in Greek, and with his twin, Phobos, he would follow their father, the god Ares, into battle.

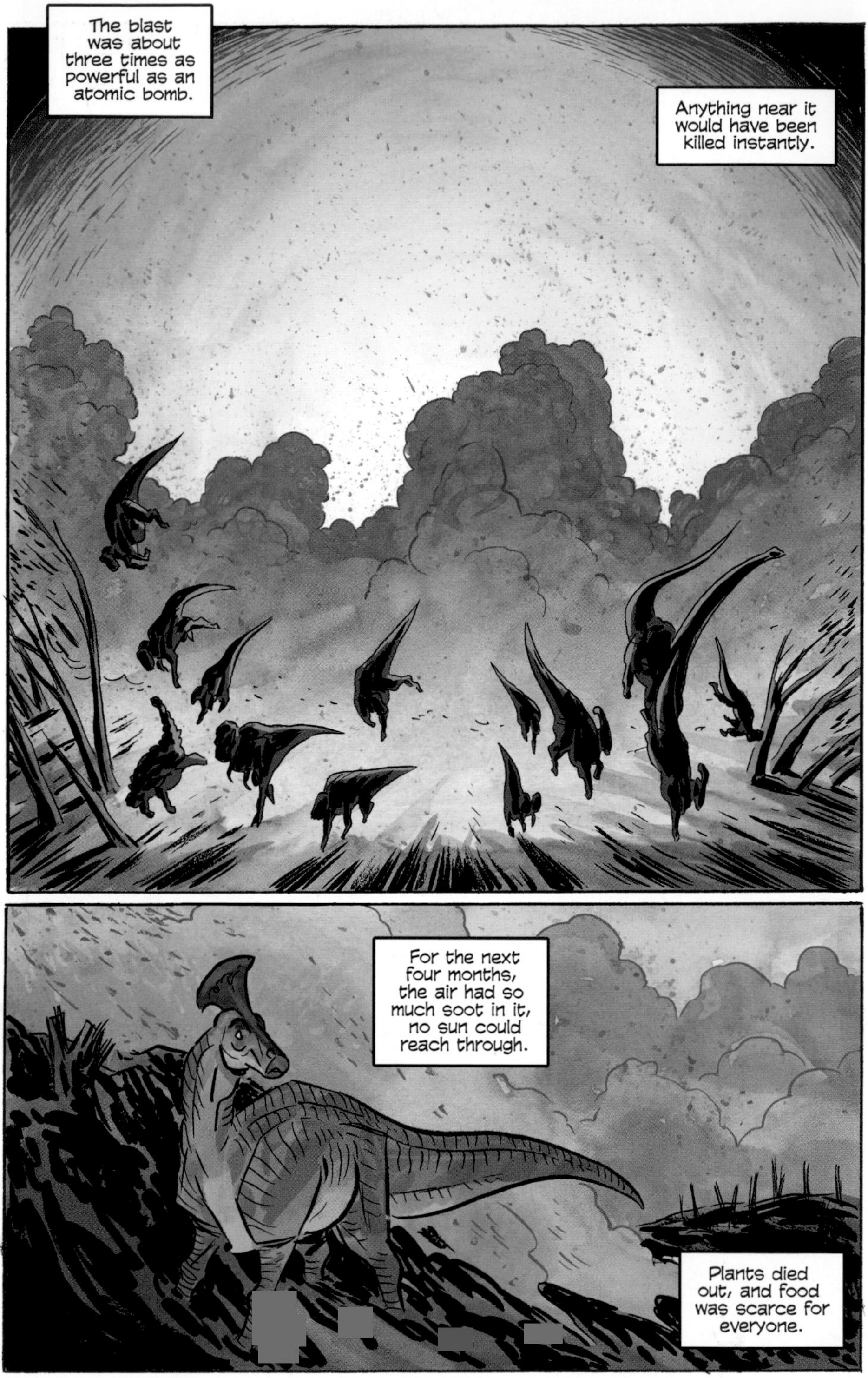
The blast was about three times as powerful as an atomic bomb.
Anything near it would have been killed instantly.
For the next four months, the air had so much soot in it, no sun could reach through.
Plants died out, and food was scarce for everyone.

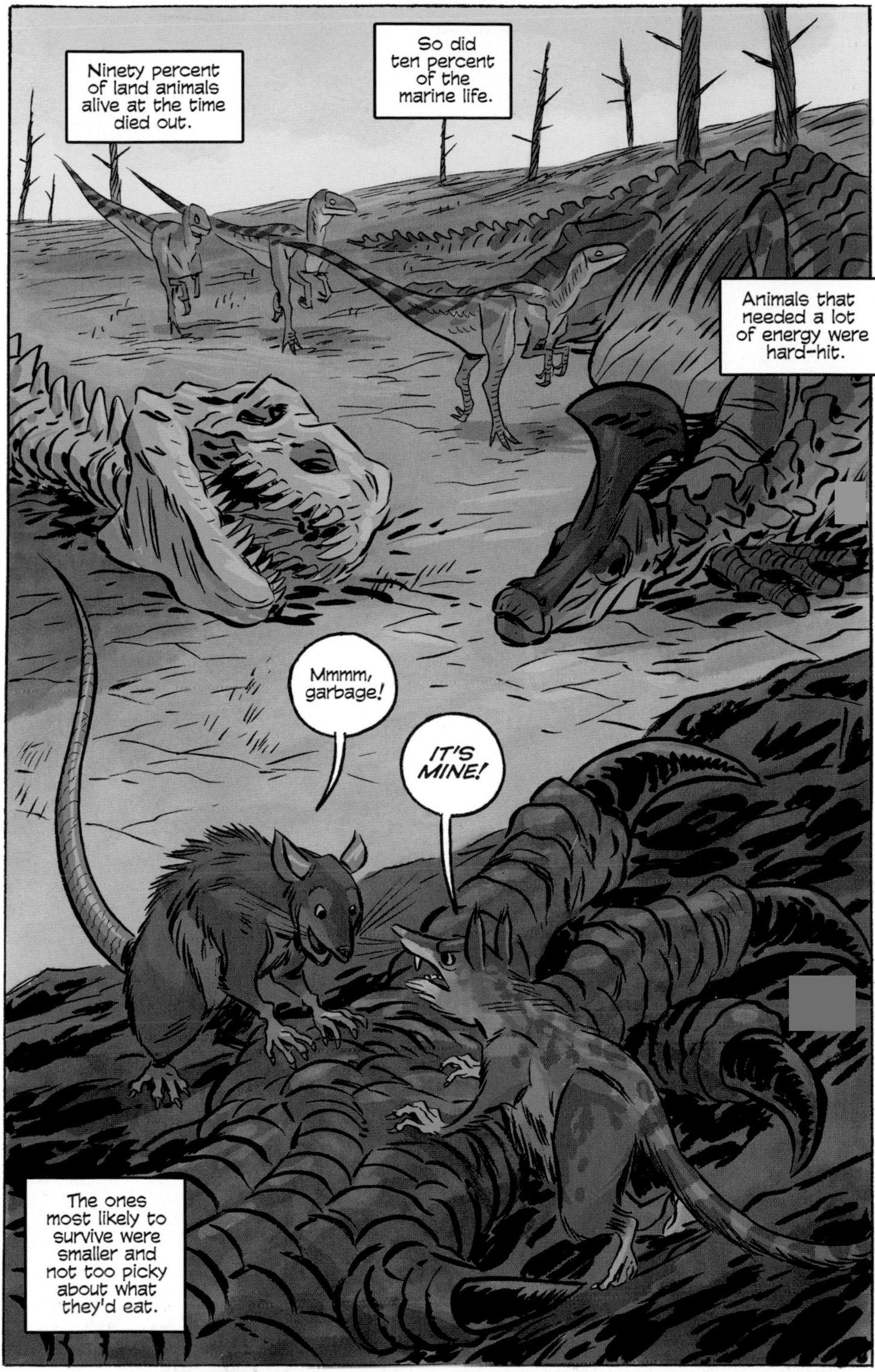
Ninety percent of land animals alive at the time died out.
So did ten percent of the marine life.
Animals that needed a lot of energy were hard-hit.
Mmmm, garbage!
IT'S MINE!
The ones most likely to survive were smaller and not too picky about what they'd eat.

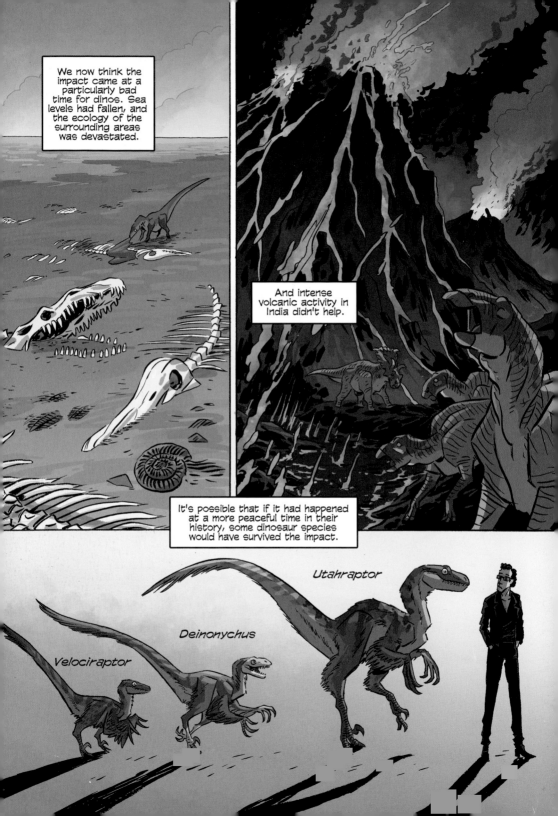

We now think the impact came at a particularly bad time for dinos. Sea levels had fallen, and the ecology of the surrounding areas was devastated.

And intense volcanic activity in India didn't help.

It's possible that if it had happened at a more peaceful time in their history, some dinosaur species would have survived the impact.

Utahraptor

Deinonychus

Velociraptor

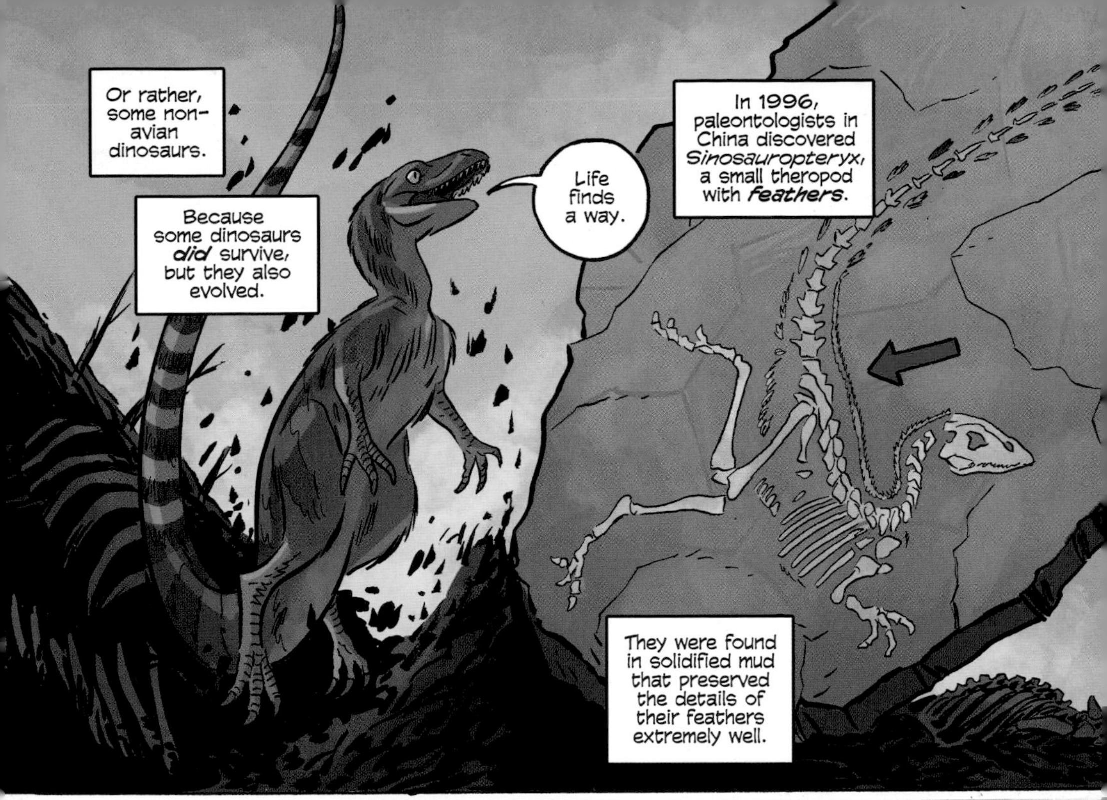
Or rather, some non-avian dinosaurs.
Because some dinosaurs *did* survive, but they also evolved.
Life finds a way.
In 1996, paleontologists in China discovered *Sinosauropteryx*, a small theropod with ***feathers***.
They were found in solidified mud that preserved the details of their feathers extremely well.

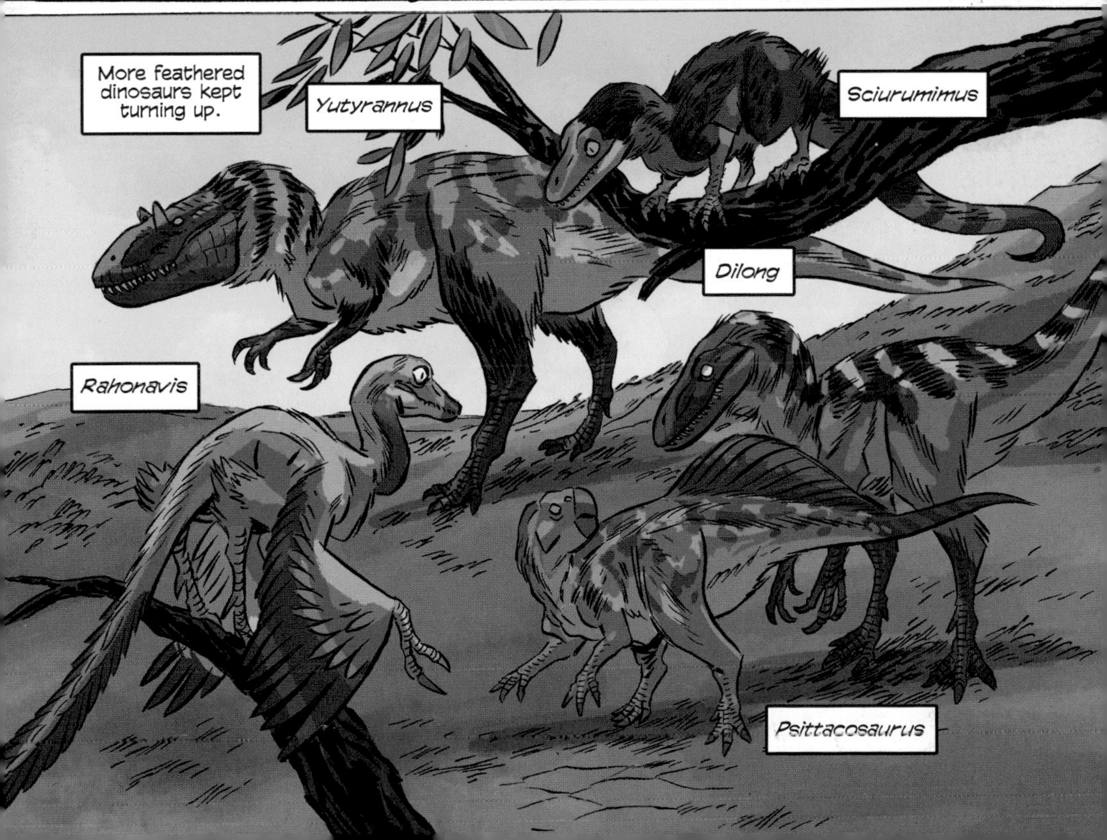
More feathered dinosaurs kept turning up.
Yutyrannus
Sciurumimus
Dilong
Rahonavis
Psittacosaurus

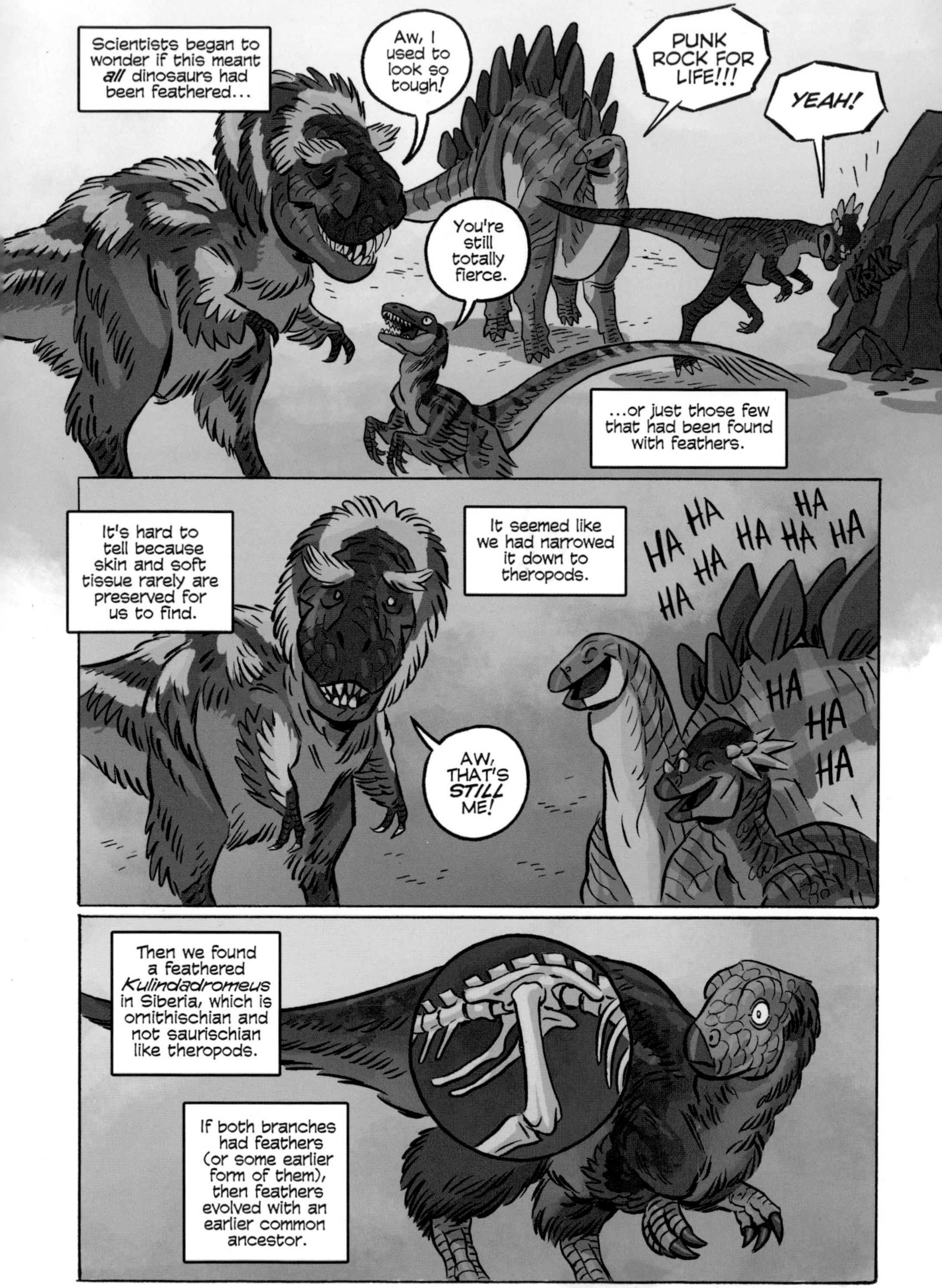
Scientists began to wonder if this meant *all* dinosaurs had been feathered...
Aw, I used to look so tough!
PUNK ROCK FOR LIFE!!!
YEAH!
KRAK
You're still totally fierce.
...or just those few that had been found with feathers.
It's hard to tell because skin and soft tissue rarely are preserved for us to find.
It seemed like we had narrowed it down to theropods.
HA HA HA HA HA HA HA HA HA HA HA HA HA
AW, THAT'S *STILL* ME!
Then we found a feathered *Kulindadromeus* in Siberia, which is ornithischian and not saurischian like theropods.
If both branches had feathers (or some earlier form of them), then feathers evolved with an earlier common ancestor.

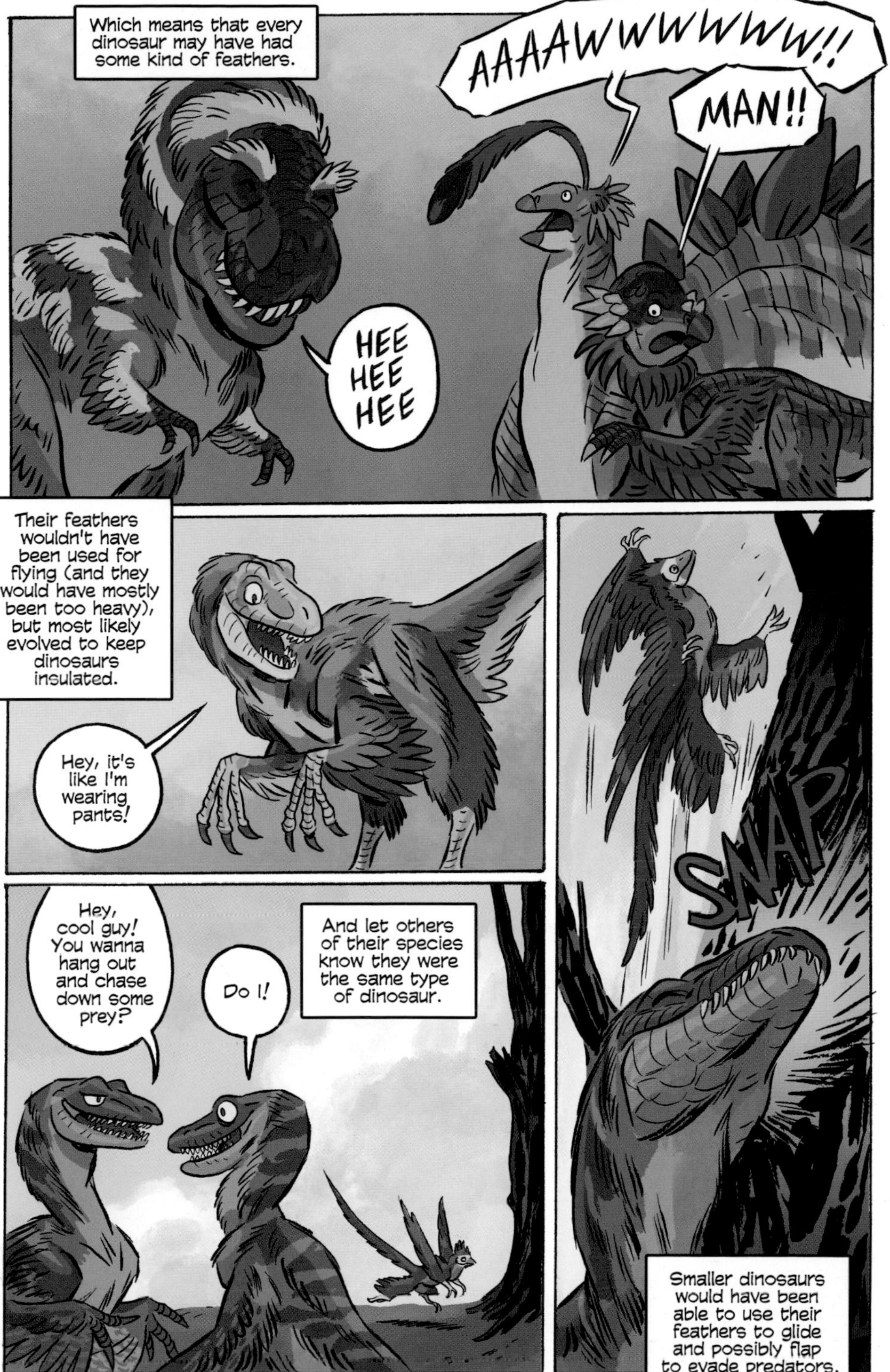

Which means that every dinosaur may have had some kind of feathers.
AAAAWWWWWW!!
MAN!!
HEE HEE HEE
Their feathers wouldn't have been used for flying (and they would have mostly been too heavy), but most likely evolved to keep dinosaurs insulated.
Hey, it's like I'm wearing pants!
Hey, cool guy! You wanna hang out and chase down some prey?
Do I!
And let others of their species know they were the same type of dinosaur.
SNAP
Smaller dinosaurs would have been able to use their feathers to glide and possibly flap to evade predators.

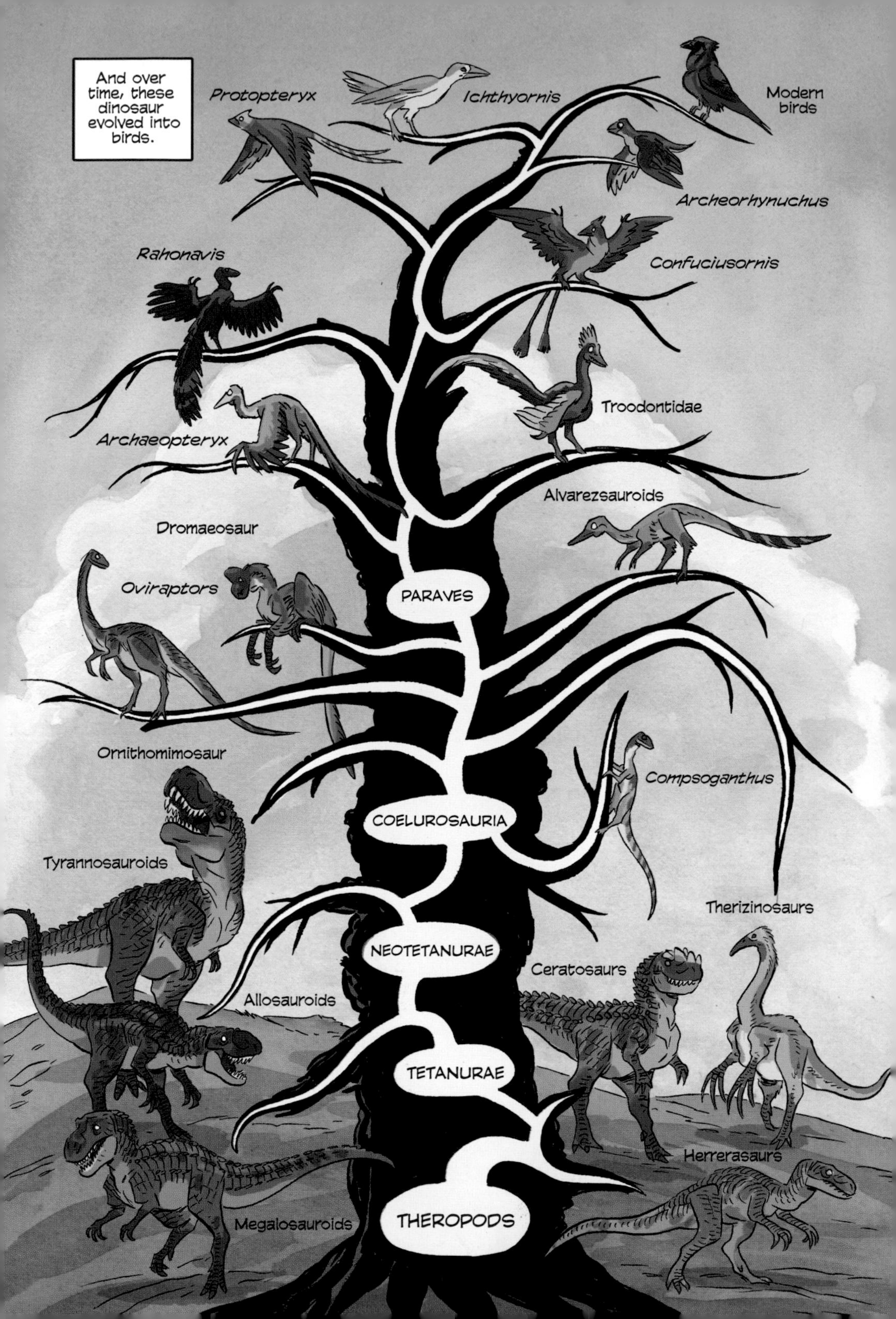

And over time, these dinosaur evolved into birds.
Protopteryx
Ichthyornis
Modern birds
Archeorhynuchus
Rahonavis
Confuciusornis
Troodontidae
Archaeopteryx
Alvarezsauroids
Dromaeosaur
Oviraptors
PARAVES
Ornithomimosaur
Compsoganthus
COELUROSAURIA
Tyrannosauroids
Therizinosaurs
NEOTETANURAE
Ceratosaurs
Allosauroids
TETANURAE
Herrerasaurs
Megalosauroids
THEROPODS

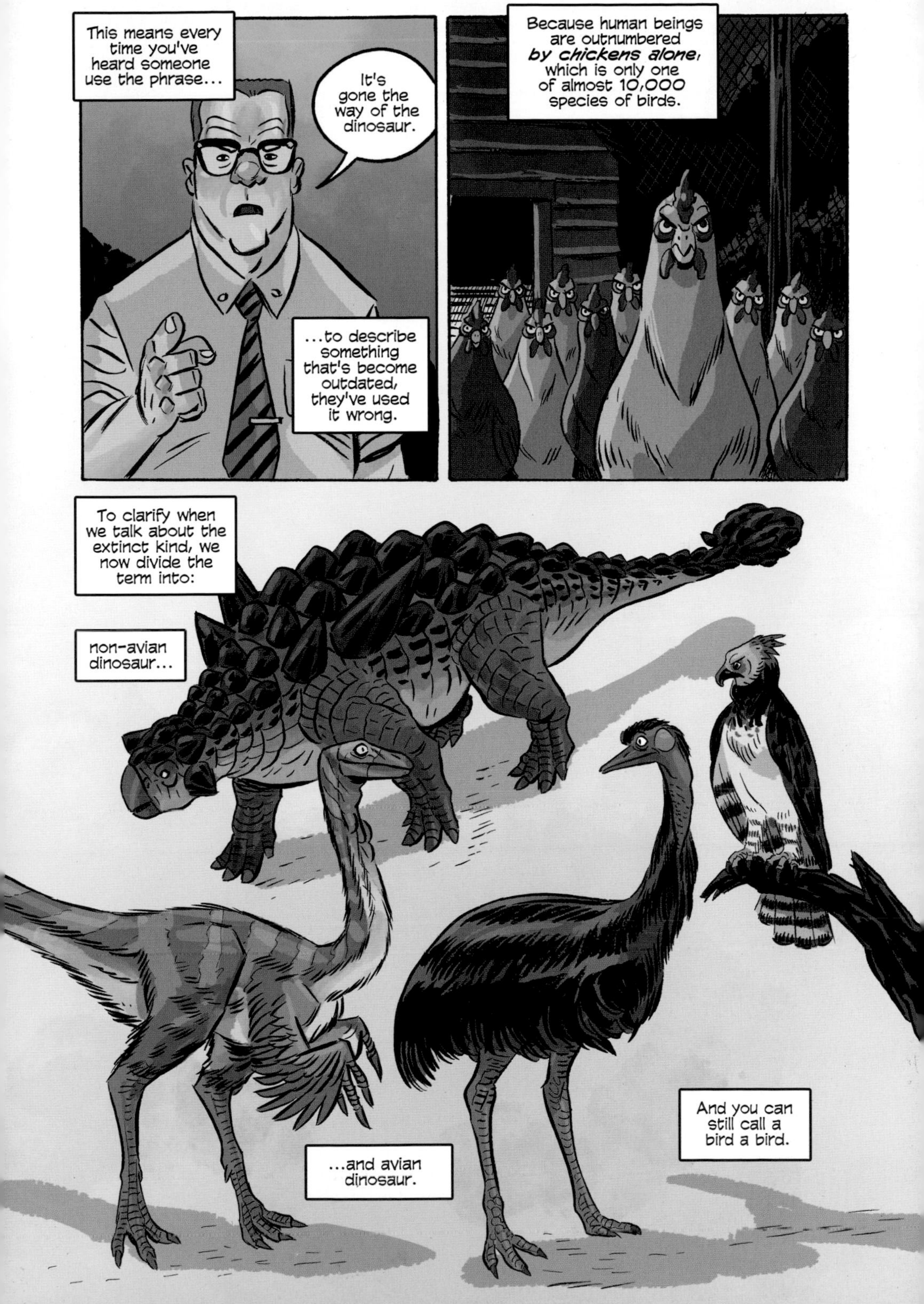
This means every time you've heard someone use the phrase...
It's gone the way of the dinosaur.
...to describe something that's become outdated, they've used it wrong.
Because human beings are outnumbered ***by chickens alone***, which is only one of almost 10,000 species of birds.
To clarify when we talk about the extinct kind, we now divide the term into:
non-avian dinosaur...
...and avian dinosaur.
And you can still call a bird a bird.

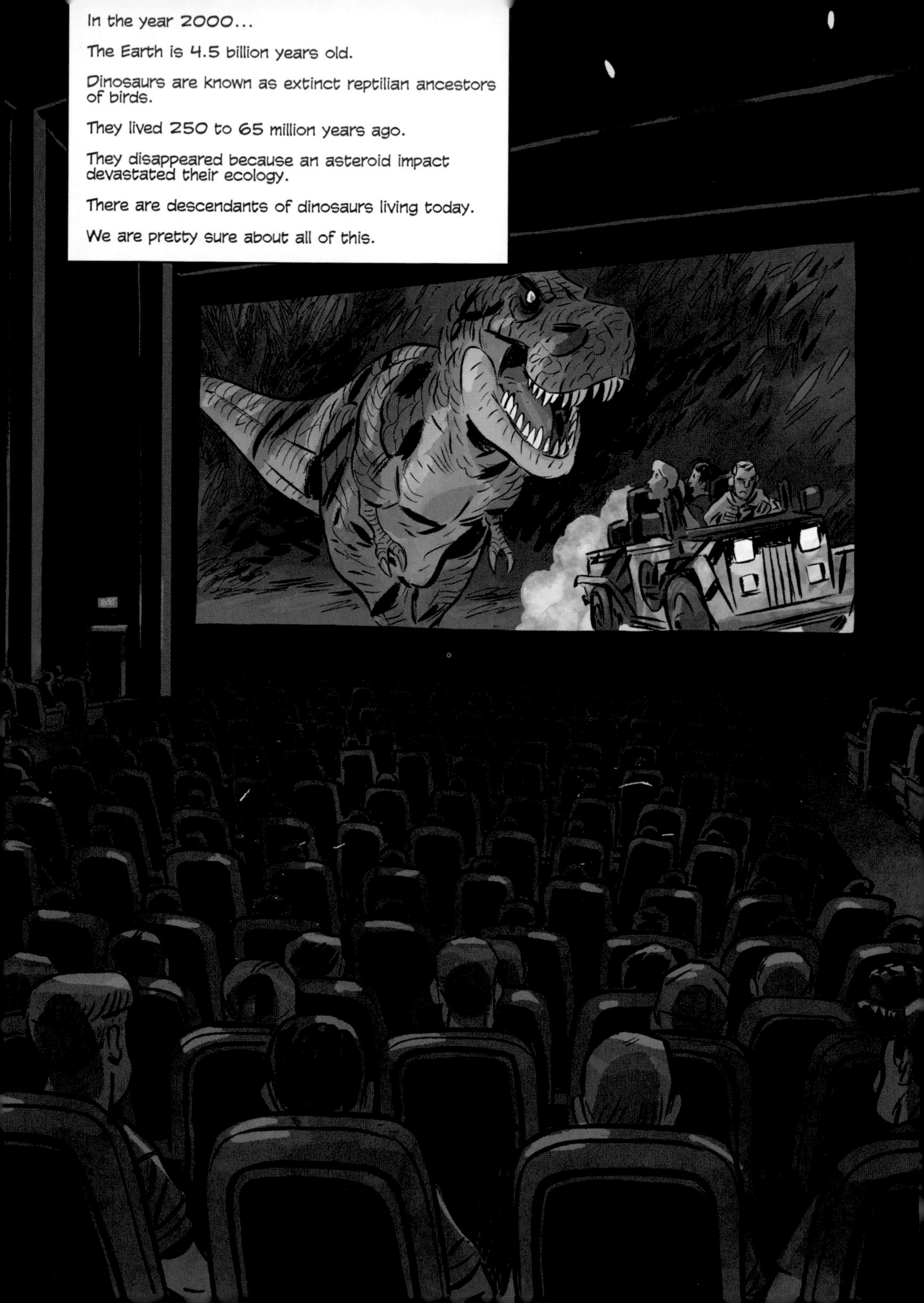
In the year 2000...
The Earth is 4.5 billion years old.
Dinosaurs are known as extinct reptilian ancestors of birds.
They lived 250 to 65 million years ago.
They disappeared because an asteroid impact devastated their ecology.
There are descendants of dinosaurs living today.
We are pretty sure about all of this.

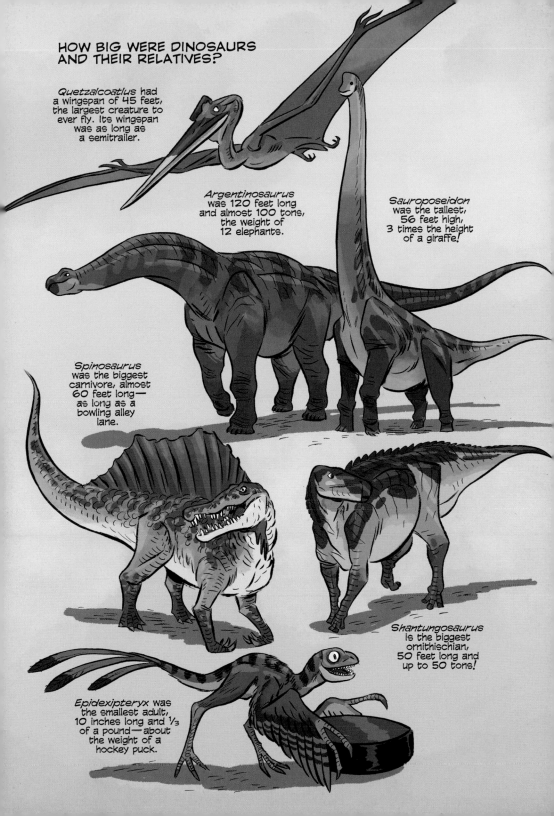

HOW BIG WERE DINOSAURS AND THEIR RELATIVES?

Quetzalcoatlus had a wingspan of 45 feet, the largest creature to ever fly. Its wingspan was as long as a semitrailer.

Argentinosaurus was 120 feet long and almost 100 tons, the weight of 12 elephants.

Sauroposeidon was the tallest, 56 feet high, 3 times the height of a giraffe!

Spinosaurus was the biggest carnivore, almost 60 feet long— as long as a bowling alley lane.

Shantungosaurus is the biggest ornithischian, 50 feet long and up to 50 tons!

Epidexipteryx was the smallest adult, 10 inches long and ⅓ of a pound—about the weight of a hockey puck.

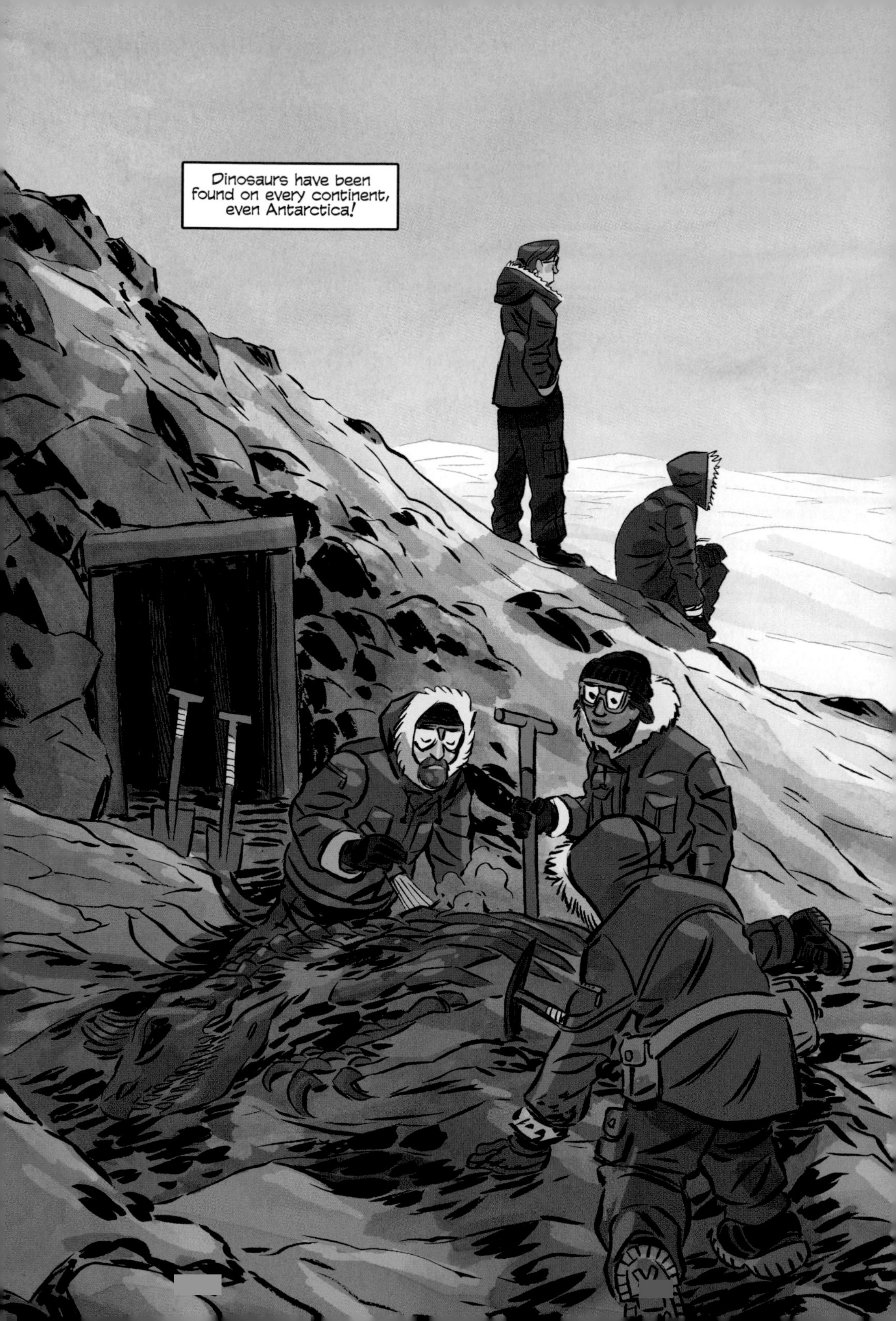
Dinosaurs have been found on every continent, even Antarctica!

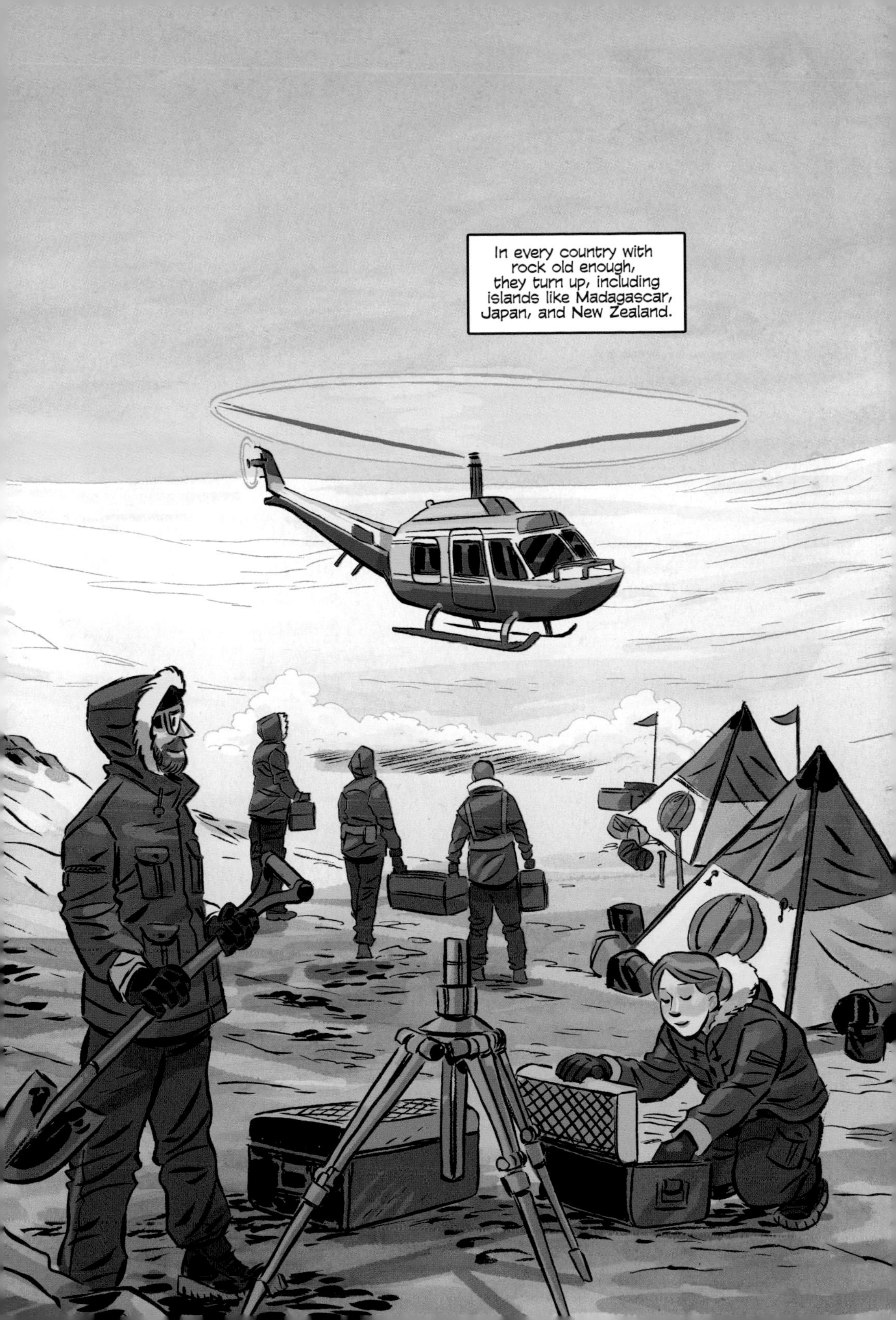
In every country with rock old enough, they turn up, including islands like Madagascar, Japan, and New Zealand.

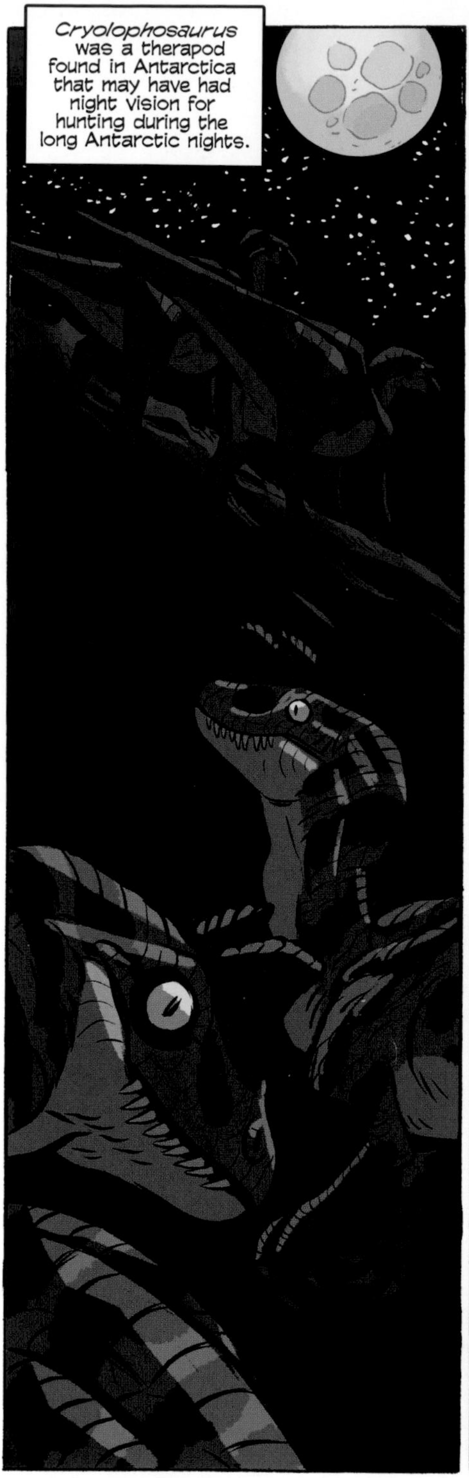
Cryolophosaurus was a therapod found in Antarctica that may have had night vision for hunting during the long Antarctic nights.

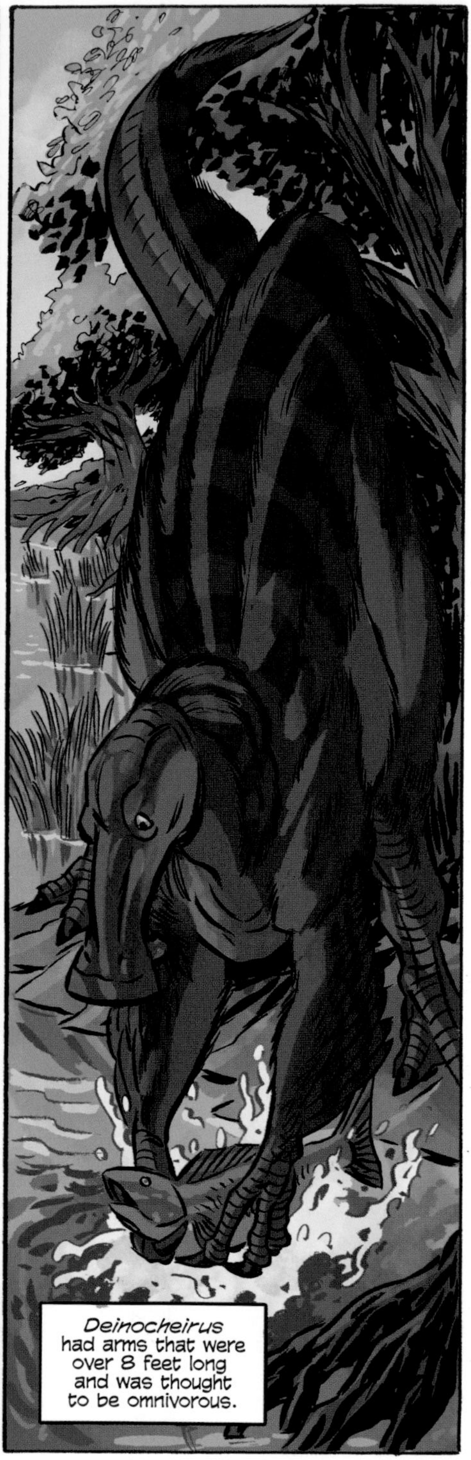
Deinocheirus had arms that were over 8 feet long and was thought to be omnivorous.

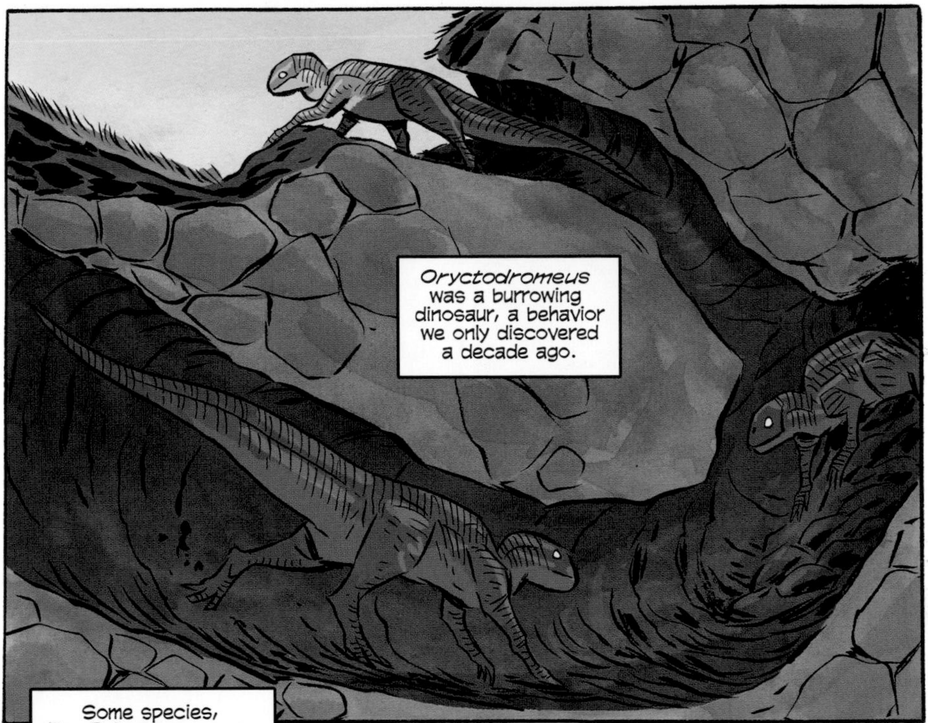
Oryctodromeus was a burrowing dinosaur, a behavior we only discovered a decade ago.

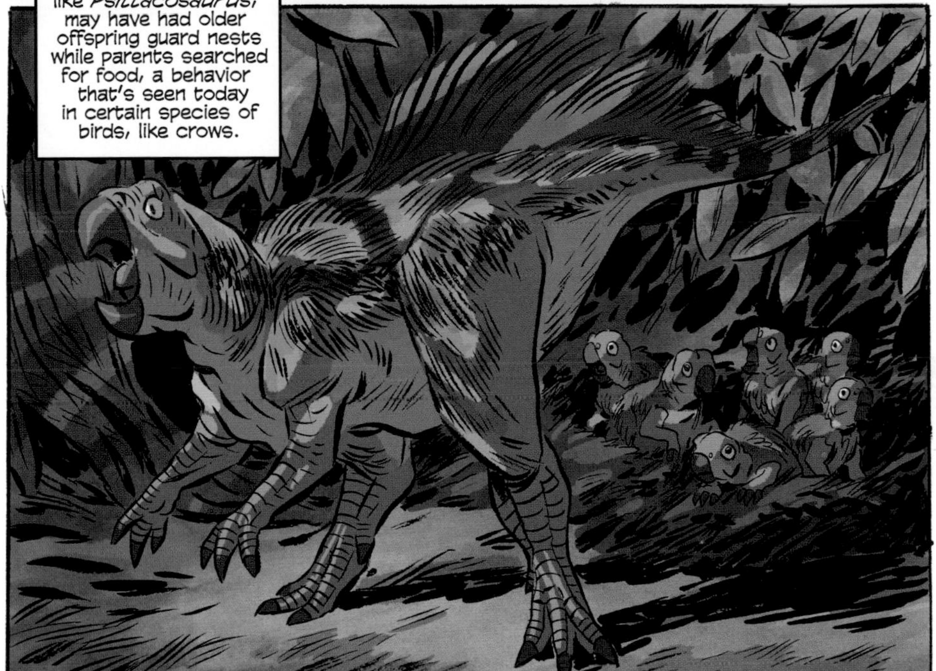
Some species, like Psittacosaurus, may have had older offspring guard nests while parents searched for food, a behavior that's seen today in certain species of birds, like crows.

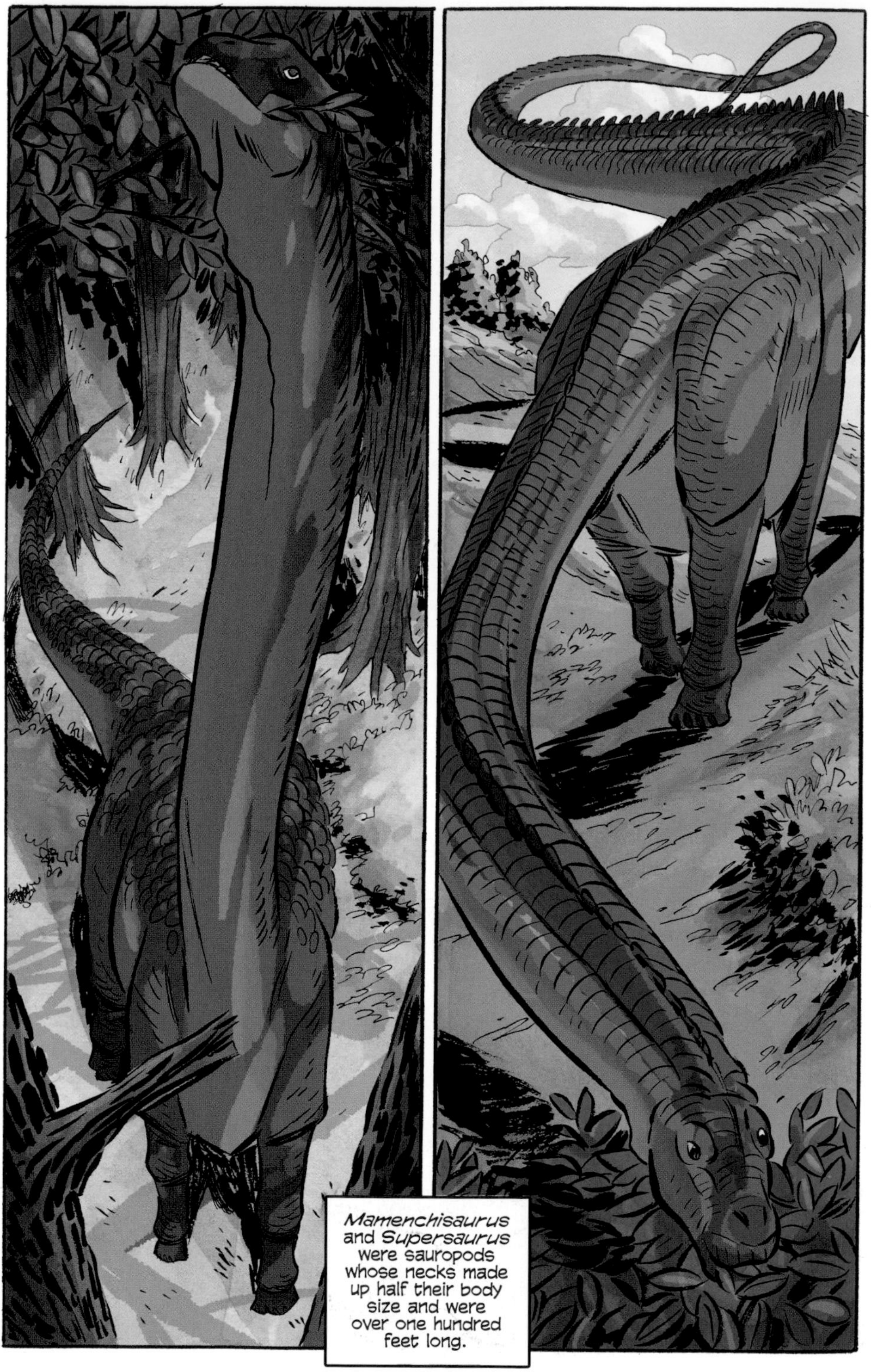
Mamenchisaurus and *Supersaurus* were sauropods whose necks made up half their body size and were over one hundred feet long.

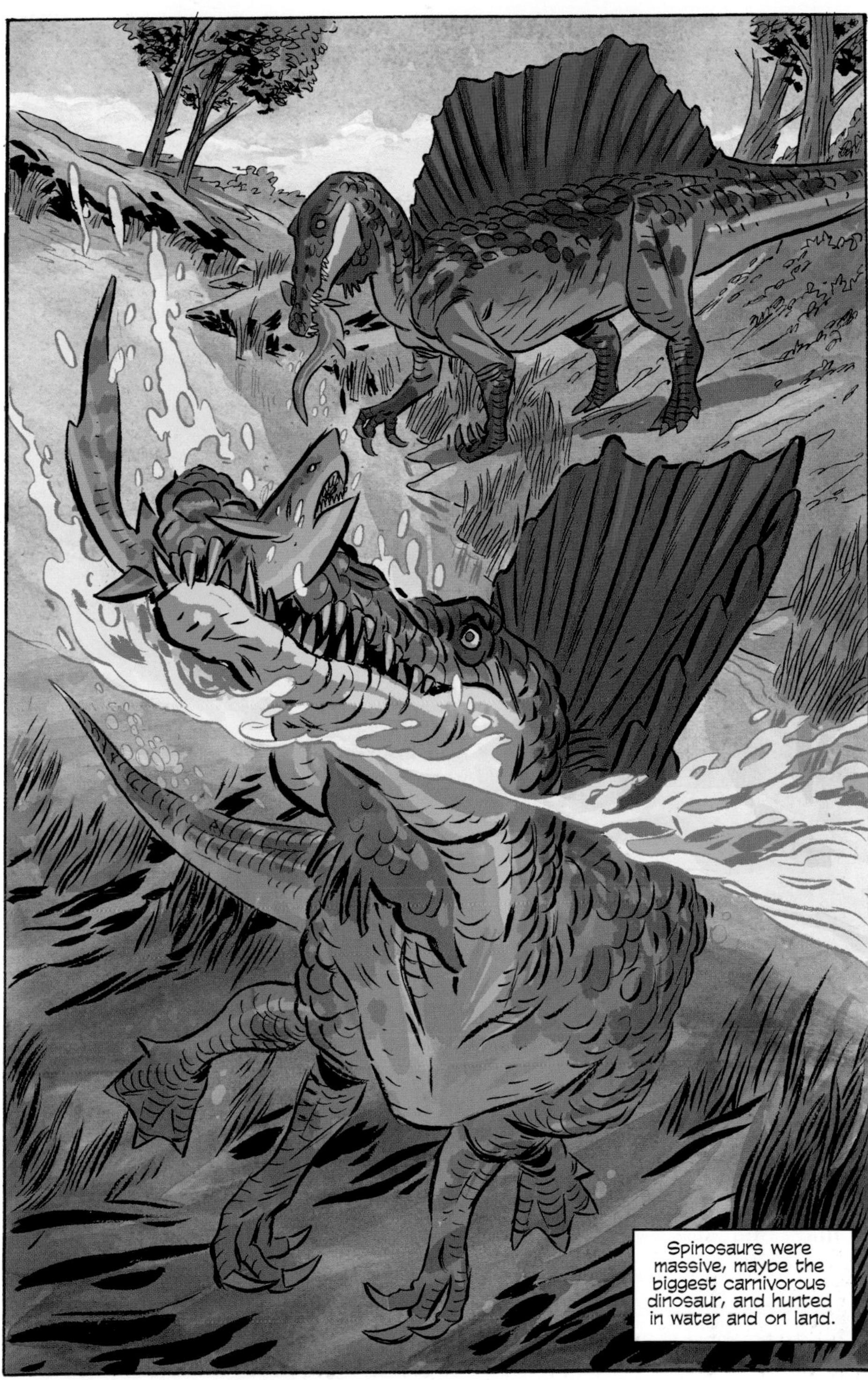
Spinosaurs were massive, maybe the biggest carnivorous dinosaur, and hunted in water and on land.

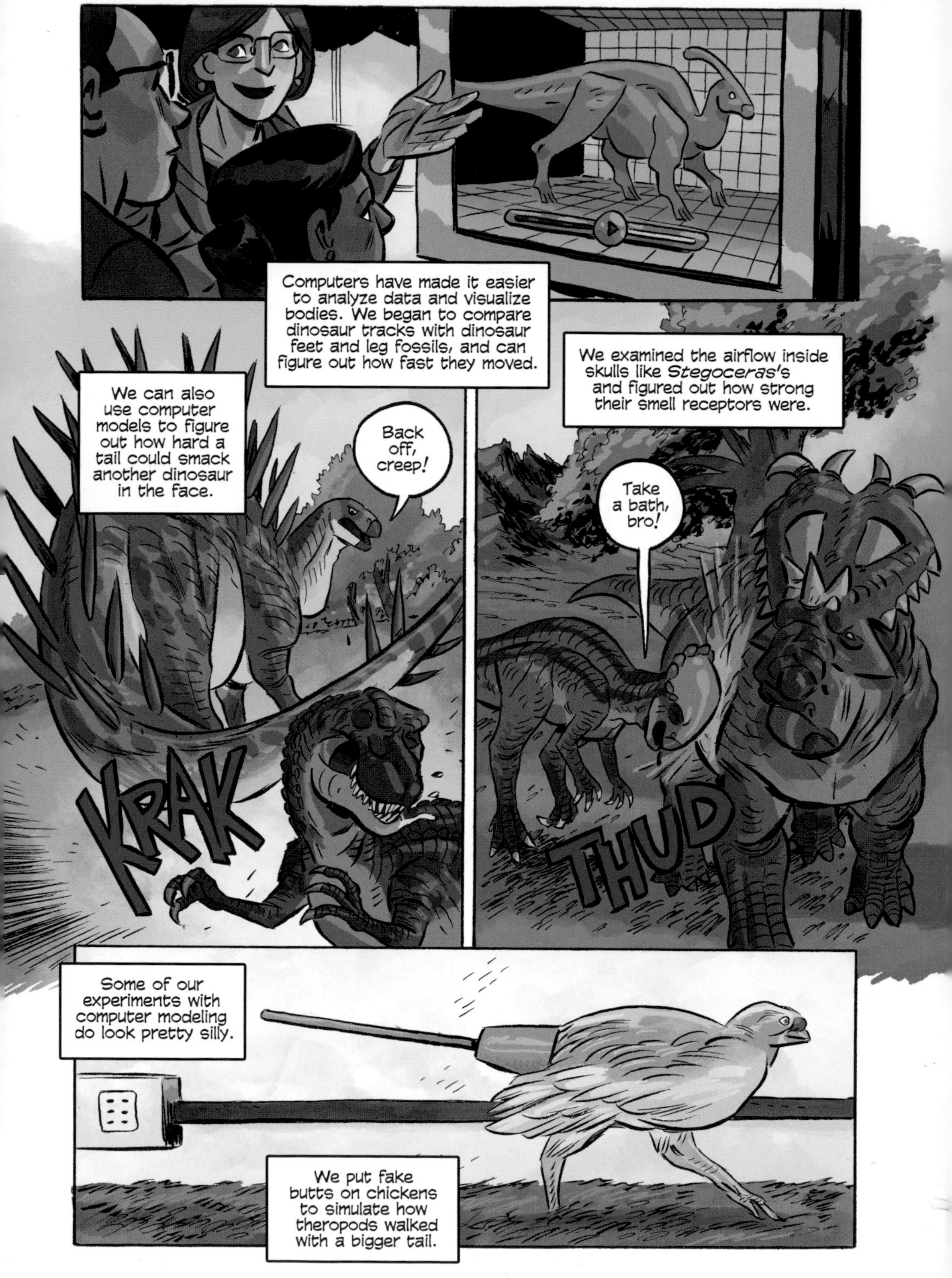

Computers have made it easier to analyze data and visualize bodies. We began to compare dinosaur tracks with dinosaur feet and leg fossils, and can figure out how fast they moved.
We can also use computer models to figure out how hard a tail could smack another dinosaur in the face.
Back off, creep!
KRAK
We examined the airflow inside skulls like *Stegoceras*'s and figured out how strong their smell receptors were.
Take a bath, bro!
THUD
Some of our experiments with computer modeling do look pretty silly.
We put fake butts on chickens to simulate how theropods walked with a bigger tail.

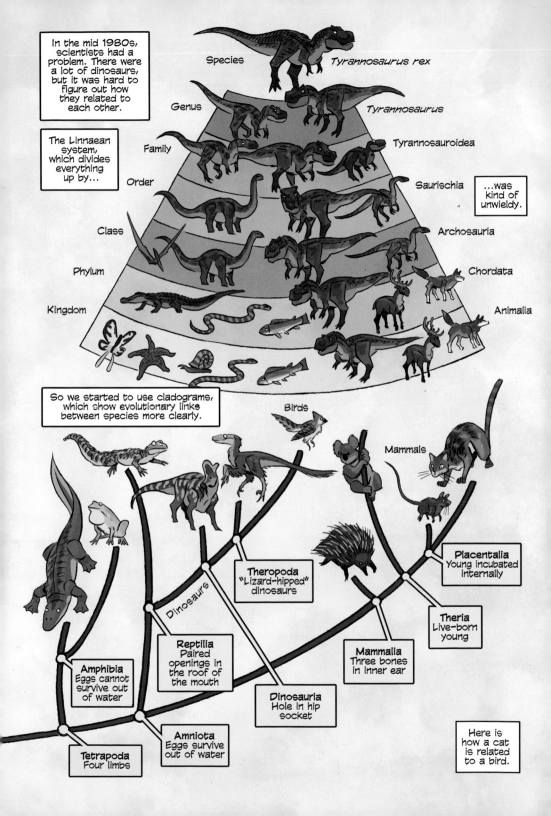

In the mid 1980s, scientists had a problem. There were a lot of dinosaurs, but it was hard to figure out how they related to each other.

The Linnaean system, which divides everything up by...

...was kind of unwieldy.

Species — *Tyrannosaurus rex*

Genus — *Tyrannosaurus*

Family — Tyrannosauroidea

Order — Saurischia

Class — Archosauria

Phylum — Chordata

Kingdom — Animalia

So we started to use cladograms, which show evolutionary links between species more clearly.

Birds

Mammals

Placentalia
Young incubated internally

Theropoda
"Lizard-hipped" dinosaurs

Theria
Live-born young

Dinosaurs

Reptilia
Paired openings in the roof of the mouth

Mammalia
Three bones in inner ear

Amphibia
Eggs cannot survive out of water

Dinosauria
Hole in hip socket

Tetrapoda
Four limbs

Amniota
Eggs survive out of water

Here is how a cat is related to a bird.

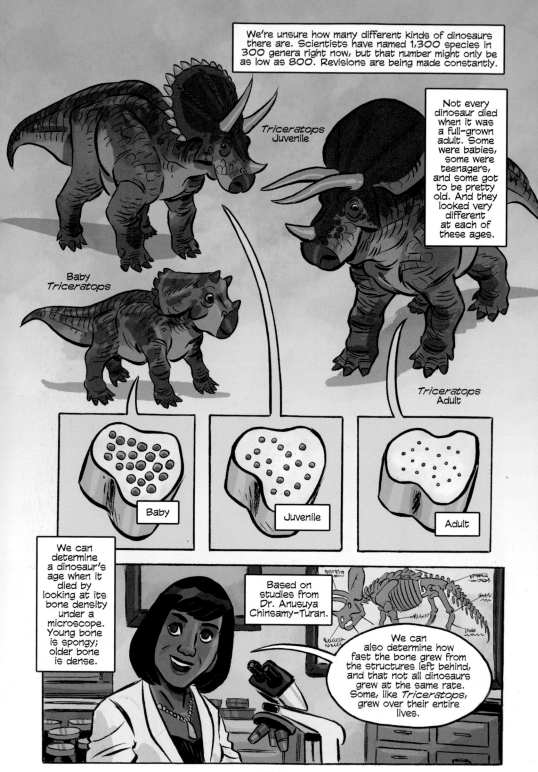

We're unsure how many different kinds of dinosaurs there are. Scientists have named 1,300 species in 300 genera right now, but that number might only be as low as 800. Revisions are being made constantly.

Not every dinosaur died when it was a full-grown adult. Some were babies, some were teenagers, and some got to be pretty old. And they looked very different at each of these ages.

Triceratops Juvenile

Baby Triceratops

Triceratops Adult

Baby

Juvenile

Adult

We can determine a dinosaur's age when it died by looking at its bone density under a microscope. Young bone is spongy; older bone is dense.

Based on studies from Dr. Anusuya Chinsamy-Turan.

We can also determine how fast the bone grew from the structures left behind, and that not all dinosaurs grew at the same rate. Some, like Triceratops, grew over their entire lives.

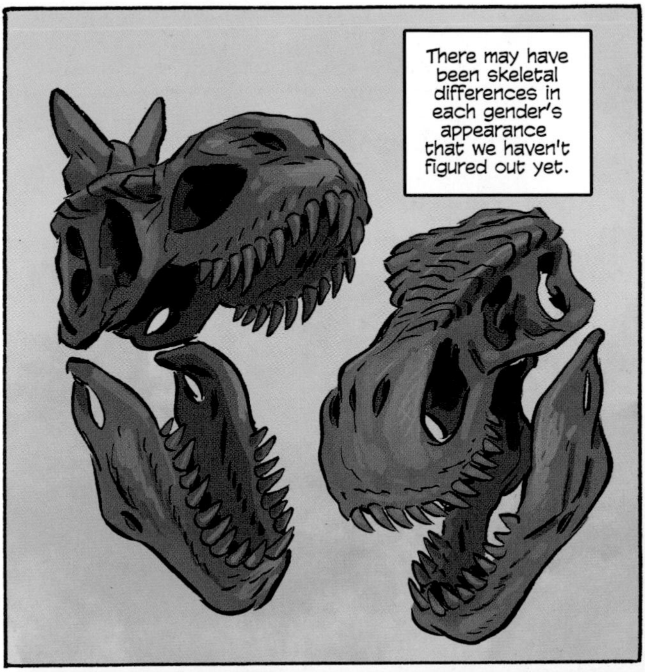
There may have been skeletal differences in each gender's appearance that we haven't figured out yet.

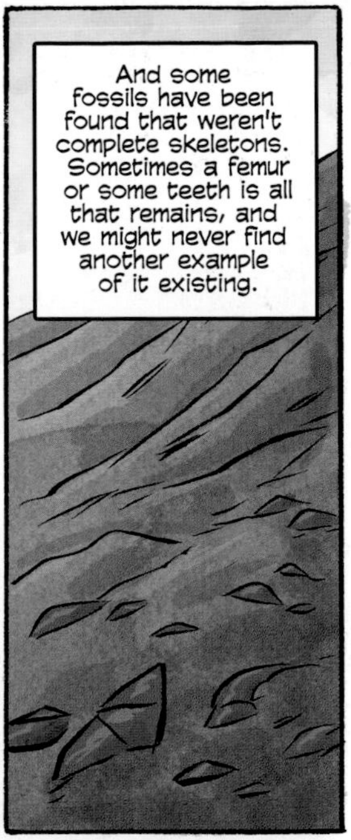
And some fossils have been found that weren't complete skeletons. Sometimes a femur or some teeth is all that remains, and we might never find another example of it existing.

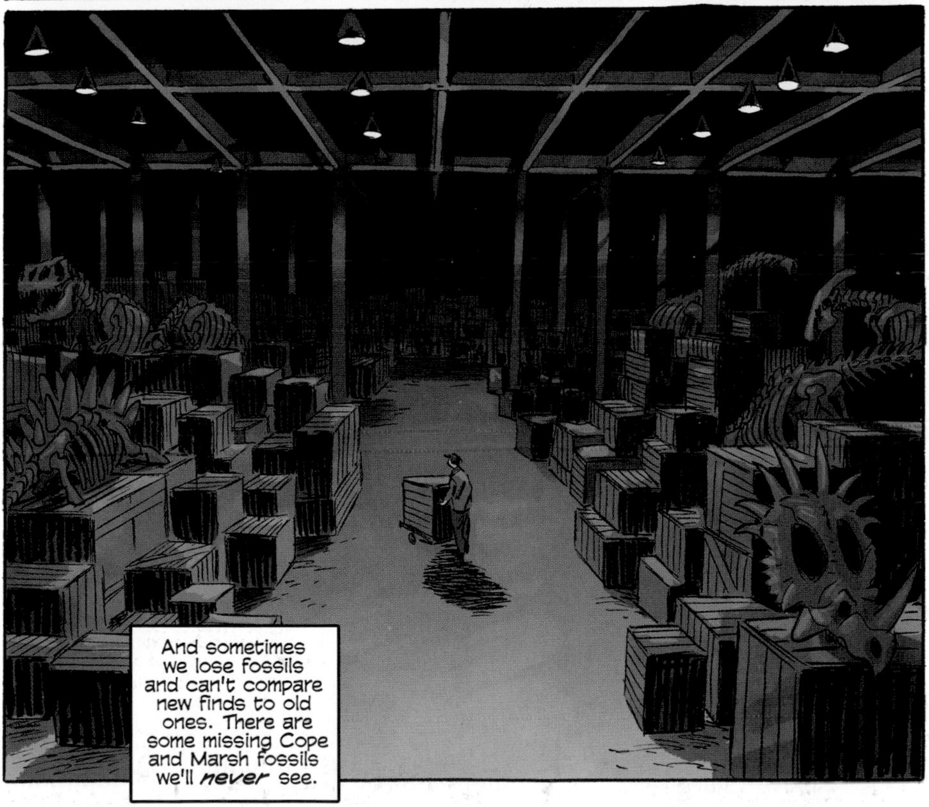
And sometimes we lose fossils and can't compare new finds to old ones. There are some missing Cope and Marsh fossils we'll *never* see.

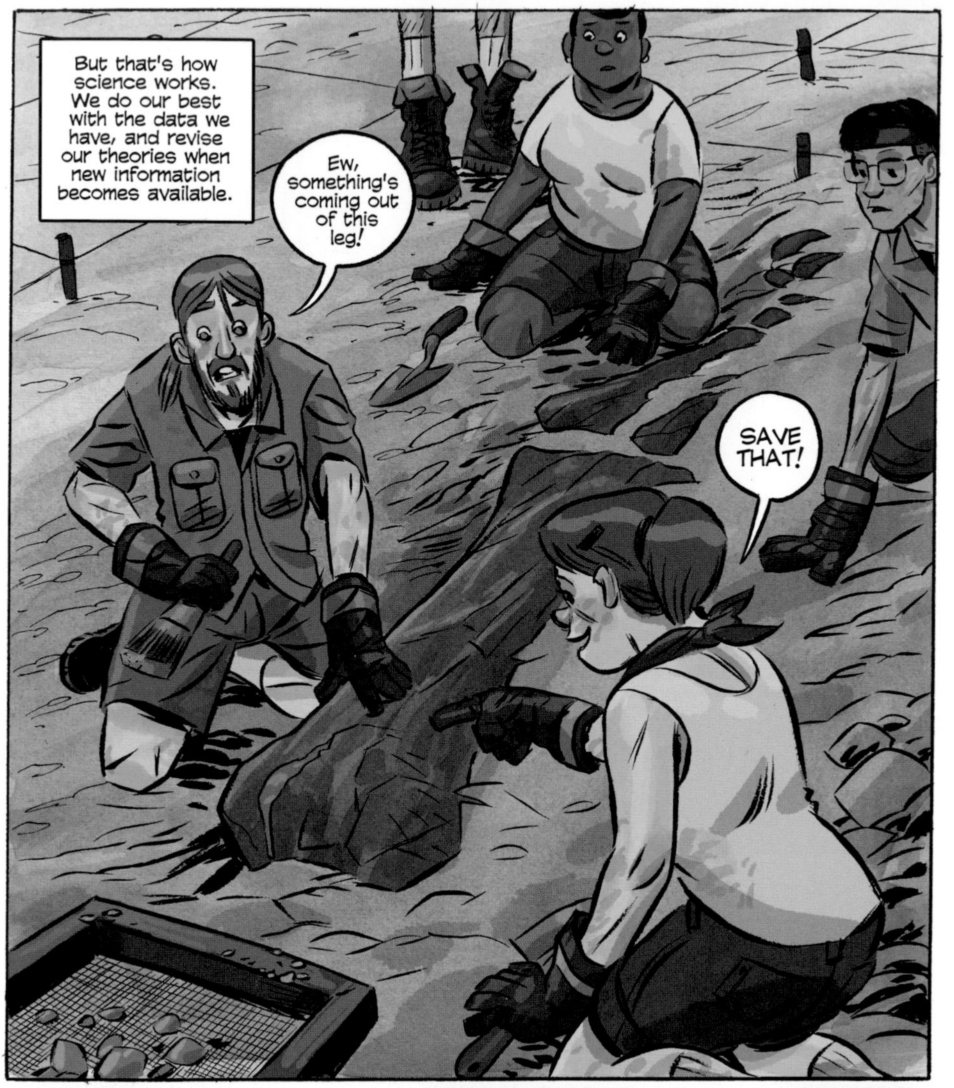
But that's how science works. We do our best with the data we have, and revise our theories when new information becomes available.
Ew, something's coming out of this leg!
SAVE THAT!

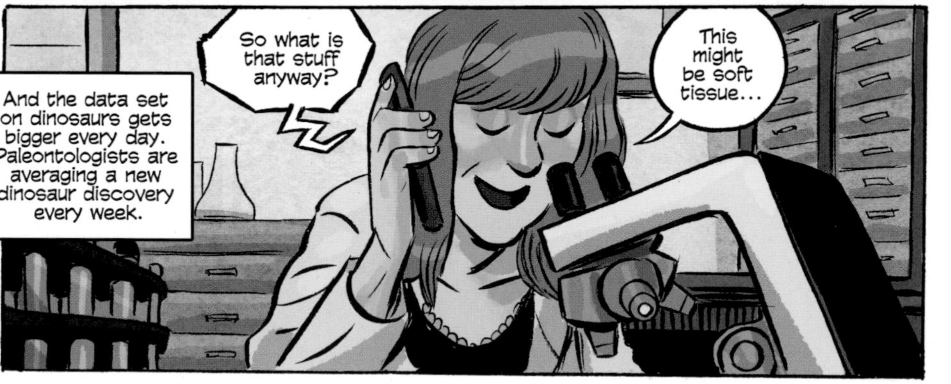
And the data set on dinosaurs gets bigger every day. Paleontologists are averaging a new dinosaur discovery every week.
So what is that stuff anyway?
This might be soft tissue...

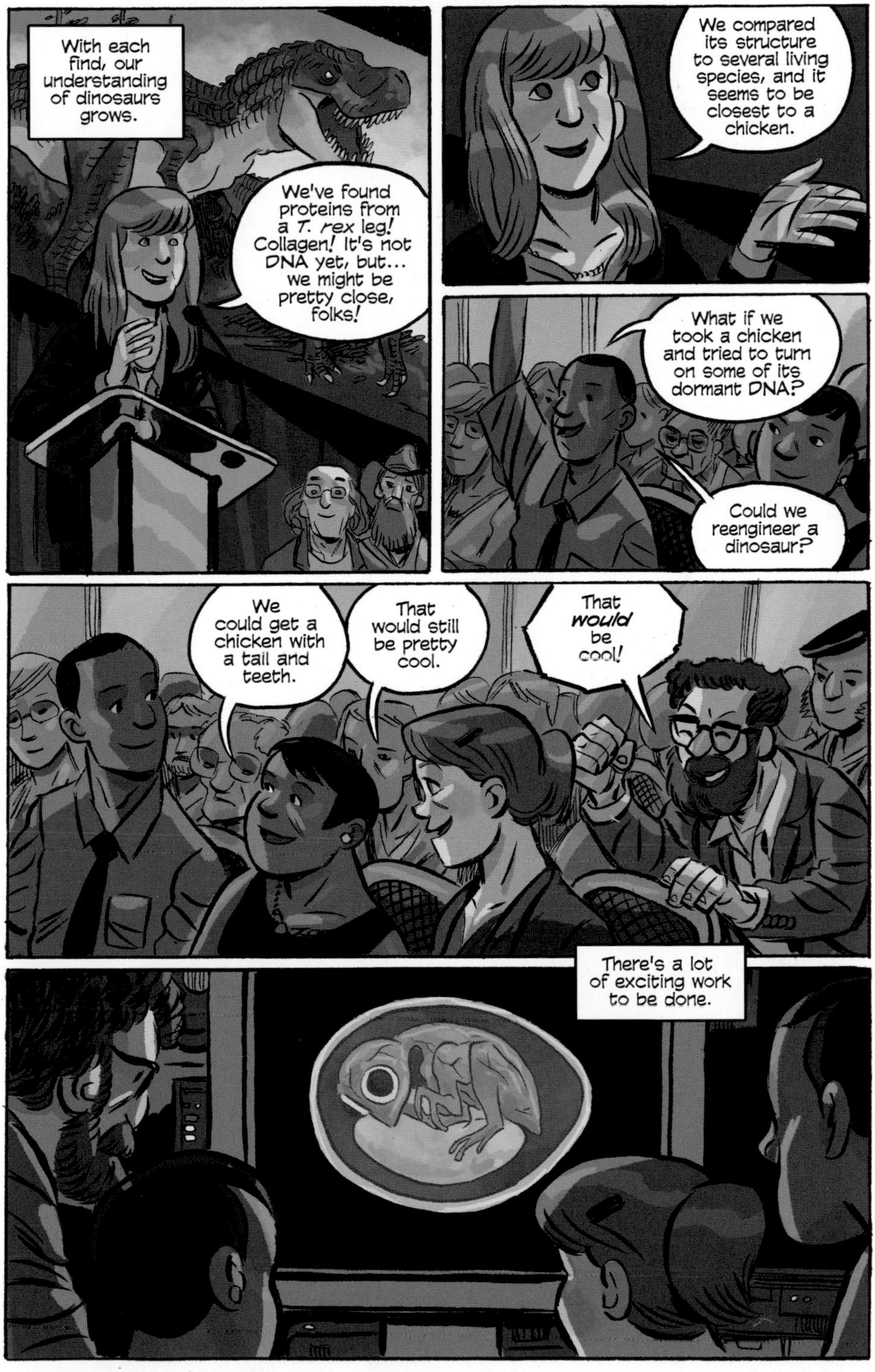

With each find, our understanding of dinosaurs grows.
We've found proteins from a *T. rex* leg! Collagen! It's not DNA yet, but... we might be pretty close, folks!
We compared its structure to several living species, and it seems to be closest to a chicken.
What if we took a chicken and tried to turn on some of its dormant DNA?
Could we reengineer a dinosaur?
We could get a chicken with a tail and teeth.
That would still be pretty cool.
That ***would*** be cool!
There's a lot of exciting work to be done.

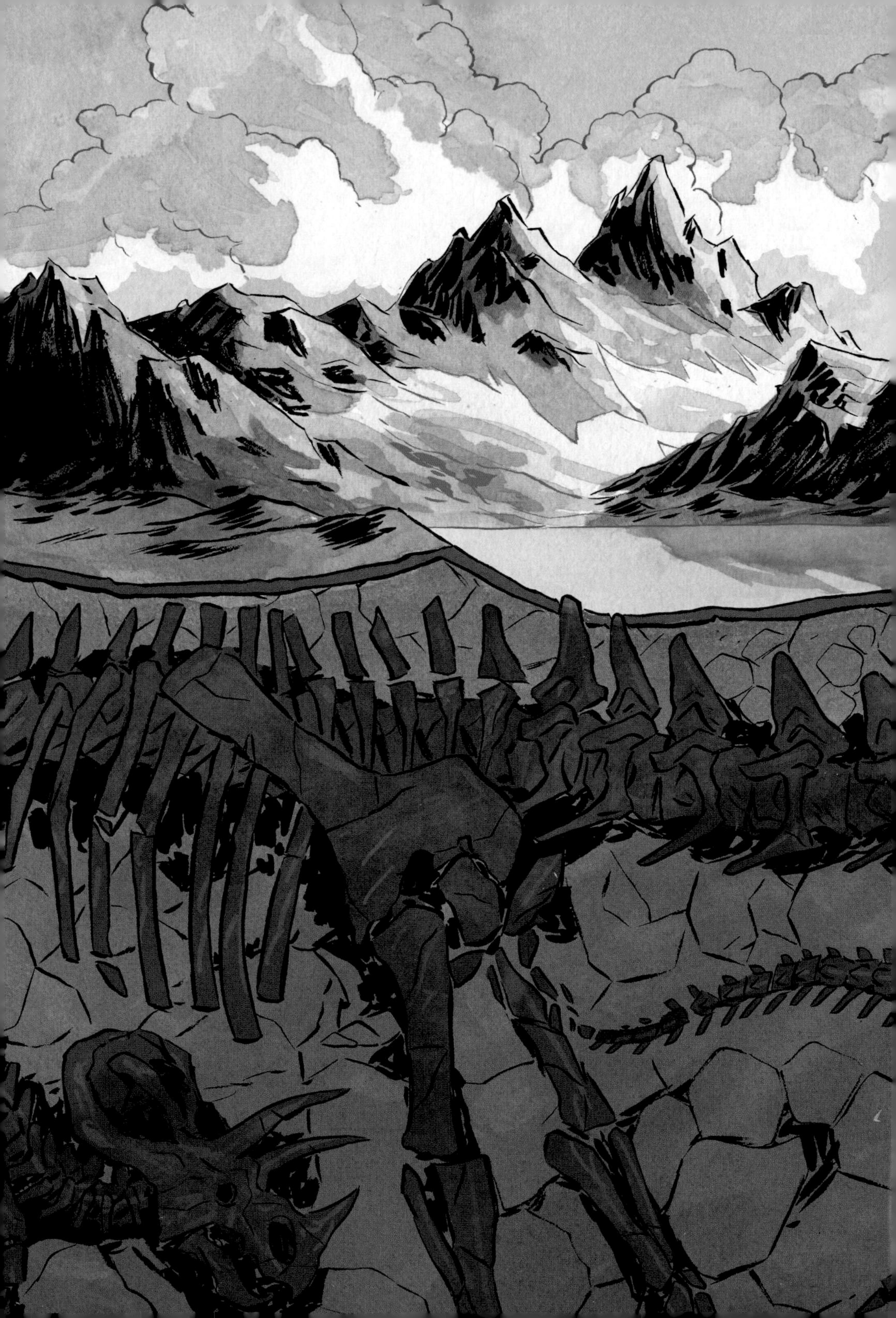

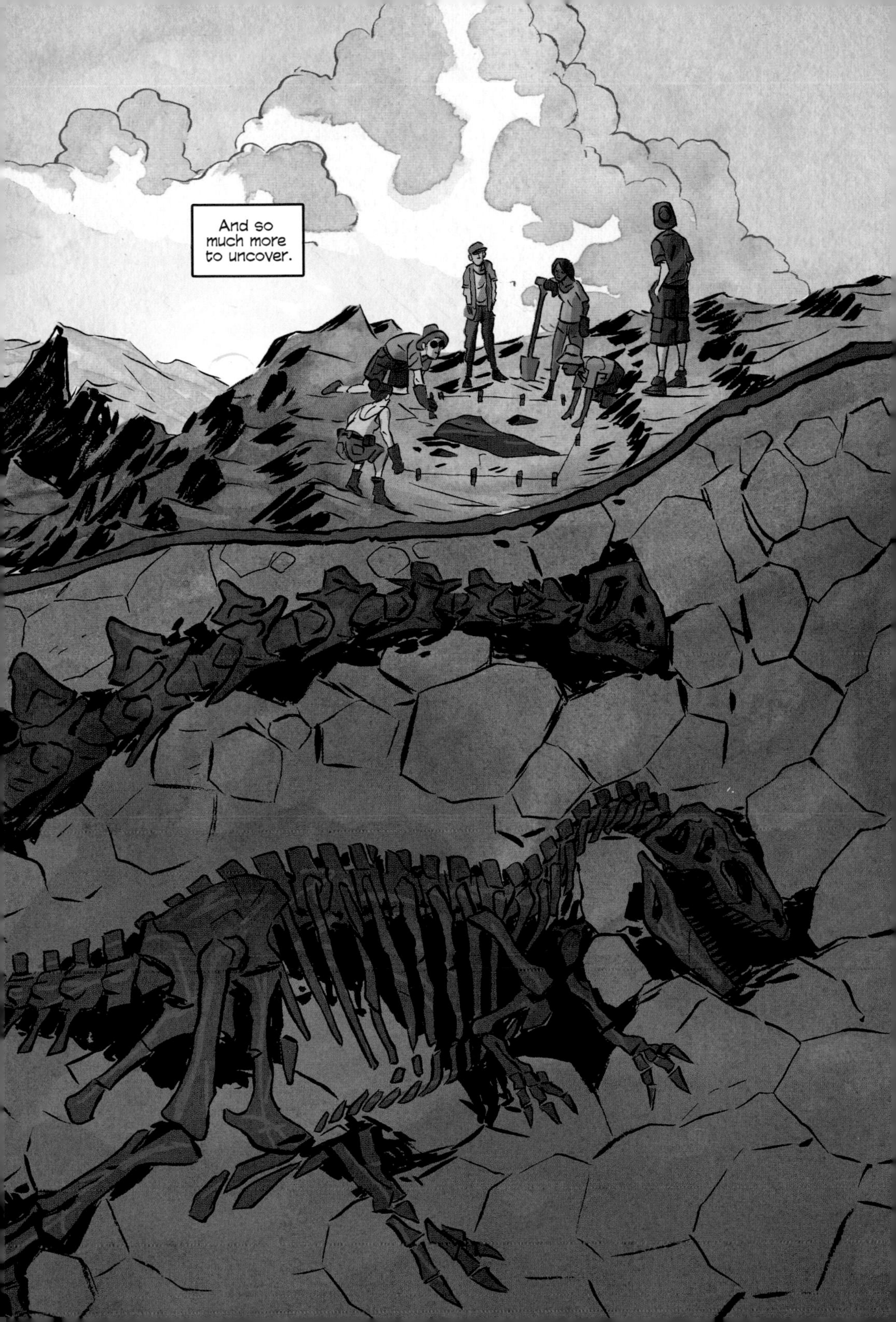
And so much more to uncover.

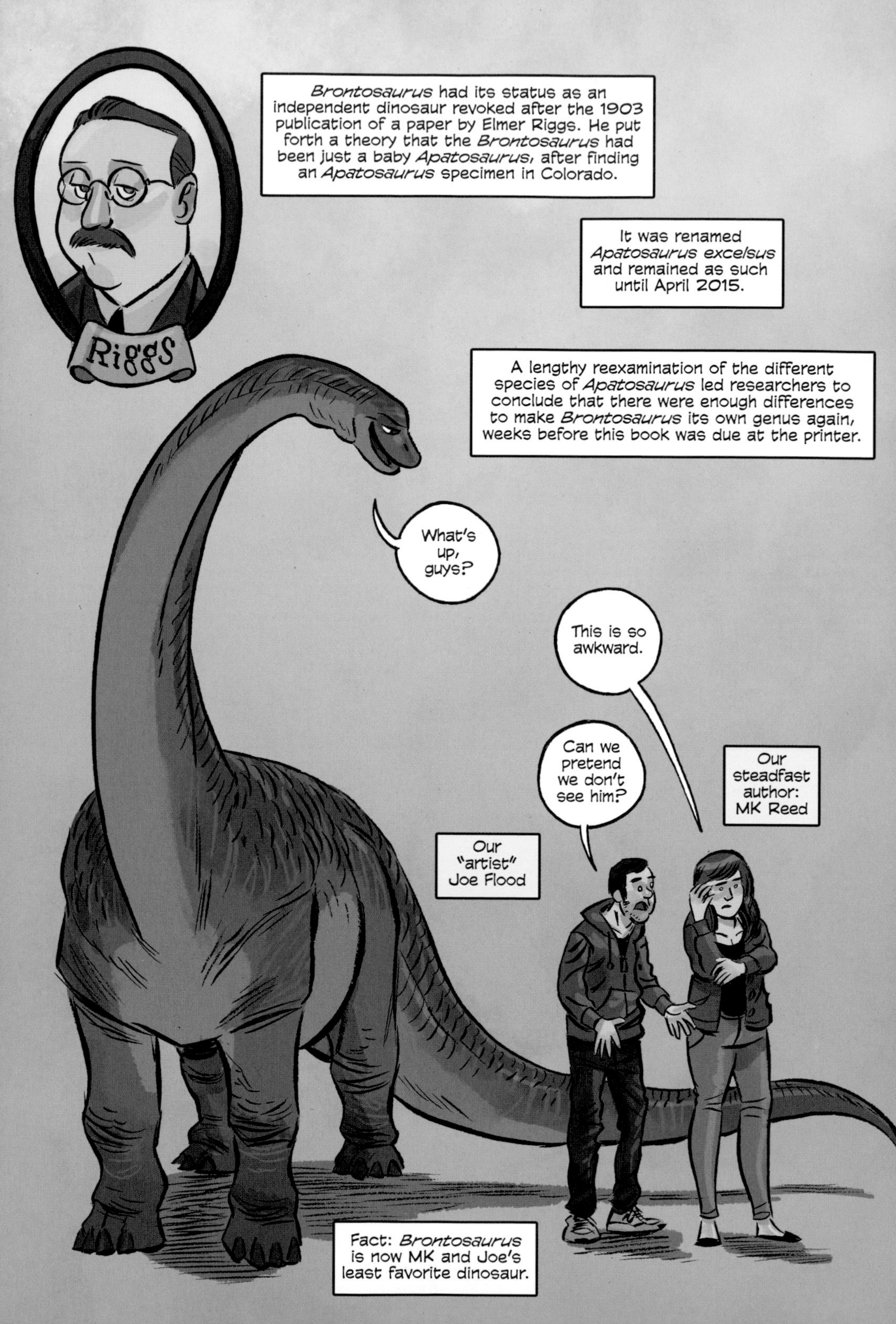

Riggs
Brontosaurus had its status as an independent dinosaur revoked after the 1903 publication of a paper by Elmer Riggs. He put forth a theory that the *Brontosaurus* had been just a baby *Apatosaurus*, after finding an *Apatosaurus* specimen in Colorado.
It was renamed *Apatosaurus excelsus* and remained as such until April 2015.
A lengthy reexamination of the different species of *Apatosaurus* led researchers to conclude that there were enough differences to make *Brontosaurus* its own genus again, weeks before this book was due at the printer.
What's up, guys?
This is so awkward.
Can we pretend we don't see him?
Our steadfast author: MK Reed
Our "artist" Joe Flood
Fact: *Brontosaurus* is now MK and Joe's least favorite dinosaur.

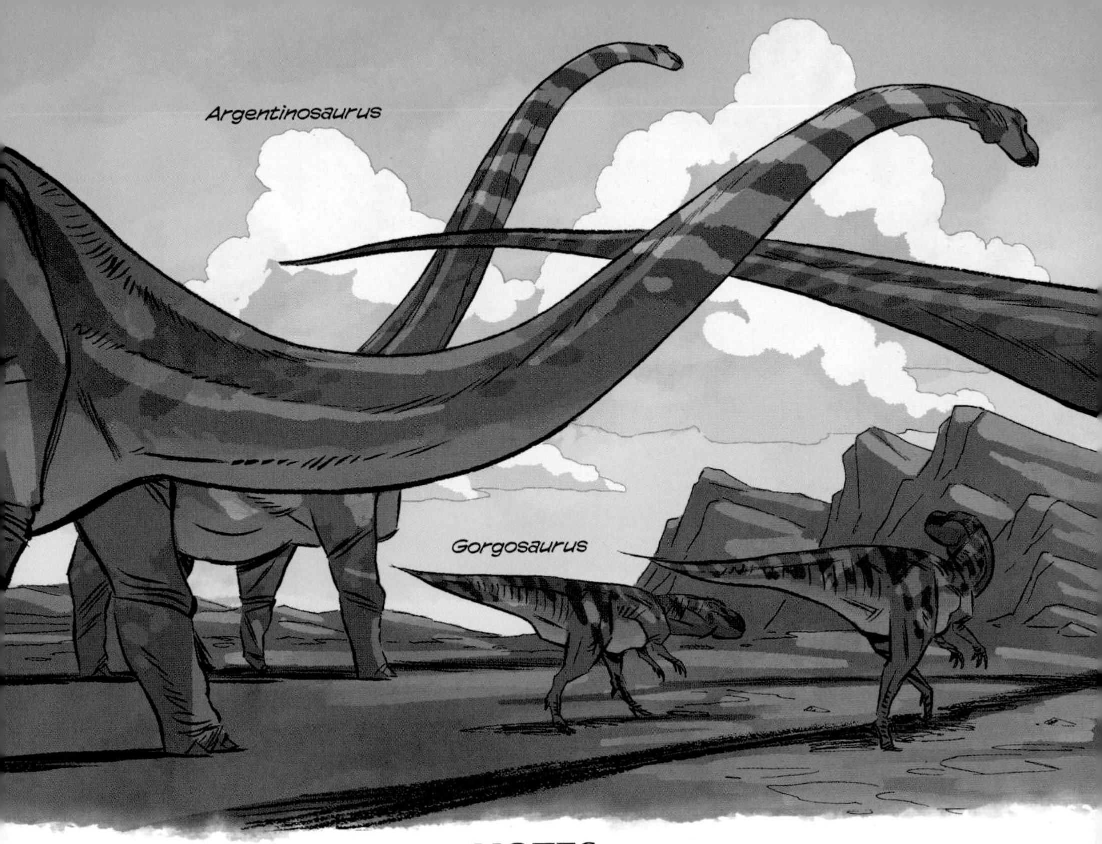
Argentinosaurus
Gorgosaurus

—NOTES—

p. 34 Plesiosaurs are no longer part of Ichthyosauria.

p. 51 The validity of *Agathaumas* as a genus is debated.

p. 51 *Edaphosaurus* lived in the late Carboniferous to early Permian periods (around 300 to 275 million years ago), 25 million years prior to the Mesozoic era, when dinosaurs lived. It predates dinosaurs, and it's an earlier ancestor to both dinosaurs and mammals.

p. 59 The original name for this specimen was *Archaeopteryx siemensii*, but it is commonly referred to as "the Berlin Specimen." As *A. siemensii* is the first name in the record, *A. owenni* is invalid.

p. 60 The Odontornithes book would later be called a waste of taxpayer money in Congress and used to oust Marsh from the US Geological Survey. It was a huge scandal.

p. 65 This explanation is slightly simplified; one isotope of uranium decays to another isotope at a steady rate, and the ratio between them is what's actually measured.

p. 70 Roy Chapman Andrews's spying mostly involved reporting on the political climate of the countries he visited back to the United States. He was more of a field reporter than a James Bond type, but Andrews is part of the inspiration for Indiana Jones. He wrote several books about his adventures and discoveries, and was the subject of comics in the 1950s as well.

—GLOSSARY—

Avian dinosaur
 birds, after discovering they are descended from dinosaurs

Carnivore
 Animal that eats meat

Cololite
 Fecal matter inside the intestines/body that has been fossilized

Coprolite
 Fecal matter that has been excreted and has been fossilized

Ectotherm
 Animals that absorb heat from their environment, also referred to as cold-blooded

Endotherm
 Animals that create their own internal heat, also referred to as warm-blooded

Fossil
 A previously living thing that has been preserved in sediment and turned into rock over a very long time, or an impression left in rock by something once alive

Herbivore
 Animal that eats plants

Non-avian dinosaur
    any species of *Dinosauria* except for the clade of Aves; every dinosaur
    that isn't a bird

Omnivore
    Animal that eats both plants and meat

Paleontology
    The study of fossilized animals and plants

Permineralization
    The process through which living tissue becomes a fossil, involving
    the absorption and hardening of minerals

Petrification
    The process through which organic matter becomes hard like stone

Sediment
    Very tiny pieces of dirt and rocks

Strata
    Layers of sediment that can be told apart by changes in color and
    texture due to variations in their components over thousands of years

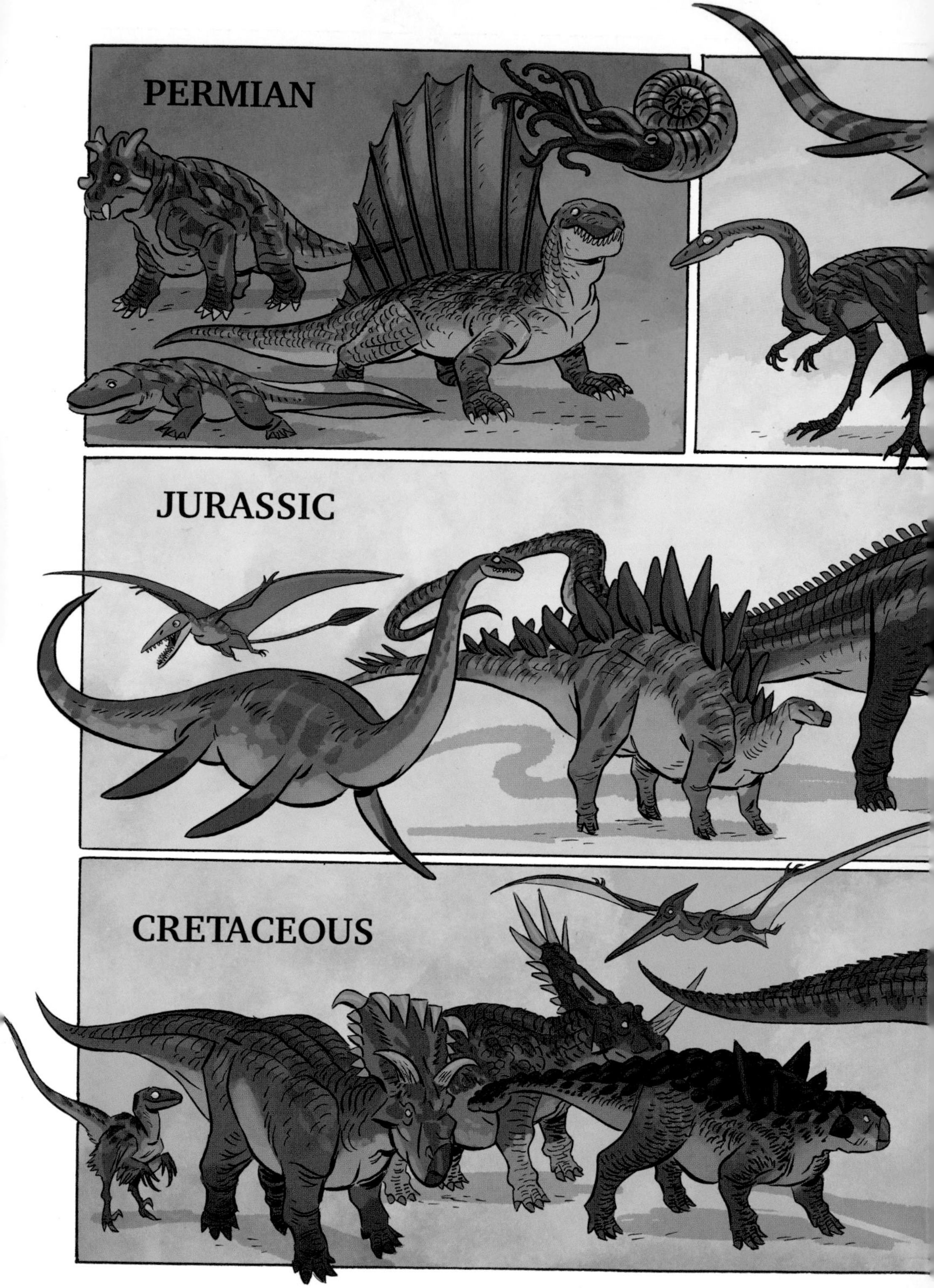
PERMIAN
JURASSIC
CRETACEOUS

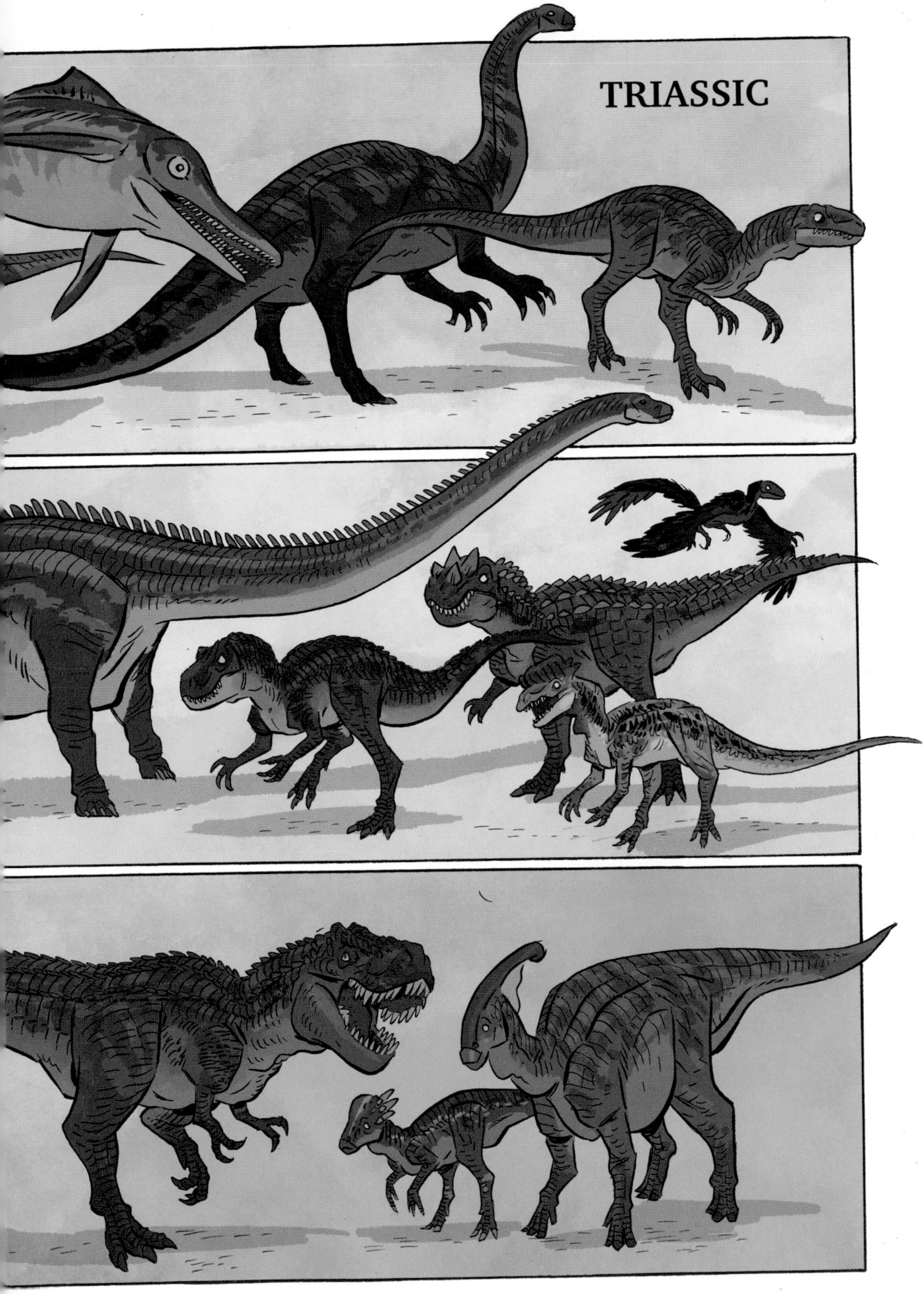
TRIASSIC

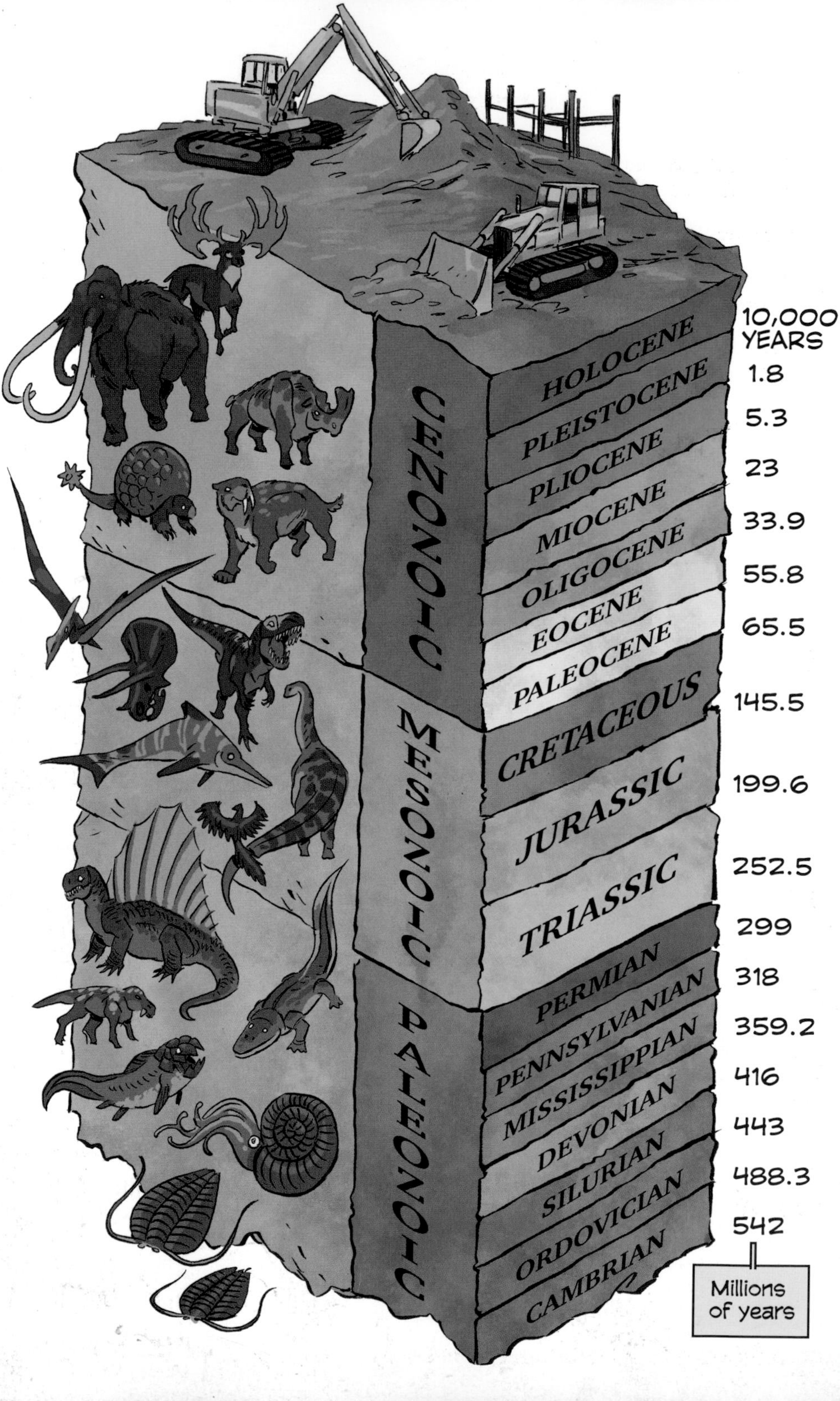

CENOZOIC
MESOZOIC
PALEOZOIC
HOLOCENE
PLEISTOCENE
PLIOCENE
MIOCENE
OLIGOCENE
EOCENE
PALEOCENE
CRETACEOUS
JURASSIC
TRIASSIC
PERMIAN
PENNSYLVANIAN
MISSISSIPPIAN
DEVONIAN
SILURIAN
ORDOVICIAN
CAMBRIAN
10,000 YEARS
1.8
5.3
23
33.9
55.8
65.5
145.5
199.6
252.5
299
318
359.2
416
443
488.3
542
Millions of years

—FURTHER READING—

Ottaviani, Jim, and Big Time Attic. *Bone Sharps, Cowboys, and Thunder Lizards*. Ann Arbor, MI: General Tektronics Labs, 2005.

Lambert, David. *Eyewitness Books: Dinosaur*. New York: DK Publishing, 2010.

Benton, Professor Mike. *The Kingfisher Dinosaur Encyclopedia*. New York: Macmillan, 2010.

Holtz, Dr. Thomas R., Jr., and Luis V. Rey. *Dinosaurs*. New York: Random House Children's Books, 2007.

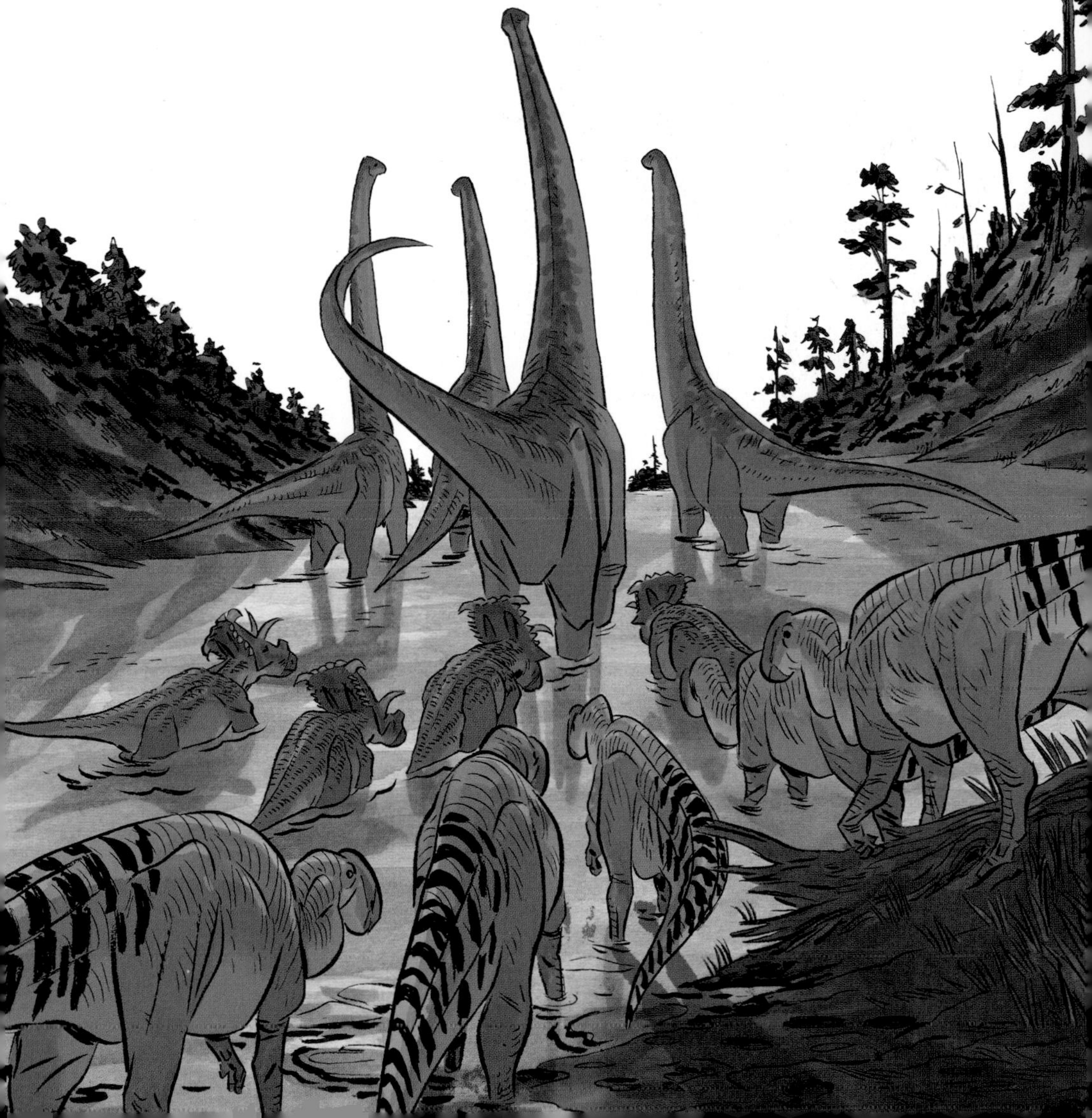

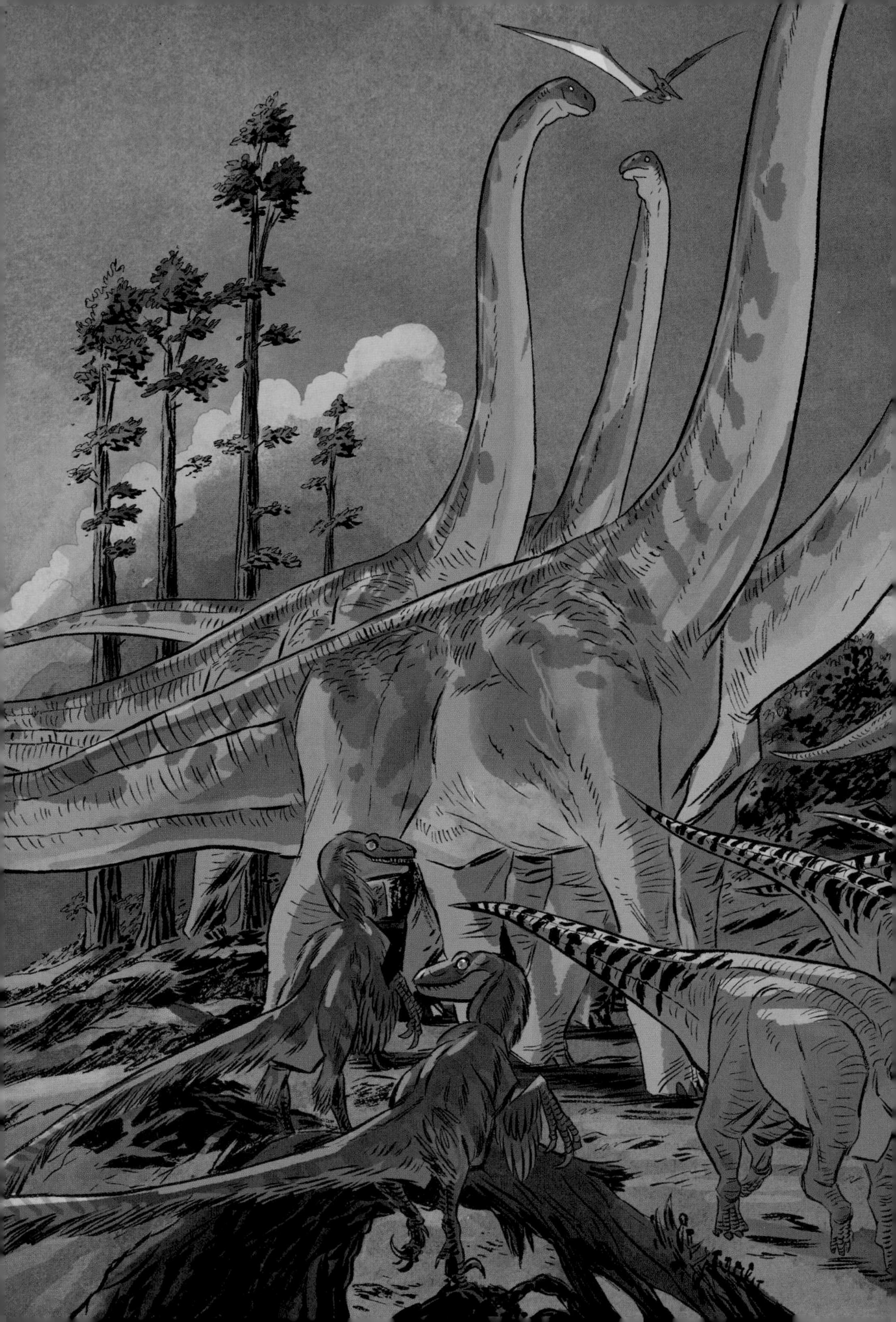